Praise for *Positive Discipline A–Z*

"In the most user-friendly format possible, *Positive Discipline A–Z* offers hundreds of specific suggestions for our parenting toolboxes, suggestions that are oriented not toward making our kids 'pay' for their mistakes, but toward learning life skills and developing healthy self-esteem for the future. A winner!"

—**Michael L. Brock, educator and author of** *School-Smart Parenting* **and coauthor of** *7 Strategies for Developing Capable Students*

"Knowing these authors is synonymous with understanding that things can always get better, and they have proven that again with their revised and expanded edition of *Positive Discipline A–Z*. Parents looking for insight into troubling childhood and teen behaviors will discover within these pages sound, practical information and advice. Applying these principles will truly improve the quality of life for each member of any family!"

—**Suzanne J. Smitha, M.S., school psychologist**

"More than any other book, I recommend *Positive Discipline A–Z* to my clients for the immediate help they need with everyday parenting problems. It is entirely consistent with the principles of healthy, respectful family relationships I am teaching them to create."

—**Barbara Mendenhall, marriage, family, and child therapist**

"When my twin boys were born, I bought your books *Positive Discipline Birth to Three, Positive Discipline for Preschoolers,* and *Positive Discipline A–Z.* As my babies became toddlers I watched various TV programs on discipline. I did have an issue with one of my boys biting the other as he was nearing two. I decided to get firm with him and put him in the corner for biting as suggested on the TV programs. After two months he was worse than ever and we were both stressed and his brother was all bitten. I decided that this really was not worth it so I took out the Positive Discipline books I had always followed before watching the TV. I bought some teethers for each of them so we had no fighting over them, with the instructions that he was not to bite his brother but bite the teether. Each time he went to bite I told him gently not to bite his brother but to bite his teether. It was better by the end of the day and within two days he was much calmer and we hardly had any incidents. Now we maybe get one bite a week, which is brilliant. I have since decided that I should have stuck with your books and not listened to the TV. I will never stop using your Positive Discipline techniques again. My children are happy and boisterous and a joy to be around. And I feel much more comfortable with the techniques than I did putting them in the corner. It's a big thank-you from us all."

—**Amelia, mother of Hamish and Finley, age two**

Also in the Positive Discipline Series

Other Books by the Authors

Raising Self-Reliant Children in a Self-Indulgent World
H. Stephen Glenn and Jane Nelsen

Parents Who Love Too Much: How Good Parents Can Learn to Love More Wisely and Develop Children of Character
Jane Nelsen and Cheryl Erwin

Positive Time-Out: And Over 50 Ways to Avoid Power Struggles in the Home and the Classroom
Jane Nelsen

Serenity: Eliminating Stress and Finding Joy and Peace in Life and Relationships
Jane Nelsen

Pup Parenting
Lynn Lott, Jane Nelsen, and Therry Jay

Chores Without Wars
Lynn Lott and Riki Intner

Do-It-Yourself Therapy
Lynn Lott, Riki Intner, and Barbara Mendenhall

Seven Steps on the Writer's Path
Nancy Pickard and Lynn Lott

Madame Dora's Fortune Telling Cards
Lynn Lott, Rick Naymark, and Jane Nelsen

POSITIVE DISCIPLINE

A–Z

COMPLETELY REVISED AND EXPANDED THIRD EDITION

1001 SOLUTIONS TO EVERYDAY PARENTING PROBLEMS

JANE NELSEN, ED.D., LYNN LOTT, M.A., M.F.T.,
AND H. STEPHEN GLENN

THREE RIVERS PRESS • NEW YORK

Published in the United States by Three Rivers Press, an imprint of the Crown
Publishing Group, a division of Random House, Inc., New York.
www.crownpublishing.com

Three Rivers Press and the Tugboat design are registered trademarks of Random
House, Inc.

Earlier editions of this book were previously published by Prima Publishing,
Roseville, California, in 1993 and 1999.

Library of Congress Cataloging-in-Publication Data

Nelsen, Jane.
Positive discipline A–Z: 1001 solutions to everyday parenting problems / Jane
Nelsen, Lynn Lott, and H. Stephen Glenn.—3rd ed.
p. cm.
Includes bibliographical references and index.
1. Discipline of children. I. Lott, Lynn. II. Glenn, H. Stephen. III. Title.
HQ770.4.N435 2007
649'.64—dc22   2006020784

ISBN 978-0-307-34557-8

Printed in the United States of America

Illustrations by Paula Gray

Design by Cynthia Dunne

10 9 8 7 6

Third Edition

To our loved ones
and
to parents everywhere
who want to show their love
by empowering and encouraging
their children

CONTENTS

CONTENTS

PART 2:
POSITIVE DISCIPLINE
SOLUTIONS A–Z

CONTENTS

HOW TO USE THIS BOOK

Positive Discipline A–Z begins with twenty-seven basic Positive Discipline parenting tools and principles in Part 1. In Part 2 you will find many suggestions for dealing with just about every behavior challenge you can think of. Many of these suggestions will refer back to the basic tools.

You may be tempted to skip directly to a problem you are having and bypass Part 1. But read Part 1 first—you will gain more knowledge by taking the time to review the twenty-seven basic parenting tools and principles before attempting to solve a particular problem.

You may also be tempted to read only about the problems you are having. But if you read all the subjects in the book, even if they don't concern you now, you'll gain the wisdom and creativity to deal with any situation. Plus many of the suggestions for a specific subject will give you ideas for everyday parenting that will help your children gain courage, confidence, and life

skills. And each subject contains a section on how to prevent these problems from happening. Don't wait until you have the problems to read about them.

When you tackle a problem, choose the suggestion or combination of suggestions that feels right to you. Put what you say into your own words so you don't sound like an insincere parrot. Whenever possible, involve your child in working on solutions. It can be fun to read the suggestions "with" your child and choose the one that both of you think will work the best. Involvement invites cooperation and the development of life skills. Since no two children are the same and since relationships change constantly, be flexible and thoughtful.

When you are unable to calm down and be objective, this book can serve as an impartial and wise friend. Sometimes just reaching for the book gives you time to cool off a bit. When you calm down, you become less hooked into the problem and can approach it more rationally and lovingly.

Share parenting with your partner. Children benefit from having all their parents involved in their upbringing and discipline. Beware of one parent becoming the "keeper of the wisdom of parenting" while the other parent takes a backseat. There's plenty of work for both parents to be involved in raising their children.

Keep the bigger picture in mind. The long-term purpose of parenting is to help your children develop healthy self-esteem and the life skills they need to be effective, happy, contributing, and respectful members of their family and society. All the Positive Discipline parenting tools and all the suggestions in this book are designed to do just that.

INTRODUCTION

What parent hasn't wondered what to do when their child has a temper tantrum in the grocery store, or won't eat dinner, or bites another child, or won't go to bed at night, or refuses to get out of bed in the morning? What parent wouldn't love to have nonpunitive solutions that work much better than punishment to help children learn self-discipline, cooperation, responsibility, and problem-solving skills? Here's a book that addresses just about every parenting problem you can imagine, for children of all ages, in alphabetical order so your particular concerns can be found easily.

When you flip to the pages that answer your parenting questions, you'll find solutions for what to do now, as well as suggestions on how to prevent the problem in the future. You'll also find information to help you understand more about yourself and your child's development. On top of that, each section is loaded with parenting pointers that could be generalized to solve other problems and to help you understand what your children are learning in response to your actions. Every topic includes a vignette (Booster Thoughts) so you can see how other parents applied the suggestions.

As you get the Positive Discipline principles under your belt, you can gain the kind of self-confidence, problem-solving skills, and healthy self-esteem that allow you to tap into your heart and deepest wisdom to find personal answers.

You may want to hang this book around your neck as a quick, easy reference while you learn to stop reacting and become a proactive parent. In no time you'll be thinking of this book as a kettle of alphabet soup that can be nourishing to the physical and mental health of your family. Keep it simmering at all times. Let the aroma permeate your home. Enjoy!

PART 1

WHAT IS POSITIVE DISCIPLINE?

As a parent you have a big job. You're the one who helps your children grow up to feel a sense of belonging and connection to the family. You teach your children social and life skills. You help your children feel loved. You find ways to ensure that your children feel special, unique, and important. You keep your children safe.

How do you do that? With discipline. Perhaps you think of "discipline" as a means of control through punishment, but Positive Discipline is not about punishment or control. Rather it is about instructing, educating, preparing, training, regulating, skill building, and focusing on solutions. Positive Discipline is constructive, encouraging, affirming, helpful, loving, and optimistic. As children don't come with directions, parents need to find an approach that gives them a sense of confidence.

Positive Discipline begins at birth and lasts a lifetime. That's right, it's never too early or too late to use Positive Discipline, because it is based on mutually respectful relationships in which you respect your child and you respect yourself. If parenting advice focuses only on the needs of the child and not the needs of the adults, it isn't *mutually* respectful. That kind of parenting encourages dependence and a lack of courage. If parenting advice focuses only on the needs of the adult and not the needs of the children, that's also not mutually respectful—it encourages submission, fear, and rebellion.

With Positive Discipline, the emphasis is on a balance of firmness and kindness, and on providing respect for both adults and children. Positive Discipline, because it is neither permissive nor punitive, brings hope, increased skills, and love to your family.

The more tools you have, the more you can teach your children. Part 1 is a reference to give you an understanding of the twenty-seven basic tools of Positive Discipline. These twenty-seven tools are referred to throughout the book, so be sure to read Part 1 before starting on the specific problems.

BE KIND AND FIRM

Many parents are plagued with guilt. That's because they are either too controlling ("I'm the boss") or too permissive ("Call me milquetoast"). Some parents are a combination of controlling and permissive, vacillating between the two extremes but not being consistent. Positive Discipline parents are neither. They practice firmness coupled *with* kindness. Which of the following styles fits for you?

> **The Boss:** You have all the power and your kids should obey you simply because you're the parent.
> **Milquetoast:** Your children are the center of the universe, so they have all the power.
> **Kind and Firm:** Your child is part of your family, not the center of the universe. You know your child's personality and can create boundaries without breaking your child's spirit.

Still not sure which is your style? Here are more clues. Both the boss and milquetoast act instead of being *pro*active. That means that they wait till something happens and respond to it in the moment. Kind and Firm parents take a step back, observe and think before they act. They work on ways to *show* their child what to do instead of constantly saying YES! or NO! The Boss often looks for blame or fault and relies on punishment as the primary discipline tool. Kind and Firm parents look for solutions instead of blame and realize that the person who can and must change first is the parent. By changing yourself even in the smallest ways, you can positively influence your child's behavior.

Milquetoast parents spend a lot of energy on what they shoulda, coulda, or woulda done. They tend to feel sorry for their children when they mess up, and are unwilling to let a child learn from his or her behavior. If this is your style, your child is parenting *you* instead of you providing leadership for the family. You are overprotective and you lack faith in your child's ability to learn and grow. You are not giving your child many opportunities to develop the belief "I am capable." Guilt is your middle name.

When you use the tools of Positive Discipline, you become the Kind and Firm parent, and you banish guilt from your life. You give yourself and your child permission to make mistakes, to be imperfect, and to try again, and again, and again. Why? Because you know that mistakes are the best teacher and that it is human to make them.

Kind and Firm parenting happens one step at a time. Reflect on your strengths and the strengths of your family. Then think of the areas you'd like to improve, and work on one issue at a time. That way you won't overwhelm yourself or your children.

DECIDE WHAT YOU WILL DO, AND THEN DO IT

The heart of Positive Discipline is learning to change *yourself* instead of trying to control others and make them change. If you've been busy trying to control your children, you probably haven't considered the possibility that you can deal with problems by controlling your own behavior and deciding what you will do instead of what you will try to make your children do.

Once you begin to focus on changing your behavior, you soon realize that actions must accompany your words and you have to follow through on your decisions. So that you don't paint yourself into any corners, it's best to think before you open your mouth. Rather than saying

things you don't really mean and finding yourself in the middle of the muddle, take a step back, and give the matter your full attention. This will help you ignore minor interruptions and deal with the ones that are really important to you.

Here are some examples of "Deciding What You Will Do" in action:

- A mother of an eleven-month-old baby who struggled through diaper changing decided to stop fighting with her child. Instead she said, "I need your help. I'll wait till you are ready to lie still while I change your diaper." Each time her child struggled, she stopped, and without speaking, waited quietly until her baby stopped wiggling. The minute the wiggles stopped, she went back to the diaper change. It took a few times before her child started to help with the process and stay still. She showed no anger, but simply waited patiently, keeping her child safe on the changing table.

- Another parent found that she was repeating herself all the time, and she realized that no one seemed to be listening to her. After some thought, she told her children that she would make sure she had their full attention and then say things one time. If they had questions, she'd be happy to answer them, but she was no longer going to repeat herself. She stuck to her guns, and soon noticed how much better her children listened when she said something. If they weren't paying attention, they would ask one of their siblings what Mom had said.

- A parent noticed that his kids were putting off their homework until just before bedtime, and then asking for help. He told them he would be available to help with homework every night between seven and nine. The first time one of his kids came to him at 9:30 to start studying for a test, he smiled and said, "I know you need my help, and I am happy to help you between seven and nine any night of the week. This time you're on your own." It is so easy for a parent to feel sorry for a child at this point, or think it is best to give more chances (after the "I told you so" lecture). But you can make the problem much better if you have the courage to follow through on your commitment, because you are allowing your child to learn from her behavior. Keep in mind that this only works if you skip the nagging, reminding, and lectures.

- Many parents have learned how to avoid unsafe driving by pulling the car to the side of the road and waiting quietly until the children settle down. Shopping trip tantrums have been avoided when parents take their children to sit in the car the moment the whining or tantrums start. All the parent says is, "We'll go back as soon as you are ready." Others have sidestepped fights and crying jags by clearly stating that they don't make

loans and sticking to it, allowing their children to learn to budget their allowance. Saying and meaning that the car doesn't move until everyone is buckled safely into the seat belt puts a stop to endless power struggles.

It's very tempting to repeat yourself, remind, and explain instead of following through with action. Kind and Firm parents save their words to talk about how wonderful their children are, or to engage in conversations about interesting topics, or to explain how life works.

ACT, DON'T TALK

Another variation on the "decide what you will do" method of parenting is acting instead of talking. Listen to yourself for one day. You might be amazed how many useless words you say. Or listen to parents bargaining with their kids at the grocery store, begging them at the department store, nagging them at the park, and explaining endlessly to them when it's time to move from point A to point B. Over 75 percent of the problems parents have with young children would probably disappear if parents talked less and acted more. Children tune parents out because parents talk too much.

This parenting by words ("Do this" "Don't do that") is a way parents mistakenly turn power over to children who tune them out and don't do a thing they say.

These parents then label their children as disobedient instead of acknowledging that they themselves are not using effective parenting skills. It is perfectly okay to take children by the hand and start walking, or lift them up and carry them to bed, or set them in the tub when they are having a fit about taking a bath. It is disrespectful to yell, nag, lecture, beg, order, and threaten. Give up counting to three; just zip your lips and act. You'll be amazed at the results.

If you decide to act more and talk less, your children will begin to notice the difference. Instead of asking your children to be quiet over and over, you can try waiting quietly for them to give you their attention. If children are fighting over a toy, quietly remove it and put it where they can't reach it. You don't need to say a word for them to get the idea that they can have the toy back when they stop fighting over it. If your child is banging his fork on the table or reaching for an object you don't want the child to have, ask the child to stop once. If the child persists, remove the object instead of repeating yourself incessantly.

Here's the biggest "parenting by words" mistake—asking your children if they would like to do something that you know they need to do. You've done it, and you've heard it from other parents. "Would you like to buckle up your seat belt?" "Would you like to come to dinner?" "Would you like to make your bed?" The answer is usually "No, no, no!"

To avoid this problem say instead: "It's time to buckle your seat belt." "It's dinner-time." "We make our beds before we leave the house." "Thursday is the day we wash our sheets." "Here's what we need to do. We pick up the dishes and bring them to the dishwasher when we're done eating." If you practice talking to your children this way when they are young, there are many things that they will accept as the way things are done in their family. They won't challenge the decisions, because that's the way it is, and not everything has to be a debate or a discussion.

Another act-don't-talk tip is to make sure you are in the same room before you make requests of children. If you can see the whites of their eyes and establish eye contact with them, you have a better chance of getting through. You have to get their attention before children can hear what you have to say. Action is a great tool for this. Notice how much quicker you get results if you stand up or move toward your children while you are talking instead of sitting in an armchair yelling instructions across the room.

USE FOLLOW-THROUGH

Follow-through can greatly reduce frustration and conflict with children while teaching them many valuable life skills. Follow-through is a form of action and a powerful way to get your children to listen and cooperate. When you use follow-through, you are being extremely proactive as a parent.

Here's how follow-through works. Instead of jumping into the middle of a problem, you watch for the patterns and then pick your battles. When you decide you are ready to improve a situation, follow these steps:

1. Give the matter your full attention;
2. Acknowledge your child's feelings and grant the child his wish in fantasy ("I wish we could give you what you want");
3. Tell your child what to do instead of what not to do or,
4. Work out a solution with your child's help;
5. Say how you feel and set your limit;
6. Follow-through with action.

Here's an example of follow-through. Shelly bugged her mom every time she tried to talk on the phone. Even though her mom gave her a turn to talk to the caller, Shelly persisted in begging to talk more or longer, and if she couldn't, she pinched, bit, and hit her mother. Mom decided to give the matter her full attention since the problem was reoccurring. She thought about choices she could follow through on. She picked a time when there were no phone calls and said to Shelly, "I know you wish you could have my attention or talk to the people who call here. I understand, and I wish you could talk as long as you like, but that's not always possible."

Then she asked Shelly if she had any suggestions of how to be more helpful when Mom needed to talk uninterrupted.

Shelly said, "I want to talk and I don't want you to talk instead of playing with me." Once more Mom said, "I understand how you feel, but here's what we need to do. When I answer the phone, I'll let you know if it is someone you can talk to. If it's not, please color in your book or play with your Legos until I'm off the phone. I know it might be hard to wait, but I have faith that you can do it and help me out so I can finish my calls. I feel upset when I am trying to talk to someone and I can't concentrate because you want my attention."

Then Mom told Shelly exactly what would happen and set her limit. "Shelly, if it's too hard for you to wait, I understand, but I need to feel safe while I'm on the phone. If I don't feel safe because you are biting or hitting me, I'll take the phone out on the deck and finish my call."

The next time the phone rang, Mom did exactly as she said she would. She asked the caller to hold for a minute and told Shelly that this wasn't a call for her. She walked Shelly to her Legos and then proceeded with her call. When Shelly approached, yelling "I want to talk," Mom stepped out onto the deck with the phone and talked while she held the door shut.

What does the child learn? She learns that you mean what you say and that you respect yourself and her. She learns that she can be cooperative and responsible. She learns that it is okay to feel frustrated, but that she can't always have her way. She learns give and take.

Many adults will ask why a smack on the butt wouldn't be easier and as effective. While punishment may solve the problem in the moment, it doesn't teach any of the skills that follow-through does and it is abusive and disrespectful. When children are punished they feel mad or guilty. When they feel guilty, they may develop the belief "I am bad." When they feel mad, they may develop the belief "I'll show you." This is not what parents want their children to learn just because punishment is quicker.

REPLACE PUNISHMENT WITH INFORMATION AND OPPORTUNITIES TO LEARN FROM MISTAKES

There is no place for punishment in Positive Discipline. Why? Hundreds of research projects have demonstrated that punishment is *not* the most effective way to teach positive outcomes. Instead it hurts, it makes others feel bad, and it uses fear as a motivator.

Then why would so many parents use punitive or abusive methods? Simple. They believe it works and that they are "doing something" instead of allowing their children to "get away with" misbehavior. Punishment provides a release for their anger and frustration. Others use punishment because they are conditioned from past experiences and lack the knowledge and skills to use different methods. They

believe that a spanking or grounding or taking away privileges is the best way for children to learn. They are convinced that children must suffer to learn.

Many parents use punishment because it gives them a sense of being in control—especially when the punishment temporarily stops the problem. They don't want to be permissive and so they think the only alternative is punishment. When these parents step back and take an objective look, they notice that they are punishing for the same behavior over and over again. That is a pretty good clue that punishment doesn't work in the long term. If this description fits you, you'll be happy to know that in this book you can learn many respectful discipline methods that are neither punitive nor permissive.

Still other parents use punishment because human nature is to take the path of least resistance. It is almost impossible to break an old habit until you have something new to replace it. Ever try to quit smoking or lose weight? The human mind abhors a vacuum. It's easier to start something new than to stop something you are used to and replace it with nothing.

Very little constructive learning can be done with anger and the output of negative energy. When your children think you are angry with them, they often behave *worse*. Discipline, to be effective, needs to be rational and loving (kind and firm at the same time). While it is fine to tell your child you are angry about a particular behavior, it is counterproductive to scream out a punishment in anger. There's a big difference between the two.

All through this book, we'll share many options of ways to replace punishment with respectful learning opportunities. Positive Discipline methods focus on teaching children that their behavior affects others and that if they are hurting others, an adult will help them stop. They also learn that feeling a certain way about a situation isn't an excuse to avoid dealing with the needs of the situation. Here are a few examples to consider.

- Your child spills his juice. Punitive parents would scream, hit, or take the juice away with anger, but you grab a cloth for you and one for your child and say, "Let's clean it up together."

- Your child plays too roughly with the dog. Punitive parents scold, argue, nag, threaten, and yell. You separate the two and tell them both, "You two can try again later when you are ready to play more gently."

- Your child forgets to do a chore. Punitive parents take away a privilege, and the chore still remains undone. But you find your child, make eye contact, and say, "Time to do that chore." If your child says, "Later," you say, "I'd like you to keep your agreement. It's time to do the chore now."

- Your toddler hits you. Punitive parents hit back, yell, or threaten. You take your toddler's hand and gently pat yourself with it saying, "Pat, pat, pat. Be gentle."

- Your child is playing roughly with a toy. Punitive parents use emotional blackmail, saying things like "You're such a baby. You're selfish. You're so clumsy," hoping that the insults will encourage their children to do better. But you take the toy, put it in a safe place and say, "Let me know when you're ready to try again and play more gently." If your child says "I'm ready" and continues playing roughly, put the toy away and say, "I'll let you know when I'm ready to try again."

You'll notice that parents using Positive Discipline don't ignore problems. They are actively involved in helping their child learn how to handle situations more appropriately while remaining calm, friendly, and respectful to the child and themselves.

IMPROVE YOUR COMMUNICATION SKILLS

Part of your job as a parent is to give information, but a bigger part of your job is to help your children learn to think for themselves. This can be accomplished by learning to listen with new ears. Listening is the most difficult communication skill a parent can learn. Here are some tips to help you become a better listener while helping your child become a better thinker.

Ask "Curiosity" Questions

Too many parents tell children what happened, what caused it to happen, how they should feel about it, and what they should do about it. Telling discourages children from developing their wisdom and judgment skills, consequential skills, accountability skills, and the wonderful gift of seeing mistakes as opportunities to learn. Telling them what, how, and why teaches them *what* to think, not *how* to think. Teaching children what to think instead of how to think is very dangerous in a society filled with peer pressure, cults, and gangs, because your child simply looks to the next "expert" for direction instead of using critical thinking skills.

It is important to remember that why, what, and how questions are appropriate only when you have a genuine interest in wanting to know what the child thinks and feels. Don't ask until you are ready and willing to listen.

You help children develop thinking skills and judgment skills by asking them, "What happened? What is your perception of why it happened? How do you feel about it? How could you use this information next time?"

The following example shows how a parent asked questions instead of lecturing when her eight-year-old's bicycle was stolen.

Juanita came into the house crying, "I can't find my bicycle. Someone must have stolen it."

Mom: *"I'm so sorry. I can see how upsetting that is for you. Tell me what happened."*

Juanita: *"I left my bike on Sally's front lawn, and now it is gone. I hate people who steal bikes. That is so mean."*

Mom: *"Yes it is. It is too bad we can't control everyone in the world and make them be nice."*

Juanita: *"Yeah!"*

Mom: *"Since we can't control others, can you think of anything you could do in the future to protect your possessions?"*

Juanita: *"Well I better not leave my things out."*

Mom: *"Sounds like you learned a lot from this painful experience. Maybe later you would like to talk about what you will need to do to get another bike, and how you will take care of it so this doesn't happen again."*

Juanita: *"Can't we talk about that now?"*

Mom: *"I think we are both too upset now. How long do you think it will take for us to feel good enough to talk about it rationally?"*

Juanita: *"How about tomorrow?"*

Mom: *"Sounds good to me."*

When children tell you something, you may be tempted to defend yourself, explain yourself, give a lecture about how the child should feel or solve the problem. Instead of jumping in and taking over, this is a great opportunity to help your child think things through and get in touch with feelings. You can help your child explore deeper by asking, "Can you tell me more about that? Could you give me an example? Is there anything else you want to say about that? Anything else?" It helps to ask "Anything else?" several times until your child can't think of anything else to say. Trust your instincts from this point. Your child may feel better having been listened to and taken seriously and that is all that is needed. You could also ask, "Would you like my help to brainstorm possibilities for solutions?" But avoid the attempt to help your child if she doesn't ask for your help.

Practice Reflective Listening

Another way to help your child feel heard and to think things through is to hold up a mirror by listening reflectively. Your job is to reflect back to your child what you hear. It is best to use words that are a little different from your child's so you don't sound like a parrot, but do stick closely to what your child is saying.

Here's an example. Your child says, "I hate Karen." You say, "You hate your best friend?" Your child says, "Yes, because she talked about me behind my back." You say, "She said something to others that she wouldn't say to you?" Your child says, "Yes."

At this point, you could say, "I'm glad you told me how you feel. Would you like a hug?" This would be more effective than

either trying to fix the situation or giving a little lecture on how your child should try to be friends and forgive and forget. It's tempting, but by allowing your child to express her feelings without your judgments, you are allowing her to learn on her own, and thus you are doing a better job parenting. In this example, the child got a hug from her mom and the next day she and her friend were best buds once again.

Develop a Feeling Vocabulary

If you want your children to learn about feelings and develop emotional intelligence, start by listening to your children's feelings without trying to explain them away or fix them. Your children learn that it is okay to have feelings and to express them. If your child is acting out a feeling instead of stating the feeling, that is, having a temper tantrum instead of talking about what he is angry about, you can help your child identify the feeling by naming it.

The trick is to use feeling words. Feelings can usually be described by one word: happy, hurt, comfortable, scared, hungry, sleepy, angry, sad, helpless, hopeless, irritated, embarrassed, ashamed, joyful.

Here's how it works. Your child is frustrated with a puzzle and can't get the pieces to go together. He throws the piece across the room and starts to cry. You say, "You're feeling upset because the puzzle is difficult. You don't like it when the pieces don't go together easily, do you?"

Your child may be acting upset, but he doesn't know that he is having a feeling called upset and it has a name and that it is okay to have a feeling. By naming it you are teaching your child a feeling vocabulary.

You could go another step and ask your child if he'd like some help with the puzzle or if he would like to try again and turn the piece until it fits. Or you could let your child be upset with the piece and say, "Maybe you'll want to try again later when you feel better."

You can also share *your* feelings using the same approach. When your child hits the dog, you could say, "I'm feeling worried that you'll hurt the dog or that the dog might bite you and I wish you would be gentle with the dog." If saying how you feel doesn't improve the situation, you can always go back to using action, separating the child and the dog and letting them know that you are uncomfortable with the way they are playing and they can try again later.

Listen with Your Lips Closed

There's a lot that can be said without ever speaking a word. When your child is talking to you, you can avoid lecturing or taking over the conversation by listening with your lips closed. You may be surprised how much your children will talk more when you talk less, peppering the conversation with expressions like "Hmm," and "Uh-huh."

Use "I Notice" Statements

Don't ask setup questions. A setup question is one to which you already know the answer and still ask for the purpose of trapping your child: "Did you do your homework?" "Did you brush your teeth?" "Did you clean your room?" Instead of asking setup questions, use "I notice" statements. "I notice you didn't brush your teeth. Let's do that now." "I notice you didn't do your homework. What is your plan for getting it done?" "I notice you didn't clean your room. Shall we call in the fire department for a big hose or hire a maid with your allowance?"

If your child says, "Yes I did," you can say, "My mistake," or "Great, I'd like to see it." If your child is deceiving you, work on the power struggle or revenge cycle (read about the four mistaken goals of behavior below).

CREATE REASONABLE EXPECTATIONS FOR YOURSELF

Have you noticed that once your children arrived, your time was no longer your own? Today parents try to be superparents, involved in every aspect of their children's lives. They want their kids to be involved in activities and excel at school, have healthy self-esteem and be protected from the trials and tribulations of life. On top of this, many parents are single parents or working parents or both. They may be parenting children from different families as the result of divorce and remarriage. They could be living at home with their parents or have their adult parents living with them. The demands on today's parents are extreme.

That's why it is important to take care of yourself and to set your expectations lower so you can achieve them. Your house may not look like *House Beautiful*. You may not have time for elaborate meals. Golf and tennis may have to wait until the children are older. When you adjust your lifestyle to allow time for your children's basic needs for love, time, and training, you may not be able to get things done as quickly or effortlessly as you once could. Cut yourself some slack. It might take a week to do what you could do in an hour and that's just fine. Hire out what you can and delegate as much as possible. Use child care so you can run errands without the kids. Learn to involve your family members in helping with the logistics of life. Take time for training them so everyone can pitch in together. (For more detailed information on involving others in caring for themselves and others, see Lynn Lott and Riki Intner's *Chores Without Wars,* Taylor Trade Publishing, 2005.)

Set your house up for the children so you don't have to worry about safety. It's okay to limit certain activities to certain parts of the house, that is, eating at the table, crayons at the table, ball games outside, roughhousing in the family room, etc.

Be realistic about your budget. Know the difference between your children's wants and their needs. You don't have to buy designer clothes or vacation in an expensive resort to fulfill your children. They can learn to save and help buy those extras that they crave. It is not their birthright to be provided with TV sets, phones, cars, cell phones, iPods, computers, and more. In fact too many things can turn your kids into materialistic junkies who don't know how to be happy without "things."

HOLD FAMILY MEETINGS

One of the best ways to involve the family in the logistics of life is through the family meeting. While family members are learning how to solve problems, they are also learning communication skills, cooperation, respect, creativity, expression of feelings, and how to have fun as a family. The family meeting is a time set aside once a week on the same day. (Some families call this special time a family meeting; others call it talk time or special time, because some of the family members may not find the word *family* acceptable, such as in a newly blended family.) Whatever you call it, it's a place where family members sit down together and talk about whatever is on their minds. Most family meetings have an agenda, usually consisting of appreciations, old business, problem solving, scheduling, and a fun activity together. During this time family members can air feelings, compliment one another, and have conversations.

Make sure there are no other distractions, such as TV or phone calls. Sit around a table or in the living room. If a family member chooses not to be involved, hold the get-together without them and let them know they are welcome to join at any time. Set a time limit for your meeting, from fifteen minutes to a half hour. Items not completed can be handled at the next family meeting.

During the week, post an agenda. A good place is on the refrigerator where everyone can see and write on it. Use the agenda as a reminder list for issues that are important to discuss that might be forgotten by the day you hold your meeting. In addition to serving as a reminder, the posted agenda allows you to postpone dealing with issues until everyone is present to help solve the problems and figure out what to do.

Start each family meeting with compliments and appreciations so everyone gets an opportunity to say and hear something positive. Depending on the age and skill level of family members, you can take turns leading the meeting and writing down agreements made. After compliments, the chairperson calls off items on the agenda and helps family members take turns practicing respectful communication. The easiest way to do this is to go around the table twice, giving each person two turns to state his or her opinion or feelings about the issue without being interrupted. If the person has nothing to say, it's okay to say, "I pass." This is a good time for them to practice their problem-solving skills by sharing their opinions, listening to feelings, and offering solutions.

It is important that everyone in the family agrees before a change is carried out. Until you reach a consensus, you might have to live with things the way they are. In some families, what this means is that the parents decide until everyone in the family can come up with an agreeable alternative. Some subjects need to be discussed for several weeks before a family can come to a consensus.

Brainstorming (generating a list of suggestions without evaluation) creates more choices everyone can consider. Instead of seeking a perfect solution, suggest that family members choose one idea from the list of brainstormed suggestions to try for a short time. Set a time to meet again to evaluate the solution and discuss what everyone learned by trying it out.

Family meetings work best when everyone focuses on solutions rather than blame. No one should be in trouble at a family meeting and everyone should be listened to and taken seriously. Holding a conversation without having to fix anything is a great tool for bringing about family cooperation and harmony.

OFFER LIMITED CHOICES

Whenever appropriate, give children a choice between at least two acceptable options. The key words here are appropriate and acceptable. There are many times when a choice is not appropriate, especially for younger children. It is not appropriate to give them a choice about whether or not they want to brush their teeth, go to school, hurt someone else, or be in a dangerous situation such as climbing on the roof. Acceptable means that you are willing to accept either option the child chooses, such as "Save your money or do without." "Practice the piano or give up lessons." "Go to bed at 8:15 or 8:30." "Put your dirty clothes in the hamper or wear dirty clothes." Some parents are not willing to let their children do without or wear dirty clothes, so they should not offer those choices.

Younger children respond well to limited choices. If you say, "Would you like to hold my right hand or my left hand when we cross the street? You decide," your child feels a sense of power while you are still teaching and protecting. It is especially empowering to add, "You decide."

As your children get older, the choices need to be much broader or you invite power struggles. For instance with a teen you may ask, "Would you like me to set a curfew for you or would you like to be involved in that decision?" Most parents tell teens when the curfew will be without engaging the child in conversation and listening to the child's point of view. Not only is this disrespectful, but it creates rebellion. If you and your child are miles apart about what time a curfew should be,

you could always agree to negotiate in small steps which you try out for a week or two at a time.

SET LIMITS

Parents must set limits for their young children and involve their older children in helping to set limits. Your job is to set the parameters, like the sides of a bridge. When your children are younger, the limits are tighter. As the children get older, the limits expand and children can be involved in setting those limits. Part of the art of parenting is to know when to loosen the limits. Usually your children will help you with that decision, either through conversation or action. If you practice the communication skills we've offered and hold regular family meetings, your kids will show you when they are ready for more freedom and will be involved in setting new limits that are mutually respectful.

If you observe your children, you'll see that they push the limits you've set, over and over and over, in spite of any consequences. Often your kids are ready to take on more responsibility before you are ready for them to have it. An example of this is the mother who taught her son how to cross the alley carefully, always looking both ways for cars while holding her hand. One day he told her he could cross the alley without her help. She wasn't ready to loosen the hold, but he insisted that he was going to play with his friends on the other side of the alley and he could look for cars all by himself. Because of her fears, she told him she'd let him give it a try, and then she hid in the bushes, so she could jump in front of a moving vehicle if need be. Of course being well-trained, he crossed by himself with ease and safety.

Positive Discipline parents set limits using natural consequences, logical consequences, and routines. Natural consequences are simple and very effective in the learning process. They happen naturally. When you stand in the rain, you get wet. When you're wet, you think, "I'll run inside and get my umbrella or raincoat." No one has to tell you to do it in advance. Frequent nagging about natural consequences usually produces children who can function properly only when bossed, reminded, or nagged. You've interfered with the natural order and robbed your child of the opportunity to learn from the consequences of her choices.

You can practice using natural consequences by teaching yourself to wait and watch before you act to see what your child will do if you don't intervene. You can always intervene after the fact, because there is no inherent danger when you allow for a natural consequence. Your child won't die of pneumonia if a few sprinkles fall on her. If she doesn't seem to mind getting wet, you could always say, "Honey, I'd like you to run inside and get your raincoat, because we need to wear our coats when it's raining." It might be even more effective to say, "Honey, what

do you need to do to keep from getting wet?" This invites your child to think for herself and feel "in charge of herself" when she comes up with the obvious answer. Children learn naturally if parents can resist the urge to control, rescue, or punish them for their choices.

There are times that a natural consequence would be too dangerous or inappropriate for helping your child learn a life skill or lesson. In these cases, logical consequences can work. The difficulty is that many parents grossly misunderstand logical consequences and try to disguise punishment by calling it a consequence. Punishment is what happens when a child makes a mistake and you feel a need to pound it home so the child learns by suffering. The point of logical consequences is to help kids learn for the future instead of paying for the present or the past. Allowing children to experience the consequences for their choices can help them learn valuable life lessons. They can learn it is okay to make mistakes and try again.

When you truly understand how to set up and follow through with a consequence, you often feel guilty or bad. You may be suffering more than your child. In fact that's a sure sign that you are using a consequence. If your child consistently forgets to bring a lunch to school and expects you to drive it over, you say, "I'm sorry you forgot your lunch. Perhaps your friends will share with you. I won't be able to bring your lunch to school today." Most likely you'll be worrying about your child starving to death, but the reality is that your son or daughter is probably eating better, because friends are giving them all the healthy foods from their lunches that they don't like to eat.

Consequences allow your child to learn from his or her choices and behaviors. If you and your teen agree that he can use your car as long as he replaces the gas, he'll learn something if he doesn't do that and you stick to your agreement. Most parents would prefer to lecture, or give just one more chance, or rescue, or scold rather than say, "When you've come up with the cash to replace the gas you used, you're welcome to use my car again." Too many parents think that is harsh and unfair and that their children are suffering because they aren't being rescued, especially if your son has an important commitment that he needs to drive to in your car. You would be better off inconveniencing yourself and driving your son or letting him hitch a ride with a friend or take his bike than bailing him out. Allowing him to learn from one little inconvenience saves him years of problems because he never faced the consequences of his own behavior.

The consequences that work best are those you set with your child's involvement. Asking your child what would be a good solution (often a better word to use than consequence) and working together to agree on one is far more effective than arbitrarily creating a consequence. The following example shows how a parent involved his kids in setting up a conse-

quence (or "solution") by asking questions about playing ball in the house.

Dad asked, "What problems do you think we might have if you continue to play ball in the living room?"

The kids thought for a minute and came up with several answers: "We might break things. You might get mad at us. We might get the dog too excited. We might be too noisy. We might have fun."

Then Dad asked, "What suggestions do you have for solving these problems?"

The kids suggested that it would be better to play ball outside unless they were playing with a Nerf ball. Even then they thought it would be a good idea to stay out of the living room.

Dad asked, "What do you think would be a related, respectful, reasonable consequence if you guys don't keep your agreements to be respectful while playing with the ball?"

The kids agreed that it would be okay to send them outside to finish playing or to put the ball away and they could try again another day.

Because the children were part of the solution, they were much more cooperative when their parents later followed through with the agreement. Children don't have to suffer to learn. But it's okay to be empathetic when you follow through, as the father in the following situation did.

Eight-year-old Brent was angry and pouting because he had to sit on the grass for ten minutes instead of continuing to play in the pool. Even though he had agreed in advance that this is what would happen to anyone who was running and pushing others into the water at the pool, he was not happy. His dad sat next to him and said, "I know it's tough to have to wait, but you'll be able to try again in no time. Can I bring you a glass of lemonade while you wait?" Brent said, "No, thanks," with a sullen expression, but then he asked, "Hey, Dad, how about bringing me an orange instead?"

The trick is to focus on one problem at a time. Ask other family members for their ideas. Use limited choices when their ideas are not appropriate. For example, if your child says, "I don't want to do it at all," give a limited choice such as "You may do it before breakfast or before dinner. Not doing it at all isn't one of the choices."

ESTABLISH ROUTINES

One of the most powerful forms of limit setting that parents can do with their children is to create routines. The problem is that sometimes the routines you create aren't the ones you want. Are you normally spending two hours putting your little one to bed at night? Do you spend the early morning nagging, coaxing, reminding, and screaming to get your children ready for school? Are you doing all the work around the house and feeling resentful? Guess what. These are routines, and we're guessing you'd be happy to create

new ones where there is more give and take and spontaneity and creativity for all family members. Positive Discipline routines help eliminate power struggles and give all family members ways to belong and contribute to the family.

Establishing good routines helps parents develop long-term benefits in their families. The long-term benefits are security, a calmer atmosphere, trust, and life skills for children. Children have an opportunity to learn to focus on the needs of the situation: doing what needs to be done because it needs to be done. Children learn to be responsible for their own behavior, to feel capable, and to cooperate in the family.

Children enjoy routines and respond favorably to them. The younger the child, the more comforting the routine. Picture the preschooler who is used to crackers and milk coming before story time trying to adjust when a substitute teacher changes the order. Once routines are in place, the routine is the boss and the parent doesn't have to continually demand help.

In the beginning you create the routines. For example, first we put on our jammies, then we have a story, then we give hugs, and then it's time for sleep. This is very different from letting your very young children decide they can't go to sleep without you lying down next to them till they fall asleep. When you are kind and firm, the routines you set will work until children get a little older and are ready to push the limit. At that time even young children can be involved in creating routines that will eliminate bedtime hassles, morning hassles, mealtime hassles, homework hassles, vacations, and so forth. For example, you can ask a two-year-old, "What things need to be done before you go to bed?" If she has a problem thinking of everything, you can say something like "What about brushing your teeth?" Once you have a complete list that might include snacks, bath time, pajamas, brush teeth, choose clothes for the next morning (which helps eliminate morning power struggles), story time, hugs, help your child decide the order in which they need to be done. Create a bedtime routine chart, and then take a picture of your child doing each task and help her paste the picture next to each task. Children love seeing pictures of themselves doing each task on the bedtime routine chart.

Now the routine chart becomes the boss. In most cases your child will eagerly follow her own routine. If she forgets, you can say, "What is next on your chart?" She will be more cooperative when she can tell you rather that hearing you tell her.

Finally follow through to implement the routine with action in a firm and kind manner. Refer to her chart or list, or ask, "What was our agreement?" Resist rescuing and lecturing.

Another tip for setting up routines is to have a deadline. When planning the routine, work backward from the deadline to figure out how much time is needed to accomplish the task. For instance if you want to have house cleaning done by 2:00 P.M. on Sunday so the family can have time for an outing, think through what the tasks are, how long they will take, and what time everyone needs to start and finish on time. Notice that most routines involve the whole family. We find that routines work best when everyone works together instead of parents leaving lists of jobs for children to complete while they are away.

Here are some examples of routines:

House cleaning

Pick a time each week to clean the house together. Each family member can choose one or two rooms to clean or one or two activities, such as dusting, vacuuming, or cleaning sinks. Once everyone is trained with everyone working together, the family can clean a six-room house in under an hour.

Meal planning and preparation

One person cooks, another assists, another sets the table, another cleans up. During a family meeting each person in the family chooses at least one night for each of the jobs. Make a meal chart where each person lists what they want to prepare for each meal. The chart may include the main dish, the vegetable, the salad, and the dessert. Use this chart when making the grocery list to make sure needed ingredients are purchased.

Grocery shopping

Use the list of items needed at the store. Let each family member choose from the master list the items they want to find in the grocery store. Go to the store together and let each person gather items on their list. Meet at the checkout counter, pay, return home, carry in the items together, and put them away together.

Morning routines and bedtime routines

These are covered in the A–Z section.

Brushing teeth

When children are young, they need your help to brush their teeth. Do it with them and help them floss. As they get older, it is helpful to add tooth brushing to their list of activities they do before school (see Morning Hassles) and before bed. Some families continue the routine of everyone brushing together just before bedtime. If your children resist brushing their teeth, instead of nagging, have the dentist use a fluoride treatment regularly to help prevent decay. Star charts and bribery are disrespectful because they imply that your children won't do anything without a prize. They are also unnecessary as children like to do what is expected of them.

Many dentists and hygienists will take time to talk to your children about dental hygiene to help you out.

These are just a few examples of how some families have set up routines. It is helpful to be realistic and to understand that routines may not work perfectly at first. Children who are used to behaving in certain ways need time before they will believe their parents mean what they say. Remember it is human nature to resist change, even when we want it or know it is good for us. When you understand this, it makes it easier for you to continue following the planned routine until the resistance ends.

KNOW WHO YOUR CHILDREN ARE

We would like to see a bumper sticker that says: DO YOU KNOW YOUR CHILD? instead of DO YOU KNOW WHERE YOUR CHILD IS? Positive Discipline invites you to know what your child thinks. You don't have to agree, but you can learn a lot about what drives your child by knowing his thoughts.

How does your child feel? We hope you will ask this question often to get a reality check of what is really going on inside your child. If your daughter tells you she feels jealous of the new baby, take her feelings seriously instead of trying to talk her out of them.

What does your child want in life? What are your child's values, hopes, and dreams?

Not yours, but your child's. Get into your child's world and try to understand and respect his or her point of view. Be curious about who your child is, instead of trying to mold your child to fit your values, hopes, and dreams.

Another question needs to be asked: Do you have faith in your child? Do you believe your child is a magnificent human being who has the potential to learn and grow from life challenges? When you have faith in your children it is easier to stop trying to control and punish them and start supporting them with respectful methods that teach the life skills they need when adults aren't around, such as dealing with peer pressure.

WELCOME MISTAKES

What were you taught about mistakes during your childhood? Are these the messages you got? Mistakes are bad. You shouldn't make mistakes. You are stupid, bad, inadequate, or a failure if you make mistakes. If you make a mistake don't let people find out. If they do, make up an excuse even if it isn't true.

We call these "crazy notions about mistakes" because they not only damage self-esteem, they invite depression and discouragement. It is difficult to learn and grow when you feel discouraged.

We all know people who have made a mistake and then dug themselves into a hole by trying to cover it up. They don't understand that people are often very forgiving when others honestly admit their mistakes, apologize, and try to solve the problems they have created. (Wouldn't it be wonderful if politicians understood this concept?)

Hiding mistakes keeps you isolated because you can't fix mistakes that are hidden, nor can you learn from them. Trying to prevent mistakes keeps you rigid and fearful. There's a saying we've heard: "Good judgment comes from experience and experience comes from poor judgment."*

You have an opportunity to help your children change these crazy notions about mistakes. Tell your children that every person in the world will continue to make mistakes as long as he or she lives. Since this is true, it is healthier to see mistakes as opportunities to learn instead of statements of inadequacy.

Teach your kids to see making mistakes as an opportunity to get valuable help from others. They will be willing to take responsibility for what they have done, even if it was a mistake, because they know it doesn't mean they are bad or will get in trouble. It means they are willing to be accountable, which is a necessary step to using mistakes as an opportunity to learn.

---

*We found this quote scribbled on a bathroom wall at the Squeeze Inn Restaurant in Truckee, California.

Sometimes mistakes require that you make amends where possible, and at least apologize when amends are not possible. Inform your children that making mistakes isn't as important as what they do about them. Anyone can make mistakes, but it takes a secure person to say, "I'm wrong and I'm sorry." If a child would like to make amends for a mistake, the Three Rs of Recovery from Mistakes can help them do so.

1. RECOGNIZE the mistake with a feeling of responsibility instead of blame.
2. RECONCILE by apologizing to the people you have offended or hurt.
3. RESOLVE the problem, when possible, by working together on a solution.

If you make a mistake, the Three Rs of Recovery can help you make amends with your child. And remember don't hesitate to let them know when you make mistakes. Your children will be very forgiving and can learn from your modeling.

MAKE TIME-OUT POSITIVE

One of the most popular discipline methods used by parents today is some kind of isolation or "time-out." They use a punitive attitude and say, "Go to your room and think about what you have done." These parents believe guilt, shame, and suffering will motivate their children to do

better in the future. The truth is that kids do better when they feel better. You don't motivate kids to do better by making them feel worse through punitive time out. Punitive time out is more likely to invite children to feel bad about themselves, "I'm not a good person," or bad about you, "I'll show you. I'll get even—and I'll be more careful about getting caught."

On the other hand, positive time-out can be an encouraging and empowering experience for children instead of punitive and humiliating, and can teach a valuable life skill. We all know that there are times when it is better to calm down before we do or say something we'll regret. We've all heard the age-old advice to count to ten or to take a deep breath. Time-out is encouraging when the purpose is to give children an opportunity to take a break for a short time and try again as soon as they feel better. Encouraging time out provides a cooling-off period to help children "feel" better, because that is what motivates them to "do" better.

It is important to get children involved in creating a space that will help them feel better. It may include soft cushions, music, stuffed animals, books to read. Then let them name their space something else besides time out (since it is difficult to overcome the negative connotations about time out). Some children call it their "cooling-off spot," or their "feel-good place."

Here's how to use this space. When your child experiences a behavior challenge, ask, "Would it help you to go to your feel-good place?" If the child is too upset, and says, "No," the next question is, "Would you like for me to go with you?" (And why not. You probably need some time out just as much as your child. In fact it might be a good idea for you to be the one to take some time out first.) If your child still says, "No," you can say, "Okay, I think I'll go." Then you go to your positive time-out area. What a great model for children.

Some children enjoy having a cuddly stuffed lamb with a timer in his belly so they can take it to their time-out place with them. When they're upset, they can decide how much time they think it might take for them to feel better and set the timer (or get help to set it).* This lamb can also be used for "time for"—time for cleanup, time for leaving the park, time for homework, etc., as a fun way for children to feel some sense of control (by setting the timer) over how much time they'll spend at an activity. Also you can ask your child if you can borrow the Time-Out Lamb when you need some time to feel better.

Remember that positive time out is not the only or even the best tool in your parenting toolbox. And when you do use it, it might be more effective to have it as just one of two choices, "What would help you the most right now, to go to your feel-good place or to put this problem on the agenda?" One more word of caution. Even positive time out is rarely appropriate for children under the age of three or four years old. (For more information on positive time out, see *Positive Time-Out: And Over 50 Ways to Avoid Power Struggles in the Home and the Classroom* by Jane Nelsen, New York: Three Rivers Press, 2000.)

PUT YOUR KIDS IN THE SAME BOAT

If you have more than one child, one of the handiest words for preventing sibling rivalry, good-kid/bad-kid combinations, and hurt feelings is the word *kids*. Quite often adults get in the habit of picking on one kid instead of using the term *kids* and putting everyone in the same boat. It is difficult to really know who started "it." You may see your older child hitting his younger brother, but you didn't see what the younger sibling did to provoke his older brother. Instead of trying to figure out who starts a fight, try, "Kids, if you want to continue fighting, please take the

---

*The Time-Out Lamb is available at www.positivediscipline.com.

fight outside or to another room." If the kids are fighting over who sits in the front seat of the car, how about, "Kids, no one can sit in the front seat until you kids have figured out a plan for sharing the seat. Please work out the details on your own time." If your children respond with "That's not fair. I wasn't doing anything wrong," or "Mom, it was Tom, not me," simply say, "I'm not interested in finding fault or pointing fingers but on getting the problem remedied. I'm happy to sit down with all of you while you work it out, if that would help."

FOCUS ON SOLUTIONS AND LET YOUR KIDS FIGURE IT OUT

Adults are often prejudiced against children and don't realize how much they underestimate the ability of children to come up with solutions to problems and proposals they can live with. When adults get involved in trying to settle conflicts between children, they often escalate the situation. Kids have ways of working things out that are both efficient and effective. Kids may not always use the same methods grown-ups would, but many grown-ups have fewer skills in conflict resolution than their children. Think of the times when entire neighborhoods were at war (the parents) while the kids had already forgotten whatever they were

arguing about and were off playing happily together. Give the kids a chance to work out their problems on their own.

Many parents think it is their job to fix everything and that they are the only ones with good ideas. Try asking the kids to figure out what to do and watch their creativity at work.

In one family the kids were fighting over who got to use the Nintendo game. Dad said, "I'm putting the game away until you kids figure out a system for sharing without fighting. Let me know when you've worked it out and you can try again."

At first the kids grumbled, but later the kids said, "We worked it out. John can use the game on Mondays and Wednesdays and I get it on Tuesdays and Thursdays. Friday is a free day. We all agreed."

If the kids start squabbling again, Dad can simply say, "Back to the drawing board. The game-sharing plan seems to be falling apart. Let me know when you are ready to try again and you can use the game again."

LISTEN TO ACTIONS MORE THAN WORDS

If you want to understand people, pay more attention to what they do than to what they say. People have two tongues—the tongue in their mouths (words) and the tongue in their shoes (actions). They may say one thing while the tongues in their shoes give a different message. People may convey good intentions with their words, but their actions tell us the truth about what they are doing. This works two ways. It is important for parents to be congruent with their children, making sure that their words and actions match. If you say that you won't wash clothes that aren't in the dirty clothes basket and then you hunt through your children's rooms, picking up dirty belongings for the wash because you are worried what they will wear to school, your words and actions don't match. Your children learn very quickly that you say one thing and mean another. They will quickly learn to ignore your words when your actions don't match. On the other hand, it is also helpful to trust kids to be who they are by watching what they *do* and paying more attention to that than to what they say. For instance, your child may tell you he'll clean his room before he goes out to play, but if you notice the room is still a mess and he's off with his friends, he didn't mean what he said. When that happens, many parents would say, "I just can't trust my child." Instead if you trust your child to say what you want to hear but do what he wants, you could check the room before he goes out to play (see Use Follow-Through). Alfred Adler said repeatedly, "Watch the movement, not the words." People often say one thing and then do something else. The proof of the pudding is in the behavior. Actions do speak louder than words.

You move toward healthy communication when words and actions are congruent. When the tongues in your mouths and your shoes match, you are respectful and encouraging to yourselves and others. When they go in different directions, your communication becomes filled with double messages.

DON'T MAKE OR TAKE PROMISES

Don't make promises unless you intend to keep them and definitely will be able to. Instead of saying, "Tomorrow I'll take you shopping," wait until you are ready to go shopping and tell the children, "It's time to go shopping. Would you like to go with me?"

Promising children you'll think about something and then forgetting to get back to it is very discouraging. Instead tell the children that you aren't ready to commit just yet. They can put the item on the family meeting agenda list or they can come and get you at an agreed upon time when you will be ready to discuss the matter with them. Making promises without checking out the details of what you have promised or checking with your partner backs you into a corner and builds resentment with the kids.

If your children make a lot of promises to you, especially if they don't keep them, say to them, "I don't take promises. Show me when you are ready instead and I'll celebrate with you."

HELP CHILDREN FEEL BELONGING AND SIGNIFICANCE

The primary desire of all people is to feel a sense of belonging and significance. Everyone seeks ways to belong and be important. If your children think they aren't loved or don't belong, they usually try something to get the love back, or they hurt others to get even. Sometimes children feel like giving up because they think it is impossible to do things right and to belong. The things they do when they feel unloved and unimportant are often mistaken ways to find belonging and importance. We call these the Four Mistaken Goals of Behavior, which include:

1. Undue Attention;
2. Misguided Power;
3. Revenge; and
4. Assumed Disability (Giving Up).

Children are not consciously aware of their mistaken goals because they are based on hidden beliefs. Once you understand that children do what they do because they are discouraged, you might be able to think of ways to encourage them when they are feeling discouraged. You are much more effective when you deal with the belief behind the behavior instead of only with the behavior.

To encourage discouraged children, instead of reacting to the misbehavior, react to the motivation (coded message) behind the misbehavior. One of the best ways to figure out your child's coded message is to check in with your emotional reaction to his behavior. If your emotional reaction to your child's behavior is feeling annoyed, guilty, or worried, your child may be asking for undue attention. His behavior is annoying, but his coded message is "Notice me. Involve me usefully." Give lots of spontaneous hugs throughout the day. Schedule regular special time. Brainstorm with your child on ways to get attention that are good for everyone.

Ignore bids for attention that make you feel irritated. Instead let your child know you are feeling irritated by his demands, and tell him that if he wants attention, all he has to do is ask for it. He can ask for attention during the day by saying, "I need some attention. I'd like a hug, to play a game, to tell you something, etc.," and that you will be more than happy to give the attention.

If you react to your child's behavior with feelings of anger or frustration, those are signs that your child's mistaken belief may be Misguided Power. His behavior may seem defiant, but his coded message is "Let me help. Give me choices." Take responsibility for how you create power struggles, and share this with your child by saying, "I can see that I have been too controlling. No wonder you rebel." Ask for help in working together on solutions after you have both calmed down. This will help you create a win/win situation instead of escalating a power struggle or turning it into revenge.

If you feel hurt, disappointed, or disgusted, those feeling reactions are signs that your child's hidden motivation may be revenge. Understand that the child who is hurting you or others feels hurt. His coded message is "I'm hurting. Validate my feelings." Deal with the hurt by checking with the child about how he feels hurt. Be accountable for anything you might have done (even though unintentionally) or listen empathetically if someone else is involved in the hurt. Help your child decide what he can do to feel better. Instead of hurting back or rejecting your child, you can behave in ways that help her feel belonging and significance in a positive way.

When you feel hopeless and helpless, your child's discouragement is called Assumed Inadequacy (Giving Up). The coded message your child is sending is "Don't give up on me. Show me a small step." Don't give in to your own discouragement. Keep encouraging your child by making tasks easy enough to ensure success. Take time for training. Keep telling your child that you have faith in his ability to learn and improve. Doing this will help you automatically come up with a positive and encouraging action on your part that can help your child move forward with confidence and hope.

USE ENCOURAGEMENT INSTEAD OF PRAISE AND REWARDS

Rudolph Dreikurs, an Adlerian psychologist and author of *Children: The Challenge,* said, "Children need encouragement like a plant needs water." Encouragement is a process of showing the kind of love that conveys to children that they are good enough the way they are. Encouragement teaches children that what they do is separate from who they are. Encouragement lets

children know they are valued without judgment for their uniqueness. Through encouragement you teach children that mistakes are simply opportunities to learn and grow instead of something they should be ashamed of. Children who feel encouraged have self-love and feel a sense of belonging.

There is a difference between praise and encouragement. It's easy to praise or reward children who are behaving well, but what can you say to children who are misbehaving and not feeling good about themselves—when they need encouragement the most? Try these: "You really tried hard." "I have faith in you to handle this." "You are such a good problem-solver, I'm sure you can figure out a way to resolve this." "I love you no matter what."

Praise and rewards teach children to depend on the external judgments of others instead of trusting their internal wisdom and self-evaluation. Instead of this example of praise: "I'm so proud of you," try encouragement: "You must be very proud of yourself." Praise: "You got an 'A.' I'm going to give you a reward." Encouragement: "You really worked hard. You deserve that 'A.' "

A steady diet of praise and rewards inspires children to believe "I'm okay only if others say I'm okay." It also teaches them to avoid mistakes instead of to learn from their mistakes. Encouragement, on the other hand, teaches them to believe in themselves and their abilities to do the right thing.

You can write notes of encouragement to your children. In some families people take turns watching for encouraging things to say and do for each other. It can also be their job to have a compliment ready for other family members once or twice a week. Encouragement goes a long way to create a positive family climate.

SAY NO

It's okay to say no. If all you *ever* say is no, that's a problem, but some parents don't think they have the right to say no without lengthy explanations. For instance if your child knows that snack time is a time for healthy treats and they ask for ice cream, it's okay to just say, "No."

When they respond with, "Why not? That's not fair. Mrs. Smith let's her kids have ice cream for a snack," say, "Watch my lips, 'No.' "

"Aw come on, be nice. You're so uptight."

"What part of 'no' don't you understand?"

"Okay, fine. You're no fun."

Most children have figured out when their parents *really* mean "no." They describe that certain tone of voice or look on the face, or refer to when their parents start counting to three. Children wouldn't be children if they didn't try to get parents to change their minds, but it is perfectly appropriate to handle their manipulations with a clean, clear "no." If you feel like they sincerely don't understand your reasons for saying no, tell them, but remain firm—they don't have to agree with your reasons.

Mrs. Ramirez thought she had to convince her children to accept her reasons for saying no. This only invited them to think of better reasons for her to give in. One day she remembered to be both kind and firm at the same time and said, "Honey, I love you and the answer is no." Her daughter said, "I can't believe you," and walked away with a smile on her face. Obviously she finally did believe that her mother meant it—and that she was loved.

USE YOUR SENSE OF HUMOR

Parenting can get too serious, especially as the children get older. Think about how you feel when you are watching babies and toddlers. It seems like everything they do is cute and adorable. See if you can get to the point with your children where you can truly say, "Aren't they cute!"

Developing an "aren't they cute" attitude can help you put your child's behavior into perspective. When you recognize their behavior as age appropriate, it helps you perceive behavior that would otherwise be annoying as cute. Babies with food all over their faces and a pile of droppings under their high chairs are adorable, so how about looking at a teenager's room as another kind of age appropriate "cute"?

Think of the way your children dress as an expression of their personality instead of a statement about you and a reflection of your parenting. When kids are three they may want to dress like a superhero, at seven a baseball player, and at fifteen the uniform of the day may be baggy clothes from the Salvation Army.

Sometimes parents forget to use their sense of humor or see the humor in situations with children. It's okay not to be serious all the time. Try telling the reluctant choredoer as you read the local paper that there is an article about them in the news section. Then pretend to read how your son or daughter was interviewed and said how much they love to wash the dishes and that when they forget they're happy when their parents remind them. You can do the same with horoscopes: pretend that you are reading theirs and it says, "Today I will remember to hug my parents five times."

Nicknames can be a fun way to keep your sense of humor, as long as they aren't used as a put-down or manipulation. On a ski trip, one of the kids shot down the hill before everyone else got to the top. His nickname became "Slow-Mo Beau." His brother, who refused to ski at all, loved being called "I-Don't-Want-To-You-Can't-Make-Me-No-I-Won't-Not-Ever Don."

For those kids who have a hard time finishing what they start, try introducing them to the Beginning-Middle-End plan. Let them know they are great at beginnings and fair on middles, but you haven't seen an end in years. Later you can ask, "How are those ends coming?" Children like being joked with about their uniqueness when parents are accepting of the differences and use a sense of humor.

GET A LIFE

Too many parents try to live through their children. They want their children to accomplish the things they didn't accomplish in life—or think their children should accomplish the same things they did. They don't bother to honor the feelings and desires of their children as people.

Kahlil Gibran says it so beautifully in his book, *The Prophet*:

Your children are not your children.

They are the sons and daughters of Life's longing for itself.

They come through you but not from you,

And though they are with you yet they belong not to you.

You may give them your love but not your thoughts,

For they have their own thoughts.

You may house their bodies but not their souls,

For their souls dwell in the house of tomorrow, which you cannot visit, not even in your dreams.

You may strive to be like them, but seek not to make them like you.

For life goes not backward nor tarries with yesterday.

Getting a life means actively following your dreams while supporting your children in following their dreams. It does not mean neglecting your children or being permissive. This whole book is about teaching and guiding your children. When you have a full life of your own you will have room to enjoy your children because you will not be depending on your children.

AVOID LABELS AND DRUGS

Have you noticed that there is a tendency to label just about every "misbehavior" a mental or behavioral problem: ADHD, ODD (oppositional defiant disorder), separation anxiety disorder, strong-willed child, depression . . . the list goes on and on. The scary thing is that there is now a drug for every one of these labels. But most of these behaviors are *normal*. For example, what some people would like to label as ODD is often a natural response from a child who is being raised by a controlling parent. Even when controlling your child too much is done in the name of love, it doesn't allow them to develop a sense of belonging, significance, and the problem-solving skills they will need. In just about every case, children will give up these "behaviors" when parents use the many Positive Discipline tools described in this book.

HAVE FAITH

Having faith in children does not mean having faith that they will always do the right thing. It means having faith in children to be who they are. This means they will act age appropriately most of the time—which means they will not do the dishes or mow the lawn as promised. Instead of getting upset about this and acting disrespectfully, you can expect it and use respectful motivation methods. Have faith that you and your children can help each other learn from mistakes.

Having faith in your children does not mean they are ready to be on their own.

They still need love, support, and help in learning life skills. But when you have faith, you don't need to control and punish. Having faith gives you the patience to teach with empowering methods such as joint problem solving, follow-through, family meetings, and asking "curiosity" questions to help kids learn from their mistakes. Having faith includes keeping an eye on the long-range picture and knowing that who your kids are now is not who they are going to be forever.

MAKE SURE THE MESSAGE OF LOVE GETS THROUGH

Making sure the message of love gets through is the greatest gift you can give your children. They form their opinions of themselves through their perception of how you feel about them. When they feel loved, belonging, and significance, they have the foundation to develop their full potential to be happy, contributing members of society. Your positive influence gets through when the message of love gets through.

The simplest way to help your child feel loved is to say, "I love you," many times a day. Give lots of hugs and tickles and kisses. Plan special time together. Children need time alone with each parent. When they are young, it is important to spend a little time each day one-on-one with your children. As they get older, special time could be a weekly routine. During special time plan activities that you both enjoy. If other children interrupt, ask them to leave.

Don't forget to play with your kids. Roughhousing on the floor, going to the park, baking or cooking together, and playing games, are a few ideas. The important thing is to take time for fun. Build some pleasant memories of family fun instead of staying too serious. Family fun doesn't have to take a lot of time or cost a lot of money. What it does take is a commitment and willingness to play.

TAKE SMALL STEPS

The road to success is best taken one step at a time. If you set your sights too high, you may never start, or you may feel discouraged if everything doesn't happen overnight. If you continue taking small steps, your movement will be forward and you and your children will all benefit.

POSITIVE DISCIPLINE SOLUTIONS
A – Z

ADOPTION

"At what age should I tell my child she is adopted, and is there any way to prevent her from the possible heartache that can result from a desire at some point to search for her birth parents?"

Understanding Your Child, Yourself, and the Situation

Parents can choose to adopt a child for reasons that are political, social, philosophical, or even trendy. But there is a very large group of people who adopt because they cannot have a child of their own. Most members of this group are experiencing some form of loss—loss of the ability to conceive or carry to term, loss of birth parents, loss of child. This loss is a lifetime issue in most adoptive situations. Adopted children deal with feelings of rejection, thinking they were unwanted by their birth parents, and feelings of shame, thinking there was something wrong with them and that is why they were given away.

As a parent, when you accept that there are predictable, nonpathological issues that go with adoption, you're on your way to a win/win situation. Your openness to allow for ambivalence and your child's mixed feelings has a positive influence. Some children think they are more loved because their adoptive parents *picked* them, while other children decide that the parent is just saying that to make them feel better because they aren't good enough. Adopted children struggle with their identity—but so does everyone. Nurturing the sense of shared family culture, along with your love and strength, will help surpass any problems.

Suggestions

1. Don't hide the adoption from your child. Tell her that she is adopted before she can comprehend its meaning. You can start practicing your script even before your child arrives. "We are so lucky that we could adopt you. We wanted you so much." By the time she understands what adoption means, it will be old hat. And keep in mind that some kids understand earlier than you would ever imagine, so start as soon as possible.

2. Don't use adoption as an excuse or explanation if your child starts misbehaving.

3. Don't take it too seriously when your child says, "I hate you. I wish I could find my real mother." Children who aren't adopted go through similar phases, saying things like, "I hate you. I wish I had a different mother." Even if you think this will never happen in *your* house, it will, and when it does, it probably will hurt your heart if you take it personally.

4. Acknowledge feelings and validate them. "You're angry, and that's okay. You wish you knew more about your birth mom. You feel unhappy because all the other kids have blue eyes and you have brown eyes. It's okay to have these feelings, and we love you for the unique person you are."

5. When your child tells you that she was teased by a neighbor or school friend about being adopted, listen empathetically before using curiosity questions to help her process the experience: "What happened? How did that make you feel? What do you think about that? Why do you think your friend would say something like that? What do other kids get teased about?" Work with your child about how to respond: role-play, brainstorm, and come up with actual words and phrases.

6. When siblings complain about a brother or sister receiving special treatment because they are (or aren't) adopted, acknowledge the different ways each child joined the family and reassure the kids that each is unique, special, and loved. In addition stress similarities among your whole family, like "We all love the Giants," or "We're all computer nuts."

Planning Ahead to Prevent Future Problems

1. During a close moment, discuss possible problems before they become important. "I've noticed there is a lot of publicity about adopted children wanting to

find their birth parents. What do you think about that? Why do you think they would want to do that? What are your plans about that?" Just listen. Don't try to talk your child in to or out of her thoughts, feelings, or plans.

2. Let your child know that you will support her if she ever wants to find her birth parents—that you will understand and not feel jealous or unappreciated. Keep albums, school papers, videos, and other memorabilia so that your child can share these with her birth parents if the situation arises.

3. Your child needs to know that her birth parents gave her up for adoption because of their personal situation, not because there is anything wrong with her. Tell her that you have a lot of compassion for her birth parents who made a plan for her. Assure her that you are glad you have the opportunity to give her all the love she deserves. Repeat this often as your child goes from one developmental stage to another.

4. Remind yourself that kids act similarly at different ages and stages regardless of who the birth parents might be, and that all kids vie for their parents' attention.

5. Allow yourself the time you need to fall in love with your adopted child and don't beat yourself up if you feel different about each child. That's also normal in families where all the children are biologically related.

6. Establish a "Sibling's Day" to celebrate the day that the children became siblings. Some people celebrate "Gotcha Day" as the day the child entered the family or the day the adoption became legal.

Life Skills Children Can Learn

Adopted children can experience the love that lets them explore their feelings, thoughts, and conclusions about their origins. They can learn that it is safe to love again without fear of rejection and that upsetting events pass with time and the joy of life goes on.

Parenting Pointers

1. Wondering about birth parents is similar to nonadopted children fantasizing about having different parents (who are rich, or famous, or not so mean). This phase can pass when not taken too seriously, or when taken seriously enough to address and explore to whatever extent circumstances allow from talking openly to having contact with birth family members.

2. If your child does take it seriously, remember that it is easier for a child to love two mothers or fathers than to feel she has to choose between them. Let your child know this. Also let her know you will be a sounding board if what she finds is disappointing.

ALLOWANCE

"Should I give my children allowances for doing their chores?"

Understanding Your Child, Yourself, and the Situation

Allowances give children an opportunity to learn many valuable lessons about money. The more children understand about earning, saving, and managing their money, the less likely they are in the future to solve their money problems through tantrums, begging, stealing, selling drugs, or borrowing from you and making promises they never keep to pay you back. The amount you give them should depend on your budget. If the money is used for punishment or reward, the lessons will be negative, because that creates an arena for power struggles, revenge, and manipulation. The lessons are positive when children are allowed to have regular, unchanging allowances so they can learn life skills. Chores are a separate issue and should not be connected to an allowance (see Chores).

Suggestions

1. Do not rescue your children when they run out of money. Learn to say no with dignity and respect when they try to con

you into giving them more money after they make mistakes with their money. Say, "I know it's upsetting and hard to wait when you run out of money, but allowance day is Saturday."

2. Be empathetic without trying to fix things. You might say, "I'm sure you feel disappointed that you don't have enough money left to go to the game."

3. Offer your services as a budgeting consultant, but do not give advice unless asked.

4. Help your children explore what happened, what caused it to happen, what they learned from it, and how they will use this information in the future. This is effective only if they agree to explore the consequences of their choices, and only if you are truly curious about their perceptions. It is not effective to try disguising a lecture in the name of exploration.

5. You may choose to offer your children a loan when they run out of money and discuss the terms of how they will pay it back. (This is not the same as rescuing.) Show them how to set up a payment plan and agree together on an amount you can deduct from their allowance. Do not make the amount so high your child won't be able to manage during the week. Another possibility is to make a list of special jobs to earn money for extra items or to help pay back their loan. Don't make new loans until the first loan is repaid.

6. Don't threaten to take away or limit your child's allowance as a tactic to prevent or punish bad behavior.

Planning Ahead to Prevent Future Problems

1. During family meetings, have periodic discussions about money where you share some of your mistakes with money and what you learned (without lecturing or moralizing). Allow others to do the same. Create a sense of fun so everyone can laugh while they learn.

2. For ages two to four, give children ten pennies, a nickel, a dime, and a piggy bank. For each year, add a few more pennies, nickels, dimes, and even quarters. Kids like putting money in the piggy bank and are starting a saving habit before they know it.

3. For ages four to six, take your child and the piggy bank to a big bank and open a savings account. Every one to three months, take your child to the bank to make a deposit. It can be fun to watch the balance grow in the bankbook. (This might inspire parents to get excited about developing the saving habit themselves, if they haven't already done so.)

4. Help your children start a wish list of things they would like to save money for. They could have a separate piggy bank for wish list saving. Whenever you

are shopping and they say, "Can I have this?" you can say, "Would you like to add this to your wish list and save your money for it?" (It is seldom that they want the item enough to save their money for it, but they want it enough for you to spend your money right now.) You can even offer to pay half if they will save half. It is amazing how many shopping hassles this stops when you are kind and firm in your offer.

5. For ages six to fourteen, schedule a planning session with your child for you to decide together how much money he needs and how it should be allocated for savings, weekly needs such as lunches, and fun. You might also encourage your child to save money to give to community organizations and those in need.

6. Set up guidelines, such as "Allowances will be given only once a week during family meeting time. If you run out before then, you have an opportunity to learn what that feels like and what to do about it, such as go without or find a job to earn extra money."

7. Set up periodic times (once a year or every six months) when an allowance can be raised based on a child's thoughtful presentation of greater need. Some families raise the allowance of all the children on every child's birthday.

8. For ages fourteen to eighteen, add a clothing allowance so teenagers can learn how to plan. Children who learn to handle money from an early age can handle a clothing allowance much sooner. In the beginning, instead of giving them money, tell them the total amount they can spend on clothing; and then deduct their purchases from a running total that you keep. They quickly find out that if they spend too much on a few items of clothing, they don't have enough left for an adequate wardrobe. The clothing allowance can be given monthly, quarterly, or twice a year.

Life Skills Children Can Learn

When you start your children on an allowance, they have the opportunity to learn how to earn money, spend what they have instead of going into debt, pay their bills on time, save for what is important to them, pay back loans, and feel the sense of power that comes from knowing they are on top of their finances. Children develop their judgment skills by making good or poor decisions about money and learning from the consequences of their choices without punishment or humiliation. They learn to budget, a skill they'll use all their lives.

Parenting Pointers

1. Using money for punishment or reward is a short-term solution. Giving allowances as an opportunity to teach children about money is long-range parenting that leaves children with life skills.

2. If you don't have skills in managing money, you need to find resources to help you learn so you can teach your children. *Chores Without Wars* (Lynn Lott and Riki Intner, Taylor Trade Publishing, 2005) is an excellent source to help you do that.

BOOSTER THOUGHTS One father says, "When my daughter rushes up to me and says, 'Dad, I need some designer jeans,' I have learned to say, 'Listen, kiddo, I got into this business to cover your body, not decorate it, and I can do that for $25 to $30 at many department stores. What you need is modesty and what you want is style. The difference will require some contribution on your part because I have a lot of other pressures and issues concerning finances to deal with.' "

There was a time in America when children wore jeans because parents were poor—now parents are poor because children wear jeans.

◎

The father of a six-year-old noticed that money was missing from his wallet and dresser top. His six-year-old brought in a container filled with money and said she found it. The father was very upset and wondered why his daughter would be stealing from him.

Upon further discussion, it was discovered that the parents told their daughter she could get a new bicycle when she earned $30 toward the purchase. Her weekly allowance was fifty cents, and it didn't take her long to figure out that she would have to wait forever for the bike. Using her ingenuity, she figured out a way to get the bike quicker.

Not wanting to start their six-year-old on a life of crime, the parents decided to raise her allowance to $2 a week. They told her that if she put half of her allowance away each week for the bike, they would match it. Then they sat down with a calendar and showed her how long it would take to save $30. They said that if she didn't want to wait that long, she could do special jobs for pay that they posted on a list in the kitchen. Within a month their industrious child had saved the $30 and the stealing never occurred again.

ANGRY OR AGGRESSIVE CHILD

"My child seems so angry all the time and becomes very aggressive when she is angry. She hits her sister, argues with me, kicks and throws her toys around, and is generally in a bad mood. Even her teacher complains about how quickly she loses her temper. What can you do with an angry child?"

Understanding Your Child, Yourself, and the Situation

There is a difference between experiencing a feeling and displaying emotions, such as a temper tantrum. Anger is a feeling that follows the belief that you can't get what you want, or that you are powerless in a situation. It can also be a cover-up for hurt feelings. Children who seem angry may be frustrated with their parents, other children, themselves, life, or other people who are angry with them. Children may think that no one is paying attention to them or considering their needs. Children usually have good reasons for feeling angry, even if they don't know what those reasons are. When children are bossed and controlled and have no choices, they will probably feel angry. Children who are overprotected often feel angry. If adults abuse children either physically or verbally, children will feel angry. And if a child sees his parent reacting to a display of angry feelings by being aggressive, he will do the same. Parents often respond to anger and aggression with more attempts to control and with intimidation, making the situation worse. If you or your child feels angry, there may be a power struggle going on, and it is important to disengage from the power contest and work for cooperation.

Suggestions

1. Validate your child's feelings, "You're really angry. It's okay to feel angry, but can you tell me in words instead of actions who or what you are angry about?" Wait for the child's response and listen with interest instead of saying, "You shouldn't be angry."

2. Sometimes children can't identify their feelings when they are upset. Let your child know it is okay to wait awhile, and to talk with you as soon as he is ready.

3. You can help your child defuse her anger by finding out (perhaps through guessing) what she wants and helping her obtain it, such as, "You're angry because your sister gets to stay up later and you wish you could, too. When you are her age, you'll be able to stay up as late as she does."

4. Don't choose sides when your children fight because this is one of the primary triggers for children's anger. Instead put them in the same boat and say, "Kids, I see you are having a hard time working this out. You can take some time to cool off and try again later, or

you can both finish this fight somewhere else, or you can work it out here, but I'm not taking sides."

5. If you have children who argue, try letting them have the last word or hugging them instead of arguing back. Ask your children for their opinions instead of telling them what to do. When you recognize a power struggle, stop and say, "I don't want to control you, but I would appreciate your help. Let's see what we can work out after we calm down."

6. If your child is hurting others with his aggressive behavior, let him know you realize he may be feeling hurt and upset about something, but you can't let him hurt others. If your child is young enough, remove him from the situation and sit with him, helping him talk about what he is upset about. If he is older, say, "I love you. Come get me when you are ready to talk," and then leave. If children need to sit down together to work out a problem, sit with them while they talk.

7. Avoid reacting to aggression with aggression, which creates a power struggle and models the opposite of what you

hope to achieve. Also avoid reinforcing aggression by giving in to it.

Planning Ahead to Prevent Future Problems

1. Look for places you may be inviting anger. Are you sticking your nose into your children's business, such as lecturing about schoolwork, friends, clothing, etc.? Do you nag your children instead of setting up routines and using follow-through? Do you use punishment instead of focusing on solutions? Do you make demands instead of requests? Children respond better to "It's time for dinner" than "Come to the table now."

2. Set up family meetings so your children know there is a place and time each week where they can talk about the things that bother them, be listened to, and find solutions to problems that are respectful to everyone.

3. Use limited choices with younger children instead of telling them what to do.

4. Involve children in creating routine charts, so that the chart is the boss and not you. (See Part 1, What Is Positive Discipline?, on how to involve children in creating routines.) Children feel even more empowered when you ask them, "What is next on our dinnertime (bedtime, morning) routine chart?"

5. When your child is in a good mood, mention that you notice she is often angry

BOOSTER THOUGHTS I was doing some research in Kmart one day when I came upon the checkout stand and there was a seminar in "How NOT to Deal with Kids and Feelings" just getting under way. A thirteen-year-old who had obviously started puberty (because his feet belonged to Michael Jordan, but the rest of him was in various stages of struggling to catch up) was having a negative emotional experience of some kind. As I arrived, his father stepped in to help him with "Why are you angry? There's no reason for you to be upset! Why do you want to carry on like that?"

At that moment I wanted to be able to speak for the boy, and give the father an honest answer to his questions.

"I'm angry BECAUSE a frontal system passing through has upset the pressure gradient in ways that produce subtle changes here in my limbic system, and I ate an overabundance of highly processed starches, sugars, fats, and carbohydrates which they loaded me up with at lunchtime because they were cheap, and I am dealing with the overwhelming frustration of trying to contain those ambient calories without moving or wriggling while sitting through hours of required classes with only four minutes to get to the toilet, my locker, and the next class, and I finally got out of school with all that energy roaring through me and they immediately put me on a bus and told me to 'Sit down, shut up, roll up the windows, or I'll tell your parents.' After I stepped off the bus with all of that still roaring through me, I had caffeine and sugar in a Pepsi and theobromine in a brownie which went up through the inherited instability of my hypothalamus from three generations of alcoholics—which we haven't even discussed yet. It surged down and hit a massive dose of testosterone which is roaring through me and getting me ready for puberty and was interrupted by a constant wail of frustration and hostility from trying to anticipate adult expectations all day. It was more than I could handle so I am *angry!*"

Since this was too much for a thirteen-year-old to articulate (or even be aware of), what this one said was, "Because!"

and ask for her help to think of a way she could show her anger that won't hurt anyone. Suggest a pillow she can punch, or listening to a tape of her favorite music, or finding a special cooling-off place. For older children, suggest they write down what they are angry about or draw a picture of their anger.

6. If you are a single parent, avoid any

The father yelled, "What do you mean, 'Because'?"

The boy finally said, "I don't know," and was quiet.

What this taught the boy was that his father didn't want to thoughtfully explore the issue and ways to deal with it effectively. What he really wanted was to make the boy feel dumb, stupid, and inadequate for having the problem.

Just remember that feelings are often very complex and not clearly understood. All of the above can and do affect our feelings, even when we're not aware of it.

◎

A young man of fifteen came to a counseling appointment with his mother. She was concerned about his anger problem. He would soon be driving, and his mother was afraid that if he didn't get some help he might take it out on other drivers once behind the wheel.

The counselor asked him what he was angry about. He said that when he agrees to do a job for his mother, she takes it back and does it herself. His mother explained that she does this because it doesn't look like he is going to do it.

Her son exploded, pounding his fists on the table and screaming, "You never trust me. I told you I would do the job. Why can't you believe me?"

His mother was amazed at the intensity of her son's rage over what to her was an insignificant problem. When she realized how upset he was, she asked, "How can we work this out so we both feel good? I'm not willing to let the job go undone, and you don't want me to nag."

The counselor suggested they have a nonverbal signal between them if the mother was wondering if the son was going to remember his chore. The son said it would be okay if his mother asked him if he was still planning to do what he agreed to—just not to do the chore for him.

Often we are unaware how we are upsetting our children and treating them disrespectfully. They get angry when that happens. Usually if we ask our children what they are angry about, and are willing to listen, they'll tell us.

derogatory comments about your children's other parent. This often results in a great deal of anger within the child against one of the parents. It can also result in aggressive behavior as a way of striking back at the perceived offending parent. Do not talk to your children as if they were another adult.

7. Don't be afraid of your own anger.

Learn to say "I'm angry." You provide a good model for your children when you express those feelings in words, instead of with displays of temper.

8. Model respectful ways for dealing with your own anger. Use emotional honesty: I feel _____ about _____ and I would like _____. Model taking time out until you can calm down and handle your anger in respectful ways.

9. Limit the amount of time spent watching television as it is filled with violence. Monitor what movies your children see. Have discussions with your children about the violence in video games and in music. Make your thoughts clear, but listen to theirs, too.

Life Skills Children Can Learn

Children can learn that what they feel is different from what they do—that it is okay to feel angry, but not okay to hurt others or to act disrespectfully. Children can learn that they can have power and control over themselves and their lives. No one enjoys feeling powerless, and children prefer to know how they can contribute and succeed without having to fight for their needs.

Parenting Pointers

1. There is a difference between aggression and assertion, and it is important to help children learn this difference. Teach children to ask for what they want; listen to their opinions. Show children how to get their needs met without putting someone else down.

2. Watch out for a double standard for girls and boys. Sometimes boys are excused for rude and hurtful behavior, or girls are discouraged from being outspoken and expressing their needs. It is equally important for boys and girls to know their feelings are okay, and that behavior is separate from feelings.

3. Not all anger is displayed. You may have a very angry child who holds all his anger inside. Look for signs that might include withdrawing from the family, passive-aggressive behaviors, and drug abuse.

ATTENTION DEFICIT DISORDER

"A teacher has suggested my child might have attention deficit hyperactivity disorder. She is complaining that he gets up and down from his seat and won't pay attention. I notice the same problem at home. He has trouble concentrating and finishing things he starts. The school psychologist says he may need medication, but I hate to give my child drugs. Are there alternatives?"

Understanding Your Child, Yourself, and the Situation

The conventional thinking about attention deficit hyperactivity disorder is that it is a neurological disability characterized by a developmentally inappropriate lack of control in attention, activity, and impulsivity. (Refer to John F. Taylor's *Helping Your Hyperactive or Attention Deficit Child*, Prima Publishing, 1990, for more information on the conventional thinking.) Our research has shown that children who show symptoms of ADD or ADHD could have parents who talk too much and follow through too little. It is our hope that anyone who works with children will be very careful about assigning labels.

Do some children have a longer attention span than others? Yes. Do some children have more energy than others? Yes. Are some children more extroverted and some more introverted? Yes. Some children eat too much sugar that can cause physiological changes that create hyperactivity. Some parents and teachers use teaching and discipline methods that drive some children "crazy." Children need to learn socially acceptable behavior and skills, but the truth is that children are just different, and not every child will be able to fit expectations of what a good child is.

The disease model is one way to understand behavior. We will share another way. We know we are dealing with a very controversial subject and we're sure you will want to investigate other theories. Just be sure to include all the latest research on the serious negative side effects of drugs when you're reading about the subject. Meanwhile try some of the following suggestions and watch how much "hyperactivity" will diminish (or be dealt with respectfully) and how you can help children learn skills to handle their short attention spans and other behaviors that can get them into trouble.

Suggestions

1. Beware of the terms ADD (attention deficit disorder) or ADHD (attention deficit hyperactivity disorder) because they often are used as a catchall. Avoid labeling your child, because the label can become a self-fulfilling prophecy and you may be missing something else that is really going on with your child.

2. Make special time a priority and find ways to truly enjoy your child during this time. Be sure to notice and celebrate successes of any size, and encourage your child's areas of interest.

3. Be willing to help your child according to his or her needs based on what your child actually does as opposed to what may be expected for his or her age group or intelligence level. If your child can't learn to tie a shoe in kindergarten, use Velcro until the fingers are ready, even if it takes longer than everyone else. Do not punish your child for not being "normal."

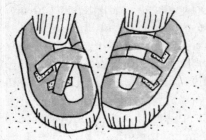

4. Use computers so your child can learn at her own pace and bypass the writing difficulties that are common. Some children who struggle with printing and writing by hand, or who agonize over spelling, excel when working on a computer. Would you expect your child to learn to tell time using a sundial before using a watch? We don't think so, yet you might balk at allowing your child to feel a sense of accomplishment by working with the computer instead of a pencil or pen.

5. Make sure you have the child's complete attention and say things only once. When the child is distracted, use simple and respectful cues like a tap on a table, a hand on a shoulder, or a one word reminder to regain focus.

6. Pay attention to ways that you may be invalidating the uniqueness of your child or putting pressure on her to perform according to your standards instead of her ability.

Planning Ahead to Prevent Future Problems

1. Use positive discipline tools to minimize misbehavior and encourage the child's best efforts. Attend parenting groups and read, practice, and review each topic in this book. Don't stray from the Positive Discipline path and don't take advice that is based on rewards or punishment.

2. One of the first things to do is notice your behavior. This isn't meant in a sense of blame; just be aware of what you're doing. Are you too busy to give your child enough time and attention for teaching and encouragement? Are you making demands instead of getting your child involved in finding solutions? Do you have too much sugar in the house? Is your child eating too much "fast food"? Do you talk too much and act too little? Does your child feel conditionally loved instead of appreciated for her strengths and uniqueness? If you notice these behaviors, you can choose to change them. When you do, you'll see big results in your child's behavior.

3. Use the mistaken goal information to understand the mistaken "belief" behind misbehavior and ways to encourage children so they don't need to misbehave. (See Part 1, What Is Positive Discipline?, for more information.)

4. To help children manage their attention span and behavior, provide extra struc-

ture for time and space. Use simple and consistent routines you create with your child. Help your child learn how to organize a place for everything close to where items are needed. Have an area near the door for things that come and go such as shoes, coats, backpacks, lunches, etc. Help children use binders, lists, and notes to keep information organized. Teach about time management with calendars, clocks, and timers. Provide special equipment like short, fat, bottom-heavy cups filled half full to minimize spills.

5. Observe your children at play to see how they prefer learning. Are they physically active? Do they prefer touch? Do they learn in short attention bursts? Use that information to create activities that emphasize your children's strengths or preferences.

6. Build your children's ability to concentrate by getting them into some kind of physical training that requires concentration, remembering sequences of moves, and physical and mental discipline. (It may be even better to do these activities with them.) Suggestions include aerobics, dance, martial arts, and sports. Help your child find activities he or she enjoys and can do well.

7. Help your child learn strategies to keep herself on track. Encourage her to use resources at school and in the community like tutors and study hall. Listen to her concerns about problem teachers and subjects and encourage him/her to research alternatives for those classes, including independent study. Be an advocate for your child. Your child's self-esteem and your relationship with him or her is more important than any grade.

8. Explore alternative learning opportunities at the school. Keep track of the teachers whom your children do well with and be prepared to discuss this with the school. The most helpful teachers are caring and flexible, while being well organized. Smaller classes and schools will also improve success. If you find that the teacher or school is not willing or able to meet your child's needs, be prepared to do whatever is necessary to protect your child from being punished for his or her difference.

9. Get your children involved in deciding what they should do at school when problems occur. Call a parent-teacher-child meeting to work together on non-punitive solutions. Some children decide it is best if they can walk around the room a few times and then return to their seats without getting in trouble. Others may need a quiet corner where they can go to spend more time on a task.

10. Prioritize your time and energy. An activity schedule that is too full or that doesn't allow for reasonable routines will soon lead to disaster.

Life Skills Children Can Learn

Children can learn that they have adults who consider their individual needs and help them learn skills so they have some sense of control over their lives. Instead of feeling like a victim of their behavior, they have a plan for controlling it. They learn it's okay to be a unique individual.

Parenting Pointers

1. Make sure you don't ignore yourself or the other children by focusing all your time and energy on one child. Take time for yourself and spend special time with the other members of your family.

2. Remember by adulthood most children with characteristics that could be labeled as ADHD have learned ways to channel their "hyperactivity" into successful careers.

BABYSITTING

"My child is five years old and has never been to a babysitter. My friends are putting pressure on me to use a sitter. They say that I'm doing him a disservice by not giving him the opportunity to get used to being with people other than his parents. I think my child will feel more secure if he gets to spend his early childhood years with me."

Understanding Your Child, Yourself, and the Situation

It is beneficial for you to be away from your children periodically, and it is beneficial for your children to be away from you occasionally. It is natural for young children to experience some anxiety at being separated from their parents, but this will go away if they have the chance to practice separation for short periods of time (see Separation Anxiety). Children develop courage and self-reliance when they learn that they can handle the separation. With overprotective parents who never leave them, they may have difficulty developing courage and self-reliance. Plus parenting a child, especially an infant, can be extremely draining, and one way to "fill your cup" is to take time for yourself away from your child and to take time as a couple without any children around.

Suggestions

1. Begin with small steps at birth. The first step is for the child to spend time in their own house with your partner or a relative while you take a few hours off and leave the house.

2. By the time your child is a month old, set up two-hour visits with a friend or relative at their place. Your child will be fine. Bring her favorite blanket and stuffed animal and go out and give yourself a break.

3. Find neighbors and/or friends who would be willing to swap child care.

4. Some parents of children as young as three months old handle babysitting by turning to infant day care. You may feel comfortable starting with two afternoons a week for a couple hours and increase the time with your child's age and your comfort level. Choose a place where the ratio of children to adults is low. (See Preschool and Day Care for information on how to find a "good" child care place.) Also look for a place where there are toddlers as well as infants. Babies love to watch older children and toddlers like to fuss over babies.

5. Our experience has been that thirteen- and fourteen-year-old teenagers often make the best babysitters. They are old enough to be responsible but usually more interested in the children than in members of the opposite sex. Of course there are exceptions. Be assertive about setting up guidelines with teenage babysitters. No phone calls from friends until the kids are sleeping. Spend time playing and reading with the children. Clean up messes. Also be clear about where you can be reached and what time you will be home.

6. Have a bag of special games and toys that you bring out only when the babysitter arrives. Ask babysitters if they have any games, toys, or books that would be a change for your children.

7. See Preschool and Day Care for hints on what to do when your children cling and cry when you leave.

Planning Ahead to Prevent Future Problems

1. Ask your friends, neighbors, church members, and school personnel whom they use for babysitters. Try them out at your home while you are there. They can play with baby while you take a bath, do a chore, or read a book.

2. Many young families get together in the neighborhood or at church or preschool and form babysitting co-ops where they take turns watching one anothers' children.

3. For kids who are four and older, get them involved in a planning session for what they will do with the babysitter: what games they want to play, what books they want to read, perhaps a popcorn party or baking frozen cookies. Plan a bedtime you can agree with and let them share or role-play how they will handle bedtime.

4. Continue to take a night off at least every couple of weeks while your children grow up. It's good for both of you.

Life Skills Children Can Learn

Children can learn that their parents like to spend some time away from them and that doesn't mean they don't love them They also learn that they are capable of

BOOSTER THOUGHTS A young working mother started her three-month-old daughter in infant day care. The day care provider complained that the little girl was too demanding and wouldn't sit quietly in her infant seat for the three hours she was there. The mother realized that this was the wrong place for her child and quickly found a place where the provider spent time holding her and letting her roll around on a quilt on the floor with plenty of infant toys.

◎

Cal and Connie couldn't wait till their mom left for work. They'd beg her to call the sitter because she was so much fun. She had a bag of costumes and put on shows with the kids and played games. There is no replacement for a fun and creative babysitter.

enjoying themselves when separated from their parents occasionally. They learn that manipulation doesn't work to stop parents from having a life separate from their children.

Parenting Pointers

1. If your children are complaining about the sitter or act afraid to go to child care, it is important to do some investigating or switch sitters to see what their reaction will be. There are some people and places that aren't a good match for your kids and it's okay to change.

2. If you are a working parent and need extended child care, make sure you find a place where the kids are fed, they have activities to do, and there is a regular routine for naps and toileting—and they are not plunked in front of a TV. Use the time in the car to visit with your kids, ask about their day, and enjoy them. When you get home, take a break and be with the kids instead of immediately beginning chores.

3. The rule of thumb for choosing a sitter is your feelings about the person and your kids' feelings about the person and not whether they are male or female. People of either gender can be a good child care provider if they are respectful to themselves and the children. Use local agencies to help find child care if you are unsure of whom to hire.

4. The babysitter's main job is to be with the children, not clean your home or do the dishes. If your kids are happy, don't make a fuss over a few messes.

BACK TALK AND DISRESPECT

"I asked my daughter to pick up her shoes. She replied, 'Why don't you. You're the mother.' I couldn't believe it. Why would she be so disrespectful? Even more important, what should I do about it? I can't just let her get away with that, but the more I punish her the worse it gets."

Understanding Your Child, Yourself, and the Situation

There are many reasons for back talk and disrespectful behavior. Sometimes children are simply testing their power—especially during the preteen and teen years. On the other hand, it could be that they feel that they have been treated disrespectfully (perhaps by parents who make demands or give orders) and are fighting back. Children might talk back to get a reaction—or may simply be having a bad day. Another possibility is that they have not been taught (by example or otherwise) respectful communication and interaction.

Suggestions

1. In a calm, respectful voice, tell your child, "If I have ever spoken to you that way, I apologize. I don't want to hurt you or be hurt by you. Can we start over?"

2. Count to ten or take some other form of positive time-out so you don't "back talk" in reaction. Avoid comebacks such as "You can't talk to me that way, young lady."

3. Use the "back talk" as information (it could tell you that something is amiss) and deal with it after you have both calmed down. Look for places where you have been turning issues into power struggles with your child.

4. Instead of focusing on the disrespect, focus on the feelings. Say something like "You are obviously very upset right now. I know it upsets me when you talk that way. Let's both take some time out to calm down. We can talk later when we feel better. I'd like to hear what you are upset about."

5. Do not use punishment to "get control." When you have both calmed down you can work on a respectful solution that works for both of you.

6. Share your feelings: "I feel very hurt when you talk to me that way. Later I want to talk to you about another way you could tell me what you want or how you feel." Or you could say, "Whoa, I wonder if I did something to hurt your feelings, because that certainly hurt mine."

7. Don't respond to demands. Decide what you will do instead of what you want to make her do. One possibility is to simply walk away. Instead of trying to control her behavior, control your own. Calmly leave the room without saying a word. If your child follows, go for a walk or get into the shower. After a cooling-off period, ask, "Are you ready to talk with me now?" This is most effective if you let your child know in advance what you will do. "When you talk disrespectfully to me, I will leave the room until we both feel better and can communicate with love and respect."

8. Use a sense of humor. Say, "I must have heard that wrong. I'm pretty sure you were meaning to say, 'Mom, would you mind picking up my shoes because I'm too lazy to do it myself right now.' "

9. If you are not too upset, try hugging your child. Sometimes children are not ready to accept a hug at this time. Other times a hug changes the atmosphere for both of you to one of love and respect.

Planning Ahead to Prevent Future Problems

1. Be willing to take a look at how you might be teaching the very thing you abhor in your child by being disrespectful to her. Have you created an atmo-

sphere of power struggles by being too controlling or too permissive?

2. Make sure you do not "set your child up" by making disrespectful demands. Instead of giving orders, create routines together during family meetings.

3. Instead of saying, "Pick up your shoes," ask, "What about your shoes?" You will be surprised how much more inviting it is to ask than to tell.

4. Once you have both calmed down, let her know you love her and would like to work on a respectful solution to what happened. Take responsibility for your part and work on a solution together.

5. Apologize if you have been disrespectful. "I can see that I was disrespectful when I demanded that you pick up your shoes. How can I ask you to be respectful when I'm not?" Let her know that you can't "make" her be respectful, but that you will work on being respectful yourself.

BOOSTER THOUGHTS From a note sent by a grateful parent: "I'm all choked up right now because my fifteen-year-old daughter just came in and said, 'Mom, are you planning to do some washing today so I can include my jeans, or should I put in a load before school?'

"It was such a respectful departure. Thank God for family meetings and calm dialogue instead of yelling, reacting, and the angry feelings we have experienced in the past."

◉

Two-and-a-half-year-old Ross threw his hat on the sidewalk and said, "I don't want to wear this hat. You get it and keep it for me."

His grandmother looked at him and said, "I'm sure there are a lot of people walking by who would love that good-looking hat. If you don't want it anymore, leave it on the sidewalk for someone else."

Ross looked shocked, put his little hands on his hips, thought for a minute, and then picked his hat up.

His grandmother said, "If you don't want to wear your hat right now, would you like to put it in the backpack? I'd be happy to open it up for you." Ross walked over, dropped the hat in the pack, put his hands back on his hips, and shuffled along the sidewalk with a grin on his face. Several bystanders gave Grandma a big thumbs-up.

6. Have regular family meetings so family members learn respectful ways of communicating and focusing on solutions.

Life Skills Children Can Learn

Children can learn that their parents are willing to take responsibility for their part in an interaction. They can learn that back talk isn't effective, but that they will have another chance to work on respectful communication.

Parenting Pointers

1. Many parents want to "set limits" and tighten controls to teach their children that they can't get away with misbehavior. This makes matters worse and does not teach respectful communication.

2. This is a good time to act instead of react. It is very tempting to get revenge by punishing when your children hurt your feelings. This models disrespect while trying to teach respect.

3. Remember to see mistakes as opportunities to learn—for both of you.

BATH TIME HASSLES

"Bath time is a nightmare at our place. My youngest screams if I try to wash her hair, *and my ten-year-old refuses to take a bath or shower unless I bodily drag him to the bathroom."*

Understanding Your Child, Yourself, and the Situation

Many young children resist bathing. (Then after they get into the tub, they often resist getting out of the tub!) When they become teens, they usually make up for lost time, sometimes showering several times a day. Infants no longer need to be bathed daily to prevent diaper rash because "wipes" are so effective. You and your doctor can decide how often is best. However at a certain age, most young children don't want to bathe at all. The more you try to force them, the worse it gets. Fortunately they won't die from dirt while you learn skills for avoiding bath time power struggles.

Suggestions

1. Young children love having a routine, especially when they have helped make a routine chart. Involvement increases cooperation. Bath time is part of the bedtime routine chart. (See Bedtime Hassles for instructions on creating the routine chart.)

2. Let reticent bathers know that it is not a choice to bathe, but that they can choose the days and time. This allows them to share the power and increases the possibility of cooperation.

3. When it is time for their bath, firmly but kindly remind them of their agreement and give them a choice: Would they like you to turn off all distractions, such as television, video games, and computers or do they want to do it? It may help to give them an egg timer to set ten minutes before bath time—again, so they can share the power and control. (Check out the cuddly stuffed animals with timers in their bellies at www.positivediscipline.com.)

4. Let children who never want to get out of the tub decide, using limited choices, if the bath should be fifteen or twenty minutes long, do they want to set the timer, or should you, and if they will open the drain or if you will.

Planning Ahead to Prevent Future Problems

1. Make bath time fun. Let the kids have special toys they can use only in the tub—anything that squirts or pours water is usually a lot of fun. Plan enough time so children can play in the tub. Sit in the bathroom with young children to make sure they are safe.

2. Young children enjoy bathing with their parents. When your child expresses his first need for privacy, it is time to allow him to bathe alone. Do not insist on

BOOSTER THOUGHTS A mother of an adopted, handicapped, three-year-old child shared that bath time was a nightmare. The little girl could speak only a few words, such as Mom. However she was bright enough to learn sign language. Her mother would put the little girl in the tub for a few minutes and then whisk her out, dry her off, and put her to bed. The little girl would kick and scream while her mother dried her off and put her to bed.

The mother attended a lecture by Stephen Glenn and realized she was not being very respectful by deciding when bath time was over. She decided to allow her child more choices. That night she put the girl into the tub and told her to call when she was ready to get out. After twenty minutes, the mother checked to see if she was ready. The little girl signed, "No." Mom checked again in thirty minutes and saw another, "No." After about forty-five minutes the little girl called, "Mom, Mom!" When her mother came into the bathroom, the little girl signed, "Out." It was the first time in two years that the little girl did not kick and scream while being dried off and put to bed.

him coming into the bath or shower with you.

3. Let children wash your hair and then you wash theirs. Use care to keep soap out of the eyes and use shampoos that don't sting. Some children do better if you wash their hair over the sink or in a shower and let the bath be a place to play.

4. For teens who want to take half-hour showers, talk about conserving water and respect for others who may also need hot water. With their help, pick a time that works for both of you and then set a shower timer.

Life Skills Children Can Learn

Children can learn good hygiene and respect for others. They can discover that a routine can be fun, and that self-care doesn't have to mean self-torture. Children can also learn that they have a right to privacy and that adults will respect that.

Parenting Pointers

1. If bath time is a drag because you are trying to rush the kids off to bed, think about making this a special time of day instead of a chore.

2. Two generations ago most people bathed once a week on Saturday nights to be civilized for church on Sunday. In much of the world bathing more than once a week is a luxury. Encourage children to bathe when necessary, but be flexible with "necessary" in order to encourage their cooperation. Kids often appreciate cleanliness more when they have experienced a serious lack of it.

BEDTIME HASSLES

"Our kids drive us crazy every night. They know it's time for bed, but they want another drink of water, one more story, the light on, the shades down, then the shades up. They keep us busy for an hour making extra trips to the bathroom and then scream like crazy when we finally refuse to come to their room one more time. The last straw happened the other night when our eight-year-old cried because he couldn't stay up as late as our ten-year-old."

Understanding Your Child, Yourself, and the Situation

There isn't a kid anywhere who doesn't try to extend bedtime at least once in a while. Wanting to belong and be part of the action is a human need. Serious bedtime problems, however, are most often created by parents who engage in power struggles. The more you involve children in the creation of routines, the more they experience organization and order. It's important for children to have input, but not to run the family. Parents who let kids work them like trained circus animals at night are clearly letting the kids call the shots.

Suggestions

1. Be available during the bedtime routine—which shouldn't take more than twenty to thirty minutes (see creating routine charts on page 56)—instead of trying to do ten other things. One reason children seek more attention is that they haven't received a good dose of your full attention.

2. Once you have given your undivided attention for at least twenty to thirty minutes of bedtime routine, stick to the allotted time for the routine. Your children know when you say what you mean and when you mean what you say. They know when there is room for argument and when there is not.

3. After your child is in bed and you have concluded the bedtime routine, do NOT lie with your child until she falls asleep. Once it is officially bedtime, it's time for you to get out of the room. Refuse to

play the power struggle game. If she leaves her room, gently take her by the hand and kindly and firmly, without talking, return her to her room. Don't explain or talk about what is supposed to happen next. Your child already knows. Actions speak louder than words, and don't leave room for argument. You may need to repeat this action several times before children learn that you mean what you say and will follow through with kind and firm action.

Children belong in their own rooms and their own beds. If they come to your bed in the middle of the night, take them gently and quietly back to their bed, give them a kiss, and walk back to your room. Do this as many times as you need to until your child knows that your bed is for you.

4. If your children have developed the habit of manipulation, it may take three to five nights of kindness and firmness (returning them to their beds, without words) before they learn they can trust you to mean what you say. Children feel more secure with parents who are kind and firm than with parents who can be manipulated or who are too firm without being kind.

5. If you have been engaging in power struggles or allowing your children to manipulate you, sit down with them and admit your mistake. Tell them that you have allowed them to form some bedtime

habits that aren't good for them or for you. This is a good time to start teaching them that mistakes are wonderful opportunities to learn, so now you can learn together how to solve the problem.

6. Some parents put locks on the outside of their children's doors to keep them in their rooms. This is dangerous and disrespectful. Keep taking your child back to her room. If you remain kind and firm, it probably won't require more than ten to twenty trips. Remember that weaning has never been easy for the "weanor" nor the "weanee," but is necessary for both to reach interdependence.

Planning Ahead to Prevent Future Problems

1. Involve kids in creating bedtime routine charts. (Each child can have his or her own.) Let them help you make a list of all the things that need to be done before they go to bed (bath, pajamas, brush teeth, pick up toys, homework, choose clothes for the next day, go to the bathroom, story time, hugs and kisses). Using limited choices, let them help you figure out how much time is needed and what time they need to start to complete everything on time. (Do they want to start at 7:00 or 7:05? Do they need one minute for getting into pjs or would they like two?) Small kids love having pictures of them doing each task pasted on their routine charts. The charts can be posted on the doors of their rooms.

2. When it is time to begin the routine, tell the kids it's time for bed instead of making demands (go brush your teeth, put on your jammies, etc). Ask, "What is first on your bedtime routine chart?" They love telling you and they feel empowered instead of engaging in power struggles.

3. Some kids find it helpful to play Beat the Clock at bedtime. Set a timer for the agreed-upon time, and let the kids scamper around getting everything done before the timer goes off. You might want to use one of the cuddly stuffed animals with a timer in its belly that can be found at www.positivediscipline.com.

4. Let the kids know that you will be available for story time ten minutes before bedtime. If they have completed their tasks, there will be time for a story; if they haven't, there is time for a tickle and a kiss, but the story has to wait until the next day.

5. For kids who think it's unfair that an older sibling stays up later, let them know it's okay to be upset, but it's not okay to stay up later.

6. As the kids get a little older, involve them in discussing bedtime and give them a limited choice, such as "You can decide if you would like to go to bed at 7:15 or 7:30."

7. As they get even older, let them pick any bedtime they like as long as the adults have "quiet-no-kid time" from 9:00 P.M. on. Bedtime means time to go to your room, not necessarily time to go to sleep. Kids are different, and some need more sleep than others. If they aren't bothering anyone else, show them how to turn off the lamp when they are through reading or playing quietly and let them fall asleep when they're ready. If they stay up too late and are tired the next morning, involve them in exploring what happened, what caused it to happen, and how they can solve the problem in the future. If they are late for school, allow them to experience the consequences with their teachers.

Life Skills Children Can Learn

Children can learn self-reliance instead of manipulation skills or dependence on someone else to help them perform the natural bodily function of sleeping. They can learn to respect their parents' need for time alone or time together without children around. They can learn that their parents will treat them with respect but will not become involved in their manipulation efforts. Children can learn that they don't always get what they want, that it is okay to feel upset about that, and that they will survive.

Parenting Pointers

1. It is better to teach children to listen to their inner voices about when they are

BOOSTER THOUGHTS One parent relates: "Our three-year-old continually came out of her room. We walked her back, and she kicked and screamed for an hour the first night until she fell asleep exhausted in her doorway. The second night she cried for half an hour. The next three nights this routine lasted ten minutes. After that bedtime became a fun time for us all with a pleasant routine filled with hugs, tickles, stories, and cooperation."

Another father found bedtime hassles ceased when he asked two questions while tucking his children in bed at night: "What is the saddest thing that happened today? What is the happiest thing that happened today?" After each question, he would listen carefully and then would share his own saddest and happiest moments of the day. This seldom took longer than two or three minutes with each child, although sometimes more time would be required. He said, "I was amazed at how much my children told me when I took the time to ask and to listen. The closeness we felt during these times seemed to help them settle down and be ready for sleep."

tired than to insist that you know when they are ready to go to sleep. It is also respectful to yourself to insist on a time the kids go to their rooms even if they don't go to sleep so you can have some time to yourself.

2. Some parents believe they are doing the loving thing by capitulating to the unreasonable demands of children. They are not thinking about the long-term effects of what this teaches children. It is not respectful to children to give them the impression that they can always have what they want. They need to learn that they can still survive disappointment and still be happy. Since you are giving your children lots of love during the bedtime routine and other times during the day, they will not be traumatized by learning that they can go to sleep by themselves. The opposite is true: they will learn the skills of capability and self-reliance.

BED-WETTING

"My eight-year-old boy still wets the bed. I've heard of all kinds of remedies from waking him up several times a night to getting a sheet that sounds an alarm. They all sound like a hassle for me or a frightening and intimidating experience for him. Any suggestions?"

Understanding Your Child, Yourself, and the Situation

If your child is four to five years old and still wetting the bed, it is cause for concern. If he or she has had many dry nights and then has a few episodes of bed-wetting, the behavior may be related to a stressor in the family, including a sign of sexual or physical abuse. Or it can be for any of the Four Mistaken Goals of Behavior (see Part 1, page 25). A child may unconsciously choose a mistaken goal when she experiences some kind of stress, such as a new baby in the house, divorce, or moving to a new location. If your child has never had a dry night, the bed-wetting can be the result of a physical condition caused by an immature bladder or a deep sleep pattern. The first thing to do is have a medical checkup to see if the problem is physical or developmental. Bed-wetting can be embarrassing for children and their family members, and often results in a lot of parental attempts to control the problem. Try some of the following suggestions instead.

Suggestions

1. If your family is going through a change that might create stress, such as the birth of a baby, moving, or a new job, spend extra time with your child to increase her sense of belonging and significance. The bed-wetting will stop when she feels secure.

2. A clue that bed-wetting is developmental, in addition to difficulty with bladder control during the day, is if the child is a heavy sleeper and has difficulty waking up in the night. Don't wake the child up unless he asks you for your help. Don't try to monitor his fluid intake before bed, or ask him if he has gone to the bathroom before bedtime. Instead let him know that some people take longer to develop bladder control, and that you are sure he will be able to handle it on his own schedule.

3. Instead of compounding the problem by using humiliation, offer positive support, understanding, and encouragement. Get into the child's world. Ask how she feels about the problem. Ask if she needs help or can handle it by herself. Listen respectfully to what she says.

4. Decide what you will do instead of trying to control what your child does. You might want to cover the mattress with a plastic sheet. You might want to make sleeping bags out of old sheets that are easy to throw in the washing machine. You may choose to stay out of his room because you don't like the smell. Whatever you do, do it with dignity and respect.

5. Offer these choices to your child as ways to improve the problem: Try to hold off on urination during the day to strengthen the bladder and experience a sense of control; ask if your child would

like you to wake him periodically during the night to empty his bladder—his choice; offer to purchase a moisture alarm that will wake him up so he can finish urinating in the bathroom; offer the help of a hypnotherapist.

Planning Ahead to Prevent Future Problems

1. Take a look at what you might be doing to create the need for undue attention, power struggles, revenge cycles, or helplessness. Many parents of bed wetters create this problem by nagging, reminding, coaxing, and trying to control the child's bladder. Stop! Instead spend special time with your child where you enjoy each other's company and play together. Get him involved in family meetings to solve problems, share feelings, and deal with hurt feelings. Give him meaningful jobs to enhance his sense of belonging and contribution.

2. Do not attempt toilet training too early. This invites behavior problems. We suggest waiting until the summer after your child reaches two and a half before you even start. Of course there are exceptions to this. Some children start the toilet training process on their own. Our point is that you shouldn't get uptight about it too early.

3. Teach your child how to use the washing machine. Even a three-year-old can handle this job. Also you could teach

him how to change his clothes and sheets in the middle of the night if he is uncomfortable. Once you have taken time for training, keep your nose out of his business and let him take care of himself however he chooses. He may choose to sleep in wet and smelly sheets and experience ridicule from his friends.

4. Share respectful stories about bed wetters so your children know it can be a common problem. Michael Landon wrote a television movie about bedwetting based on his childhood experi-

ence. We have a friend who said that in the U.S. Marines there was a special tent for bed wetters. The sergeant in charge woke the residents up every two hours.

5. If you travel or if your child wants to have an overnight, discuss with your child possibilities for dealing with the issue in public like special wetproof pants or a liner in a sleeping bag.

Life Skills Children Can Learn

Children can learn that their parents respectfully and lovingly will help them

BOOSTER THOUGHTS Here's the experience of one family: "We became familiar with our children's bladder control capabilities on family camping trips. If Josh announced that he needed to go to the bathroom, we knew we had about twenty minutes to find a suitable stopping place. If Katy said she needed to go, we knew we had about ten minutes. If Brian announced a need, we pulled over to the side of the road immediately.

Brian was also a bed wetter into his early teen years. We knew it was developmental and very embarrassing for him. At the age of fourteen, he was invited to an overnight campout with his friends. He stayed up all night because he was afraid he would wet the bed and be ridiculed. We were grateful that we knew his problem was developmental so we didn't add to his problems by hassling him. We simply gave him empathetic understanding and worked with him on many possible solutions. The funniest was our agreement that he would tie a string around his toe. Since I have to get up several times in the night to go to the bathroom, he asked me if I would pull on the string around his toe to wake him up.

Eventually we became so unconcerned about the problem, and Brian became so good about taking care of his own sheets, that we don't know for sure when he stopped wetting the bed. I think he stopped. I'll ask his wife.

deal with problems that are physical or developmental. Children can learn that what they do isn't a definition of who they are. They may be struggling with a problem, but that doesn't make them worthless individuals.

Parenting Pointers

1. Toileting is a natural bodily function. Children want to do what adults do unless it becomes a power struggle and children feel they have to win or lose their sense of self.

2. Avoid comparing your child to other children. So what if other children stay dry sooner than your child? Love your child just the way he is—unconditionally.

BITING

"How can I make my child stop biting her little friends? She probably won't have any before long. Whenever she is frustrated, she just bites."

Understanding Your Child, Yourself, and the Situation

We hope it helps you to know that biting is a temporary behavior in some children from the time of teething until around age three. Even though biting is embarrassing for parents of the biter and upsetting to the parents of the child who gets bitten, biting is not a misbehavior in most cases, but a lack of skills. Children who bite often do so when they become frustrated in social situations and do not know how to express themselves in acceptable ways. Some toddlers may bite because that is their way of exploring: "I wonder what Suzie will taste like or feel like."

Children also may bite their parents and think it's a game. It is important to deal with biting in ways that do not leave residual problems, such as children feeling they are bad or deciding it is okay to hurt others smaller than they are because adults punish by hurting them.

Suggestions

1. Do not bite the child back or wash the child's mouth out with soap. Hurting a child does not help her learn to stop hurting others.

2. When your child has a history of biting, supervise closely. Intervene quickly when disputes begin (see Fighting [Friends]).

3. Watch the child closely for a few days during play with other children. Every time she looks like she is ready to bite, remove her from the scene and say, "It is not okay to bite people. Use your words." She may not understand what you are saying, but will understand your actions. If the child is preverbal, after saying it is not okay to bite, offer a

distracting choice, "Do you want to play on the swings or with the blocks?"

4. When your child bites before you are able to intervene, comfort the biter first and then get her to help you comfort the child who has been bitten. Give her a hug and say, "Look. Sally is crying. What could we do to help her feel better? Let's put some ice on her bite and you can help me give her a hug." Some people object to this idea, but think about what you are modeling. You are teaching her to focus on comforting another child instead of hurting. She won't understand lectures; she won't understand punishment; yet she will feel the energy of compassion and helping others. When her brain develops enough to understand, she will remember the compassion instead of shame and pain.

5. Apologize to the parent of the child who has been bitten. Be honest with your feelings. "I feel very embarrassed about this, and I will do everything I can to help my child stop biting. However I do not believe punishment solves anything." Comforting the child who has been bitten, after comforting the biter, models loving ways to deal with people.

6. If you are dealing with another parent who thinks you should punish your child, stand your ground. "I can see we have different philosophies and that it would not be respectful for either of us to try to change the other." Then walk away with dignity and respect for yourself and the other person. Your child is more important that what others think of you.

Planning Ahead to Prevent Future Problems

1. Play Let's Pretend with your child. Pretend the two of you are fighting over a toy and that you are going to bite her. Stop and ask, "How would you feel if I bit you? What would you like me to do instead?" Then pretend you are fighting over a toy and let her try whatever she suggested instead of biting.

2. Brainstorm other ways to handle problems. If she doesn't have any ideas of what to do instead of biting, teach her to use your words. You can suggest things, such as telling the other child "I'm mad at you" or "Let me have a turn" or "I'll go get another toy and we'll trade" or asking an adult to help settle the problem. Then play Let's Pretend so she can practice these ideas.

3. Use emotional honesty: "I feel bad when you bite other people because I don't like to see people get hurt. I wish you would find something else to do besides bite people." Or "I don't feel safe around you right now because you are biting. I'm going to go somewhere safe till you are ready to try again."

4. If you child is preverbal, it is important to accept the fact that she needs close supervision and kind and firm distraction until she learns socially acceptable ways to handle frustration. Take comfort in knowing that she will have stopped biting by the time she goes to kindergarten—if not much sooner.

5. When you are supervising closely, you will be able to understand what your child is trying to accomplish. Verbalize her intention before showing her another way: "I can see that you want the ball. It is not okay to bite to get the ball. Let's find another ball."

6. If your child is at the teething stage and continues to want to bite, offer her a stuffed animal, a cloth, or a teether to bite. Help her find relief for sore gums by offering a frozen juice bar.

Life Skills Children Can Learn

Children can learn that it is not acceptable to hurt other people. They can learn that their parents love them no matter what they do, and adults will help them find acceptable ways to solve problems. Instead of developing a victim or bully mentality (which often happens if you comfort the child who has been hurt while shaming the biter), children can learn they are capable of solving problems in ways that don't hurt other people, and that their parents will remain lovingly kind and firm while they learn.

BOOSTER THOUGHTS Susan and her new boyfriend, Frank, spent a lot of time arguing around Susan's two-year-old, Betsy. Whenever the two would argue, Betsy would walk up to Frank and bite him. Frank thought Susan was letting her child get away with murder; Susan thought Betsy was trying to express her opinion about the arguments. What Susan and Frank both agreed on was that it was time to help Betsy find another way to express herself. First they decided to argue somewhere else. Then they agreed to really pay attention, because they could tell when Betsy was about to bite. She would get a gleam in her eye, throw her head back, and charge with an open mouth. At those times, whoever was closest would hold Betsy away from Frank and say, "People aren't for biting. If you want to bite, Mom will get you a rubber toy to bite." It only took a few days for Betsy to stop biting Frank.

Parenting Pointers

1. Some people think comforting a child who has just bitten another child is rewarding the misbehavior. It is not. Hugging gives the child reassurance of your love while not accepting the child's behavior. Hugging helps the child feel belonging and helps reduce the need to misbehave. It also shows the child an acceptable way to behave—to love the other person and tell him or her what you don't like.

2. Some parents believe you should bite a child back to teach them how it feels. Children under the age of three or four cannot understand an abstract concept such as empathy. They do understand concrete examples and will mimic what you do. By biting them back, you are actually teaching them that biting is an acceptable way to behave—even if it hurts. Biting back models revenge (which honest parents would admit is what they really want) and violence. Remember the long-term results of what you do. Do you want to teach revenge and violence or respectful solutions? Learning takes time, whether it be reading, driving a car, or social skills.

BOREDOM

"My child complains about being bored and expects me to drop everything to entertain him."

Understanding Your Child, Yourself, and the Situation

We live in a society where children are used to being entertained. Televisions, computers, and video games are major contributors to this dilemma. Children can passively sit and watch *Sesame Street* or play with a video game and be highly entertained. (It is true that *Sesame Street* is educational and that electronic games teach eye-hand coordination, but they also limit creativity, resourcefulness, and proper brain development.) Another contributor to this program is the belief of many parents that they must fix every problem their children have. Children do need your help to become involved in sports, outside interests, hobbies, and other activities (in moderation), but they do not need to be entertained or have their time controlled by parents every minute of the day.

Suggestions

1. Ask, "What ideas do you have to solve your problem?" If your child says, "I don't know," do not get hooked into giving him answers. You might say, "I have faith in you to work it out."

2. Listen with empathy and acknowledge without trying to fix the problem: "I can understand that. I feel bored myself sometimes." If your child keeps badgering you, keep listening and acknowledging with noncommittal sounds, "Umm.

Uh-huh." Eventually your child will get so bored with his unsuccessful efforts to get you to handle his problem that he will find something else to do.

3. Another possibility is to say, "That is good. Perhaps your mind and body need some quiet time. Would you like to learn how to meditate?" She will probably run the other way. However meditation could be a good practice to model for your children and to teach when they are ready.

4. Limit time for television, computers, and electronic games so children are used to being creative and resourceful instead of being passive or depending on electronic gadgets (see Electronics).

5. Tell your child that you will be happy to show him how to clean the oven or wash windows as a solution to boredom.

Planning Ahead to Prevent Future Problems

1. During a family meeting or a problem-solving session, brainstorm with your children to see how many ideas you can all come up with for things to do when they feel bored. Have each child choose his favorite things from the big list and make his own "Things to Do When I'm Bored" list.

2. The next time a child complains, say, "You might want to check your list."

3. Once a child has a plan for what to do when bored, you can give a choice: "You may either continue to be bored, or you can find something to do. I have faith that you will do what is best for you."

Life Skills Children Can Learn

Children can learn that it is up to them to take care of how they structure their free time. They can go to others for understanding, emotional support, and inspiration, but ultimately they are capable of taking care of themselves and the skills of self-reliance can begin getting exercised early in life. They can also learn that boredom is the precursor to creativity and that boredom, if allowed to happen, usually leads to some new and exciting activity.

Parenting Pointers

1. Children have a sense about when they can hook you into feeling sorry for them and try to fix things. You may have noticed that when you try to fix things

> **BOOSTER THOUGHTS** Children, when allowed to be bored for more than an hour, become so bored with boredom that they begin to use their native intelligence to find an alternative. When my child says, "Dad, I'm bored," I say, "I understand that, honey. Let me know how it works out." Then I get on with what I'm doing.

for them, nothing you do is good enough.

2. Have faith in your children. It is contagious. Your children will follow your lead and develop faith in themselves. Don't be afraid to involve your children in tasks around the house or in a routine that fills in some of their time. This will also help with boredom.

3. Your children may be bored because they need some adult help to set up programs, activities, and outside interests that they can be engaged in. There are cases where children are bored because they are being neglected by their parents and need adult help to learn about resources that are available and how to access them. Others are bored due to overstimulation.

4. Avoid the temptation to believe it is your job to protect your child from experiencing every frustration life has to offer. However don't see this as an excuse to go to the other extreme and justify neglect.

BULLYING

"My son comes running home every day from the bus stop because one of the bigger kids is shoving him and threatening to beat him up. I don't want to come off as an overprotective parent or make it harder for him by showing up at the bus stop, but I don't know how to help, and I've got to do something."

Understanding Your Child, Yourself, and the Situation

Who hasn't dealt with a bully at one time or another? Every school has them. Every neighborhood has them. They victimize others through threats and actions, sometimes making life almost impossible for children. If you are a pacifist, you may not want your child to fight back, but what other tools are you giving your child to deal with the problem? It won't go away by ignoring it.

Suggestions

1. Encourage your children to tell an adult that they are having a problem, even if

the bully is threatening retribution if they tell.

2. Suggest a buddy system so that your child doesn't have to be alone. Kids can watch out for one another, and there is safety in numbers.

3. Enroll your child in a self-defense course that stresses self-discipline, self-control, and self-esteem. When your child feels stronger and more able, he won't have to be aggressive. His confidence will come from within.

4. Observe and talk with your child to make sure that he isn't teasing or baiting someone who then responds by bullying.

5. When your children complain of being bullied, listen carefully and make sure you let them know that you are sorry they have been treated badly, that it's not okay, and that you are there to help.

6. Suggest that your child try any of these suggestions from www.familyeducation.com/whatworks: use a sense of humor, walk away, refuse to fight, make friends with the bully, let the insults go, scream, or reason with the bully.

Planning Ahead to Prevent Future Problems

1. Ask for help from the school to increase supervision and set up a zero tolerance policy for violators.

2. Suggest that the school set up a safety training and peer mediation program where bullies and their victims can talk together and show ways to engage in nonviolent conflict resolution.

3. Make your physical presence known where bullies operate. Take your morning coffee and walk to the bus stop, standing a distance away, drinking your coffee.

4. To avoid raising a bully, make sure your child feels a strong sense of belonging and knows he isn't powerless. Have regular family meetings so your child learns to focus on solutions.

5. Turn off those TV shows and stop watching movies and allowing your child to play video games that are murder simulators.

6. Be careful that you don't encourage good guy/bad guy identities in your own family. If you are constantly picking on one kid and protecting another, you could be setting up a potential victim/bully situation without realizing it. If you are physically abusive, you are teaching your child to do the same.

7. Have regular family meetings to increase the chances that your children don't become bullies because they have learned to respect differences and to focus on solutions to problems.

BOOSTER THOUGHTS Grant moved into a new apartment complex and was constantly picked on by the big kids in the complex. One day his little sister put her hands on her hips and said to the bullies, "If you don't leave my brother alone, I'm going to kiss you." The big boys scattered in all directions yelling, "Help, help. Don't let her near me."

❂

Doug's big brother Gus was a bully. Whenever his parents weren't looking, he kicked his younger brother, stepped on his toys, broke his belongings, and spit in his room. Nothing the parents did made a difference. The parents lectured Gus, threatened him, spanked him, yelled at him, and made him spend time in his room. They tried to protect Doug and fix the situations, but nothing worked.

One day Doug's father sent him to a karate school. After a year of karate, he told his big brother that he now knew how to be a lethal weapon, and that he wouldn't hesitate to use his new skills if he had to. He did a little demonstration of what he had learned so far, showing his family a series of kicks, hand movements, and flips. From that time on, Gus left him alone.

Life Skills Children Can Learn

Children can learn ways to deal with situations without being violent or being victimized. They can also understand that bullies are made, not born, and that much of their behavior is learned or a release for feelings of isolation.

Parenting Pointers

1. Don't create bullies by being disapproving, emotionally or physically abusive, or solving problems by threatening and pushing others around.

2. Teach your children nonviolent conflict resolution skills. Encourage your children to physically avoid bullies by staying out of their range, and never hesitate to ask for adult help if the situation is too difficult.

CAR HASSLES

"Is it possible to go for a ride in the car with children who wear their seat belts, don't fight, and don't talk or chew in your ear? I can hardly stand getting in the car

with my kids or my friends' kids. And what can I do to avoid being the perpetual chauffeur?"

Understanding Your Child, Yourself, and the Situation

If you recognize yourself in this picture, you aren't alone. This is a common problem for parents and children. It can even be dangerous. Who knows how many accidents have been caused by fighting children or by parents who are trying to hit their kids in the backseat while they drive. It's the law that you and your children be either belted in or in car seats. Since cars are essential transportation in most families, it is important to find ways to make car travel safe and comfortable for everyone.

Also it is important for children to be involved in healthy activities, and this requires transportation—which doesn't mean you should buy a limousine and don a chauffeur's hat. Instead use the need for transportation as an opportunity to teach respect and problem solving.

Suggestions

1. Do not start the car until everyone is in a buckled car seat or has buckled a seat belt. Each child needs to have his or her own seat and a seat belt to ensure safety in the car. Kids know when you mean what you say, and they know if they can manipulate you to give in to their demands.

2. Decide what you will do. Let the kids know that when you feel it is unsafe to drive because it's too noisy, you'll pull over until things calm down. Have this discussion at a time other than while in the car. Then if the kids start yelling or fighting, simply pull over and wait without saying a word. Do this as many times as you need to until the kids learn you really mean it.

3. If you are having car problems with kids, leave plenty of time to get to your destination so you can have time for training. When children remove their seat belts or act in ways that make driving unsafe for you, pull the car over at the first available spot and wait until they rebuckle. It is best not to say a word. When they know the rules in advance, it is disrespectful to assume they need reminding. Actions speak louder than words.

BOOSTER THOUGHTS* The Jones family is very excited. They have just finished planning a day at the beach. Seven-year-old Jason and five-year-old Jenny have promised that they won't fight. Mr. Jones has warned, "If you do, we'll turn around and come back."

Of course the kids fight and Mom and Dad do not follow through on their promise. And so the story goes. Throughout the day Jason and Jenny fight, and Mr. and Mrs. Jones make threats. At the end of the day, Mr. and Mrs. Jones are angry and threaten never to take the kids anywhere again. Jason and Jenny feel bad that they have made their parents so miserable. They are beginning to believe they really are bad kids.

Now let's visit the Smith family. They have just planned their trip to the zoo during their weekly family meeting. Part of the planning included a discussion about limits and consequences. After a discussion where the kids promise not to fight, Mrs. Smith says, "Well then, is it okay with you if we stop the car if you do forget? We don't think it is safe to drive when you are fighting, so we'll just pull over to the side of the road and wait for you to stop. You can let us know when you are ready for us to drive again. How do you feel about that solution?" Both kids agree with innocent enthusiasm.

Typically it doesn't take them long to forget their promise, and a fight begins. Mrs. Smith quickly and quietly pulls off to the side of the road. She and Mr. Smith take out magazines and start reading. Each child starts blaming the other while whining about their innocence. Mr. and Mrs. Smith ignore them and just keep reading. It doesn't take long for them to catch on that Mom and Dad must mean what they said, and they agree to stop fighting.

Mr. and Mrs. Smith stopped using words and instead followed through with kind and firm action. Because the kids are kids, they just had to test the waters one more time. When their parents started to follow through again the kids knew they meant what they said. They were left with the feeling, not that they were bad kids, but that they were clever enough to figure out a solution to the problem and that cooperation was the most effective alternative. *Kind* and *firm* are key words to remember to make follow-through effective.

---

*Adapted from *Positive Discipline for Step Families*, by Jane Nelsen, Cheryl Erwin, and H. Stephen Glenn, an e-book available on www.focusingonsolutions.com.

Planning Ahead to Prevent Future Problems

1. Equip your car with legal seat restraints for everyone in the family, and be sure to use them.

2. Introduce your children to car travel at an early age and take frequent short trips. If the trip is long, make frequent stops so the kids can get out, run around, and stretch. It may help to have a timer so the kids can see how much longer before you stop.

3. Before you get in the car, ask the kids for their ideas of what will help make the trip more comfortable and fun for them. Then let them discuss rules for safety. Children cooperate better when they are involved in creating the rules.

4. If you are going on a long trip, have the kids bring toys and books to entertain themselves. With infants an adult should sit in the backseat with the child until they have more travel time under their belt. Some families have special baskets or backpacks with toys that can be used only in the car. Others pop a video into their traveling DVD player.

5. If the kids are fighting over who sits in the front seat—and what kids don't fight over this?—let them work out a system for taking turns. Have them inform you when they are ready to put their system into effect. You do not need to know their system; they do. If the fighting starts again, they can all sit in the backseat until they are ready to try again.

Life Skills Children Can Learn

Children can learn that the car is not a place to move about or create unsafe situations and that they can cooperate to help their family be safe. They can learn that parents mean what they say and will follow through with dignity and respect. They can learn that their parents also consider their needs.

Parenting Pointers

1. Take time for training. Leave for your destination at least ten minutes early. This allows time for you to pull over and read a novel while your children test you to see if you mean what you say.
2. Everyone is expected to wear his/her seat belt. It goes without saying that you need to wear your seat belt too.

CELL PHONES

"My ten-year-old daughter insists that all her friends have a cell phone and that she must have one too. I think she's too young. My fifteen-year-old has a cell phone because I want to know where he is and be able to stay in touch with him, but he is running up a huge bill each month with his calls and text messaging. I don't want to

take the phone away, but I can't afford his habit. What should I do?"

Understanding Your Child, Yourself, and the Situation

Your kids want a cell phone to communicate with their friends, take pictures, text message, be cool, play games, and surf the Internet. You want them to have a cell phone because you are concerned for their safety and need to be in touch with them. Or maybe you are afraid they'll be upset with you if you refuse to get them a cell phone. Or worse yet, you are worried about your child being deprived. The situation is out of hand. Men, women, and children walk around with phones glued to their ears. Having a cell phone has become as important as having a toothbrush. You live in a cyberworld filled with technology that your children often seem to handle more easily than you do, but you still want to provide some guidance.

Suggestions

1. If you don't want your child to have a cell phone, say no! Include information about how and when your child will be able to use a cell phone. If your child needs to have a way to get in touch with you, purchase a prepaid phone card for your child.

2. If you do decide to get your child a cell phone, expect her to cover part of the cost. If she doesn't have the money to pay for her calls over the allotted amount, let her know you'll hold her phone for her until she has reimbursed you for the extra charges.

3. If your child has a tendency to run up charges, purchase a plan with a prepaid service that shuts the phone off except for 911 calls once the money is used up.

Planning Ahead to Prevent Future Problems

1. During a family meeting (or during a joint problem-solving session) discuss all the rules for having a cell phone that you can agree on in advance. Make sure the kids know how many minutes a month they have, how to check on how many they have used, and what will happen if they break any agreements (see Suggestion 2 above). Make sure they know when nighttime free minutes begin. Set up a system for how kids can pay for minutes used over their limit. Talk with your kids about how easy it is to accidentally use extra minutes and incur extra expenses.

2. If you decide it is okay for your child to have a cell phone, make sure he uses a headset until further research proves that cell phones *don't* cause brain tumors from the radiation emitted. Explain the potential dangers of a cell phone to your child.

3. Have your children research and report to you on what the school policy is for

cell phones and discuss that policy with your children.

4. Do not let your children drive and talk on the cell phone. Some states have fines for this, but even if they don't, your new drivers need to focus on driving.

5. Discuss cell phone manners and the importance of shutting off cell phones in movies or other public venues. Discuss why it is rude to speak on a cell phone while interacting with others.

6. Talk to your child about how to handle predators and telemarketers who may abuse the cell phone. Register cell phone numbers with state and national do not call registries.

Life Skills Children Can Learn

Kids can learn how to set priorities and budget for something that is important to them. They can also learn about responsible use and etiquette for owning a cell phone.

BOOSTER THOUGHTS The father of two elementary-school-age twins told the kids that they couldn't have a cell phone until they were in middle school. When the kids entered sixth grade, they asked again for a cell phone. Their parent said, "You need to give me ten good reasons why you need a phone." He had to laugh when the first reason was to call home. "Right," he said. "I'm sure you'll be calling us all the time." The second reason wasn't much better. The kids said that they needed a cell phone so their parents could call them, to which the parent responded, "We don't really need to call you that often." As the kids searched for more reasons, it became evident that they wanted a phone because everyone else had one.

The parents were wise. They told the kids that the minimum monthly cost for a cell phone was around $5 a week. When the kids offered to pay out of their $10-a-week allowance, the parents suggested another plan. They said that they would split the cost with the kids as long as the kids paid for any excess charges for overusage. They also suggested that there would be no credit, so if the kids owed money, the phones would stay with the parents until all excess charges were paid.

The parents also said they would pay for the basic phone, but if the kids wanted upgrades, they would have to pay for them. The kids asked if they had a choice, and the parents said, "No." And even when the kids had to go without movies and lunch money to cover their mistakes of overusage, the parents stuck to their guns. Before long the children had become responsible cell phone owners.

Parenting Pointers

1. It is not your child's birthright to have a cell phone. It is not your job to provide your child with a cell phone.

2. Don't underestimate the creativity and ingenuity of your children if you are considering adding the Global Positioning feature to their cell phones. You may be spending a lot of extra money to know where your child is . . . while the cell phone may be parked somewhere else.

CHORES

"It is a constant battle to get my child to do his chores. He always says he will, but then he doesn't without constant reminders and hassles that usually end in punishment. I feel like giving up and doing everything myself, but I know he needs to learn responsibility. Maybe he's just too young. When are children old enough to help with chores?"

Understanding Your Child, Yourself, and the Situation

It's never too early or too late. Kids need to know they are important, useful, contributing members of your family. If they don't find satisfaction in positive ways, often they find not-so-positive ways to feel important. Helping with chores builds skills, makes them feel useful, and teaches appreciation for the work that needs to be done and for those who do it. It may be tempting for parents to do everything themselves, thinking it is easier and will get done "properly." When parents take that attitude, they deprive their kids of opportunities to learn cooperation and responsibility.

Suggestions

1. Get the kids involved in brainstorming a list of jobs that need to be done to help the family.

2. Take time for training and work with your children until they learn how to do the job. When they feel ready to do the job alone, let them know you are available if they need help. Step back and don't jump in unless asked. If there are problems, work them out at a family meeting instead of criticizing at the moment.

3. Provide kid-size equipment, such as a small broom, a feather duster, or small gardening tools.

4. Create a chore time when everyone works together, rather than handing out lists of chores for kids to do. Use the "As soon as _____ then _____" formula. "As soon as your chores are done, then you can go out and play."

5. Notice the contribution instead of the quality of work done. If your very young child loses interest halfway through emptying the silverware in the dishwasher, thank her for the half she did instead of insisting she finish every last piece.

6. When accidents happen, avoid punishment. Instead focus on how to fix the problem. If your child spills the dog food, ask, "What do you need to do to fix that?" This teaches that mistakes are wonderful opportunities to learn.

7. Don't feel sorry for kids and do their jobs for them because they have a lot of homework or play in a sport. Help them organize their time to continue helping the family.

8. Sing the cleanup song as you work, or play lively music.

9. Make sure the jobs are appropriate for the age. The following list provides some suggestions. Remember to work with two- to three-year-olds instead of expecting them to do chores alone.

Two- to Three-Year-Olds

Pick up toys and put in the proper place.

Put books and magazines in a rack.

Sweep the floor.

Place napkins, plates, and silverware on the table (perhaps not correctly at first).

Clean up what they drop after eating.

Clear their own place at the table and put the dishes on the counter after cleaning the leftovers off the plate.

Wipe up their own accidents.

Help put groceries away on a lower shelf.

Unload utensils from the dishwasher.

Fold washcloths and socks.

Choose their outfit for the day and dress on their own.

Four-Year-Olds

Set the table—with good dishes, too.

Put the groceries away.

Help compile a grocery list; help with shopping.

Follow a schedule for feeding pets.

Help do yard work.

Help make the beds and vacuum.

Help do the dishes or fill the dishwasher.

Dust the furniture.

Spread butter on sandwiches.

Prepare cold cereal.

Help prepare plates of food for the family dinner.

Make a simple dessert (add topping to cupcakes or ice cream, Jell-O, instant pudding).

Hold the hand mixer to whip potatoes or mix up a cake.

Get the mail.

Five-Year-Olds

Help with the meal planning and grocery shopping.

Make their own sandwich or simple breakfast, then clean up.

Pour their own drinks.

Tear up lettuce for the salad.

Put certain ingredients into a bowl.

Make their bed and clean their room.

Scrub the sink, toilet, and bathtub.

Clean mirrors and windows.

Put white clothes in one pile and colored in another for washing.

Fold clean clothes and put them away.

Answer the telephone and begin to dial it.

Do yard work.

Help clean out the car.

Take out the garbage.

Six- to Eight-Year-Olds

Shake rugs.

Water plants and flowers.

Peel vegetables.

Cook simple foods (hot dog, boiled egg, toast).

Prepare their school lunches.

Help hang their clothes in the closet.

Gather wood for the fireplace.

Rake leaves and weed.

Take a pet for a walk.

Keep the garbage container clean.

Clean out the inside of the car.

Straighten or clean out the silverware drawer.

Be responsible for a pet, that is, caring for a hamster or lizard.

Nine- to Ten-Year-Olds

Change sheets on the bed and put dirty sheets in the hamper.

Operate the washer and dryer, measuring detergent and bleach.

Buy groceries, using a list and doing comparative shopping.

Keep their own appointments (dentist, doctor, school) if within biking distance.

Prepare cookies and cakes from mixes.

Prepare a family meal.

Receive and answer their own mail.

Wait on guests.

Plan their own birthday or other parties.

Use simple first aid.

Do neighborhood chores.

Sew, knit, or weave (even using a sewing machine).

Wash the family car.

Earn their own money (babysit, do neighborhood yard work).

Pack their own suitcases.

Be responsible for a personal hobby.

Eleven- to Twelve-Year-Olds

Put siblings to bed and read to them.

Clean the pool and pool area.

Run their own errands.

Mow the lawn.

Help a parent build things.

Clean the oven and stove.

Be responsible for a paper route.

Help do family errands.

*Planning Ahead to Prevent
Future Problems*

1. Use the family meeting to set up chore responsibilities.

2. When you are in a power struggle, say, "Let's put this problem on the family meeting agenda and solve the problem when we both feel better."

3. If the kids forget to do a chore, use a sense of humor. One mother brought a pot of soup to the table and pretended to ladle the soup into imaginary bowls. The table setter for the evening suddenly realized he had forgotten his job and ran quickly to bring the bowls before the soup hit the table.

4. Use mutually agreed upon nonverbal reminders if a chore is forgotten. Many kids like the signal of an upside-down plate at the table. When the plate is upside down, it reminds the kids that part of the routine needs to be completed before sitting down to eat.

5. For ages three to four, make a chore spin wheel. Find pictures that represent chores such as dusting, putting the silverware on the table, unloading the silverware from the dishwasher, cleaning the sink, or putting clothes in the washer or dryer. Paste these pictures around the edge of a paper plate. Make an arrow from heavy construction paper. Use a brad to punch a hole through the arrow and the center of the paper plate so the arrow spins around the plate. Let kids spin the wheel to see which chore they will do for the day.

6. For ages four to six, make a list of chores kids can do for their age level. Put each chore on a piece of paper and put them in a box for each age level. As part of the family meeting, let kids pick out two chores they will do every day for that week. They can pick new chores at the next family meeting so no one is stuck with the same chore all the time.

7. For ages six to fourteen, use a kitchen white board to list chores that need to be done that day (at least two for each child). Each child (on a first-come basis) chooses the chores he wants to do and then crosses them off the board after they are done.

8. By ages fifteen to eighteen, kids may have strong problem-solving skills. Have regular discussions at family meetings to agree on what chores need to be done and to put in place a plan that works for everyone.

9. Refrain from nagging and reminding. If a job is forgotten, ask the kids to look at the chore list to check if everything is done.

Life Skills Children Can Learn

Children can learn that they are part of the family and people need their help. They're

> **BOOSTER THOUGHTS** Three-year-old Kristin asked if she could help clean the house in preparation for company coming to dinner. Her mom asked if she would like to do the bathroom, and she said, "Yes!" Kristin took a can of cleanser and a cloth into the bathroom. When Kristin was finished, she said to her mom, "The bathroom is all cleaned up! I like helping you clean." Her mom got busy and forgot to check Kristin's work.
>
> The guests used the bathroom several times during the evening without comment. After they left, Kristin's mom went into the bathroom. To her shock, she saw that Kristin had used an entire can of cleanser. There was white powder everywhere. Kristin's mom laughed to herself as she thought about what her guests might have been thinking when they took their turn in the bathroom. She realized Kristin needed more time for training in the use of cleanser.

capable and skilled and can be useful to themselves and others.

Parenting Pointers

1. It is normal for children to avoid chores after the age of three or four. (Remember when they were two and said, "Me help, Daddy!" "Me do it, Mommy!"? Too often you discourage toddlers by saying, "No, you're too little. Go play. Go watch TV." Then you wonder why it is difficult to get them encouraged to help again.) However just because it is normal for children to avoid chores, that doesn't mean they shouldn't do them.

2. Children aren't born with the competency to do jobs efficiently and quickly. As a matter of fact, it's usually *more* work to have them help. But the extra effort it takes to involve and train children to help the family is worth it because they learn skills such as keeping commitments, planning ahead, following through, organizing their time, and juggling several tasks at a time.

3. Do not use punishment when chores are not done. Keep going back to the family meeting to work out the problems and come up with solutions.

CLOTHING POWER STRUGGLES

"What should I do when my child refuses to wear the clothes I pick out?"

Understanding Your Child, Yourself, and the Situation

You want children to learn to think for themselves, yet too often you think for your children, especially in areas where children could safely have a say, like deciding what they'll wear. You want your children to develop a healthy self-esteem, yet don't give them the opportunities to experience their own capability (a primary ingredient of healthy self-esteem). You can avoid a lot of power struggles by looking for areas where children can have positive power. Clothing is one of those areas. If you stop being concerned about what others will think if your child is not dressed "properly," you can let clothing choices be a time for your child to develop a personal style and make an identity statement.

Suggestions

1. Yes, you get to dress those babies the way you like. But soon your children will start having opinions about what they like and don't like to wear. As early as possible, allow your children to choose their own clothes. Ask yourself, "Is it more important that my children be neat and color-coordinated or capable and confident?" Grin and bear it when they leave the house in mismatched or "terrible" outfits. Allow them to experience the natural consequences of their choices and learn for themselves. They will get plenty of feedback from their peers—or they might start a new trend! If your children are interested in learning about color coordination, you can offer your help with choices and they can see you as a consultant rather than a boss.

2. As children develop stronger tastes, allow them to go shopping with you and make some choices within your budget. Get them involved in preplanning to decide what they need in advance—how many pairs of pants, tops, shoes, socks, and underwear. Help them figure out how much they have to spend so they know that if they spend too much on one item they have to give up another item.

3. When it is very important to you that your child dress a certain way (the president is coming to dinner) tell your child why it is important and ask for cooperation. Invite a bargain: "I don't bug you six days a week, so I would appreciate it if you would do this for me when it is really important to me."

4. If you are really concerned about how your child is dressing, sit in front of their school for ten minutes as the children arrive. You will probably find that your children fit in perfectly with the outfit of the day if they are picking out their own clothing.

5. If your child wears a uniform to school, and puts up a fight some mornings, or

stretches the boundaries, let your child experience the consequences of a wrong choice with the faculty.

6. All children go through periods where their dress choices may be a worry: too much black, too much skin showing, too many low-hanging baggy pants. Feel free to share your feelings with your children, as long as you listen to theirs. They'll be interested in your input as long as it doesn't sound like a lecture.

Planning Ahead to Prevent Future Problems

1. Set up a time in the evening (as part of their bedtime routine) for children to choose the clothes they want to wear the next day. When they have plenty of time to choose, they usually choose quickly. Children often use time restraints as a time to rebel. When they have limited time to choose they usually want the shirt at the bottom of the clothes hamper and insist that it be washed, dried, and ironed in twenty minutes because it is the only thing in the world that they can possibly wear.

2. During the winter put summer clothes in storage boxes (and vice versa). This reduces unreasonable choices.

3. Set up a clothing allowance (see Allowances). Children are more likely to take better care of their clothes if they know they have to last until their next clothing allowance time.

4. If children share clothing with their friends, stay out of it. Many children have found ways to extend their wardrobe by swapping. If clothing gets lost or isn't returned and your children are on a clothing allowance, allow them to experience the consequence of their behavior by waiting until the next financial installment to replace a lost item.

5. Respect the desires of your children so you don't invite rebellion. If you are worried about what your friends think about how your child dresses, ask yourself if your friends would really think you picked out those outfits.

6. Teach your children to throw dirty clothes in a laundry basket instead of rewearing them.

Life Skills Children Can Learn

Children can learn that their choices are respected so long as they are not harmful to themselves or others. They can learn from their mistakes and develop judgment skills. They can also learn that there are times when respect trumps a personal statement.

Parenting Pointers

1. Respect invites respect. When you show respect to your children, they are more likely to respect your reasonable wishes.

2. Children need to "rebel" a little to test their powers and find out who they are separate from their parents. When you

allow them to rebel in safe areas (like choosing their own clothes even when you can't stand their choices) they have less need to rebel when they get older in areas that are not safe, such as drugs. Before interfering in a choice your child is making, ask yourself these questions: Will this choice be life-threatening to my child? Is there any possibility that someday my child may need to make a choice when I'm not around? If it's not life-threatening and if you want your child to be able to make good choices when you're not around, back off.

3. Allow your children to make choices and mistakes while you are still around to give support and have some influence, instead of having them wait until they are on their own and make bigger mistakes because they haven't learned.

BOOSTER THOUGHTS We heard from a father who had a style-conscious daughter. He gave her a back-to-school clothes allotment, and she rushed out and decided that instead of several pieces of clothing, one Ralph Lauren original would be her sole purchase. Dad carefully explored the implication of that decision: "Honey, have you considered what kinds of things you will have to wear day in, and day out?"

"Yes, I have, Dad. This is real neat and real important. This is what I want."

Dad asked, "Do you understand when your next school-clothes allotment will come?" She verified that she understood it would be the following December and that it was now the beginning of September. That confirmed, she went ahead and bought her Ralph Lauren original.

Within a week she was bored stiff with the outfit, and her friends were even asking her if she washed it at least. This touched off a great round of creativity. Having no budget, she took over some extra-large T-shirts her dad had marginally worn out, got out the sewing machine, and decorated the shirts with drawstrings, rickrack and ribbons, fancy buttons, and appliqués. Somehow she made it until December. When she received her next school-clothes allotment, she bought several interchangeable outfits sans designer status in order to have a little more flexibility.

This father would have canceled out a lot of important learning if he had gone out and bought his daughter a new wardrobe while pointing out the deficiencies in her judgment. In experiencing the consequences of a choice that, at worst, could produce only inconvenience and a little embarrassment, his daughter became more confident and self-assured. When she went out to shop again, she showed better judgment and a clearer understanding of what she was doing.

CRUELTY TO ANIMALS

"My little boy kicked the cat. I was so upset. I spanked him and told him he should never be cruel to animals. The very next day he was squeezing the cat and practically choking her to death. How can I teach him to be kind to animals?"

Understanding Your Child, Yourself, and the Situation

It is normal to feel angry and indignant when you see cruelty to animals, but remember that it does not help to treat children with the same kind of cruelty. Spanking hurts children just as much as kicking hurts animals. Worse yet, the level of anger you show your child usually translates to the level of anger your child shows the animals. While it can be extremely frustrating and painful watching very young children learn to play with pets, it can also be extremely rewarding. When your children are young, get animals they can have a relationship with so they can experience the unconditional love that comes from growing up with a pet. At the same time, keep in mind that small children may show love by hugging too vigorously or experiment by kicking or poking just to see what will happen, so a certain level of vigilance, persistence, and patience on your part is needed. Help them find other ways to express their love and curiosity. Chronic sadistic acts may indicate a more serious disturbance that requires professional help.

Suggestions

1. You should definitely consider having animals living with you. It is important to teach your child how to relate to them.

2. If you are overreacting to how your child treats a pet, as in the above case, separate the child from the pet. Then cool off and apologize to your child for spanking him. Tell the truth. Tell him that you were angry about the way he hurt the cat, but that was not an excuse for you to hurt him. Your child can learn more when you explain that you were angry after you have calmed down instead of yelling in anger in the moment.

3. Get into his world and make a guess about how he felt when you spanked him: "I'll bet you didn't like it when I spanked you. It probably made you feel angry or hurt." Wait for a response, listen, and validate his feelings by saying, "I would probably feel the same way."

4. If it happens again, take quick action. Separate the cat from the child and say, "The cat is not for hitting. Be gentle with the cat. You can pat the cat or snuggle the cat. If you hit or kick the cat, the cat is going to have to go somewhere else where it is safe and you can both try again later." You may have to do this several times.

5. Allow for breaks by having a safe place where your pet can rest up for the next round. Most dogs and cats will run and

hide from a child if they are not being treated right.

6. Show your child how to pet and snuggle an animal in a safe way. Teach your child that the animal's body is precious just like his is.

Planning Ahead to Prevent Future Problems

1. Decide what you will do and tell your child, "I won't hit you anymore because I don't want you, the cat, or anyone else to experience that kind of disrespect." Model what you want your child to learn. You may also be modeling disrespectful methods with your pets, perhaps unconsciously or perhaps because you think that is the best way to train a dog or cat. Make sure you practice what you preach and stop using punitive methods with your pets. You can learn how to parent your dog using the Positive Discipline methods by reading *Pup Parenting* by Lynn Lott, Jane Nelsen, and Therry Jay, Rodale Publishing, 2006.

2. Invite your child to think by asking, "Can you remember how to pet the dog gently? Would you like to sit on the couch and I'll put the cat in your lap so you can snuggle? Shall we put the dog on a leash and take her for a walk? Would you like to try again and pet the cat gently?" Wait for a response and listen.

3. Teach your child that feelings and actions are different. It is okay to feel angry. It is not okay to do things that hurt others. Help him find acceptable actions. "What else could you do when you are angry or hurt that won't hurt other people or animals? What could we do to make the cat feel safe and you feel safe?"

4. When children hurt animals or other people, it is usually because they feel hurt themselves (unless they are too young to know that a hard squeeze hurts). See if you can guess what your child might be feeling hurt about (perhaps a new baby has joined the family, or parents are divorcing, or he was hurt by punishment). Share your guesses with him in a friendly manner to see if you're right. Work together on solutions to see if you're right.

Life Skills Children Can Learn

Children can learn how to love and care for a pet without abusing the animal. They can also trust that they won't have to suffer to learn. They can learn to be respectful because they are treated respectfully. They can learn that it is okay to try again when they make a mistake and that sometimes taking a break is the best solution for all concerned, even the family pet.

Parenting Pointers

1. Children learn what they live and you are their teacher. If they live with

BOOSTER THOUGHTS Rosie used to dress her cats in doll clothes. She would bend their little limbs this way and that as she squeezed them into their outfits. Her mother watched in horror as they scratched and bit her. The cats' behavior never discouraged Rosie, and her behavior never discouraged the cats. In fact to Mom's amazement, they lived in her room, slept under her covers, avoided the rest of the family, and ran to her like a dog would when she came into view.

Sometimes the best solution to cruelty to animals is to let the child and the animal work it out.

cruelty, they learn cruelty. If they live with respect, they learn respect.

2. Children deserve the same kind of compassion and protection from harm that you give animals.

CRYING

"My child is so sensitive that he cries at the drop of a hat. I find this so annoying. How can I get him to change?"

Understanding Your Child, Yourself, and the Situation

Feelings give valuable information about who you are and what is important. Children need to learn that it is okay to feel whatever they feel. Some children cry easily because they have a sensitive nature and this is their way of expressing themselves. Other children cry to seek attention, power,

revenge, or as a display of inadequacy. Some children cry out of momentary disappointment, anger, or frustration. And, of course, babies cry because it is their only means of communication. The key is to know your child well enough to know the difference, and to have the parenting skills to deal effectively with each situation.

Suggestions

1. Take your child on your lap (sit down next to children over seven) and ask, "Would you like to tell me about what's wrong?" Then be quiet and listen.

2. When your child has stopped talking, stifle the temptation to lecture, explain, or try to fix things for the child. Ask, "Is there anything else?" This question often encourages the child to go to deeper feelings.

3. After a long enough silence to be sure your child is through talking, and feels calmer, ask, "Would you like to brain-

storm with me on some solutions?" Many times there is no need to work on solutions. Your child simply needs comfort and to be listened to and taken seriously.

4. When your child feels too upset or hostile to sit on your lap or to talk, say, "Don't stuff your feelings. You have a right to them. Let yourself feel sad. Let me know if you want to talk about it." Then leave the room if the child is being verbally abusive to you, or say, "Would you be willing to go to your room or somewhere else that helps you feel better until you feel like being around people? If not, I'll go to my room, and you can come get me when you are ready."

5. You might use reflective listening, which can be done with your mouth shut: Hmm. Umm. Then allow him to work out the problem for himself—unless he asks for your help.

6. You could use active listening, which means hearing between the words and verbalizing his deeper feelings: You feel really angry, hurt, upset—or whatever you think he might be feeling. Again

sometimes that is enough. It can be so validating to a child to feel understood.

Planning Ahead to Prevent Future Problems

1. Start early to teach your child that feelings are okay by not invalidating their feelings. When your child says, "I'm hungry." Don't say, "No you aren't. You just ate twenty minutes ago." Say, "I'm sorry you are hungry. I just cleaned up from lunch and I'm not willing to fix any more food right now. You can either wait until dinner or you can choose something from the healthy snack shelf." This is respectful of the child's feelings and needs and your own.

2. Teach children to use emotional honesty to express their feelings: "I feel _____ because _____ and I wish _____." (I feel upset when my brother knocks over my Legos because I worked hard on that building, and I wish you would tell him to leave my toys alone.) Using emotional honesty does not mean others will feel the same or give you what you want.

3. Encourage children to put things they are upset about on the family meeting agenda so the whole family can help with solutions.

4. Your child needs unconditional acceptance for who he is. If he is sensitive, accept this personality trait even though

BOOSTER THOUGHTS Julius spent a lovely day at the beach with his grandmother. When it was time to go he turned on his "water power" and started to cry. You would think his little heart was going to break as he sobbed about having to leave. His grandmother was able to get his attention long enough to ask, "Would you like to say good-bye to the ocean?" Immediately Julius was distracted from crying so he could carry out his task to help the ocean feel better. "Bye-bye, ocean, I will miss you. I'll see you tomorrow." The tears stopped and Julius felt comforted. And so did the ocean.

he is different from you or your ideal. It will also help if you focus on the positive side. Many women wish they were married to men who were more sensitive and vice versa. Diversity in personalities is one of the things that makes the world interesting.

5. Anytime a behavior becomes a pattern, advance planning is appropriate. Tell your child that you respect his right to feel what he feels. If he would like your problem-solving help, he can let you know when he is ready. Let him know that it is not effective to try solving problems at the time when he is upset, but that you will be available if he wants your help to solve the problem later. (Helping children solve a problem when they ask for help is much different from trying to help because you feel the need to rescue or overprotect.)

6. Never compare one sibling to another, or to anyone else. This is disrespectful and discouraging.

Life Skills Children Can Learn

Children can learn that their feelings are important and others will listen to them and help them share their feelings respectfully. Children learn that feelings are not right or wrong. They are just feelings. Feelings give valuable information. Feelings are separate from actions. Children can learn that by expressing their feelings, they feel better. They learn that it is okay to feel what they feel, and that they can deal with their feelings, and so can their parents.

Parenting Pointers

1. Crying and laughing are natural, healthy processes for relieving stress—for both boys and girls. Usually people who are taught not to cry have to laugh twice as much to break even because they laugh to cover up pain.

2. Children should be allowed to cry in the interest of their mental health. However if you think they are using water power

to manipulate you, acknowledge their concern without buying into their manipulation.

3. It is not your job to fix your children's feelings. It is your job to accept that your children have feelings, to help your children name the feelings and express them in respectful ways.

DEATH AND GRIEF

"My child and I were watching the news and saw a story that involved death. My child seemed agitated and confused. How do I approach this issue?"

Understanding Your Child, Yourself, and the Situation

Death is an inescapable part of living, but in this culture we often avoid or deny the issue. The media may make death look so awful and violent that it becomes depersonalized. Even when death comes as a natural process for aging grandparents, it usually happens away from home and excludes children. These issues make it difficult for children to have a healthy understanding and perspective on death. Talking about death, though challenging, is an important part of parenting that can provide information, support, and comfort. It's also a way to find out what your children already know and what their misconceptions might be.

Suggestions

1. Don't try to hide death and dying from children. Give children permission to talk about death and dying by your ability to do the same. Help them learn to be part of it by talking openly about people who are dying and encourage children to talk with the dying person. Prepare children for what they will encounter if they visit the dying person. If visits aren't allowed, let your child call or send cards and letters. When someone dies, don't send your child away. She needs comfort too.

2. When you lose someone close to you, don't hide your grief from your children. Let them see that it's okay to be sad.

3. Allow children to participate actively in acknowledgments of death, especially of people close to them, so they can achieve a sense of completion. This includes attending funerals, wakes, and memorial services, planting a tree or creating a memory box that sits out for everyone to enjoy. Prepare children ahead of time for what they will be seeing and allow them their choice as to whether they participate or not. Let them help with planning anniversaries of a death.

4. When a pet dies, involve the children in planning an appropriate service and burial. Use this as an opportunity to discuss their perceptions of death as part of

life. Encourage the kids to express gratitude for the time they had together.

5. When children are exposed to violent death, discuss openly their fears and apprehensions. Help them identify resources they have so they don't have to feel so vulnerable. These might include praying, writing in a journal, drawing, and talking to people including teachers and friends.

6. Don't expect your children to understand about death from one conversation. Children of different ages have different life experiences, so you may need to bring up the subject often. Some children may deal with grief for five minutes, while others may hang on to fears about their own mortality or worry that they could lose both parents and have no one to care for them.

7. Children can be very literal, so don't use words like he went to sleep, he left us, he's happy now, we lost him, he got sick and died, he died because he's old. These phrases conjure up all sorts of fantasies and fears about what it means to die.

8. Explain that different people have different beliefs about death and what happens when a person dies. Stress that all views are worthy of respect.

9. When someone close to your children dies, balance the expression of pain by talking about the happy times and the good memories. Do not remove photos of the person who died or treat the death as though the person had never lived.

Planning Ahead to Prevent Future Problems

1. Talk with children about preparation for natural disasters that could happen in your area. Make sure they are prepared with a fire safety, earthquake safety, or tornado or hurricane safety plan for your home. This may help them feel less vulnerable when they know what to do. If children are worried about international events that could lead to war, encourage them to write letters to their congressmen and the president.

2. Look for signs that your child may be grieving a loss and be prepared to comfort and console. If your child asks when you will die, reassure your child that you will probably live a long time and that if something happens to you there are lots of people who love her and who will care for her. It's also okay to say, "I don't have all the answers."

3. If your child is feeling guilty or thinking he caused a death, keep communication open. Listen and reassure.

4. Watch out for comparing living children to those who have died. No living being can compete with an "angel."

BOOSTER THOUGHTS A little girl and her sister were killed in a car accident. Her classmates held a class meeting and were invited to celebrate how this little girl had touched them. Each student had a chance to share an appreciation for the girl who had died. Then the teacher asked her students, "What are your concerns now?" Some of them were afraid to go home. Many had never dealt with death before and didn't know what to do. They brainstormed and found several suggestions. One was to set up a phone tree so they could call each other, even in the middle of the night. They came up with a list of people they could talk to during the day. Many kids had different people they felt they could talk to during school hours: janitors, librarians, a lunchroom supervisor, counselors, teachers, the principal, and one another. It was decided that anyone could get a pass to go talk to someone whenever they felt the need. They decided to make circle pictures of the little girl on ribbon pins that they wore for a week in her memory. They planted a tree that they purchased and nurtured throughout the year in memory of the little girl. The kids became role models for the adult school personnel on the many alternative ways to deal with grief.

◎

Single mother Susan and her young son, Drew, were worried about who would die first, so they made a pact. The pact was that whoever died first would somehow come back and let the other person know he or she was okay, whether it was in dreams or in a special sign.

When one of Susan's friends lost a baby, Susan comforted her by saying, "I have a theory about babies who die. I think that all babies bring love, and they all have a mission. Sometimes it takes them years and years on this planet to accomplish that love and that mission, and sometimes it's accomplished while they're still in the womb. I believe that when they leave us early it's because they came and did their mission and taught us a lesson. Now it's our job to figure out what that lesson is."

When Drew's friend since second grade shot and killed himself, Drew's theory was that even though he was really sad that his friend wasn't here anymore, now he had a personal guardian angel. Drew was sure he had other guardian angels, but he didn't know them personally. Now when something good or exciting happens in Drew's life, he pictures his friend—his guardian angel—smiling and helping from above.

5. Encourage your children to make scrapbooks, photo albums, or keep journals to record their feelings.

6. When your child has experienced loss, remember that grief takes time. Do not assume that one time for expressing pain and care or one ceremony is enough.

Life Skills Children Can Learn

They can learn that death is part of life and they can face their fears about the future with help and courage. They have many personal resources for dealing with traumatic events. They can also learn to value life more when they know that death is part of it.

Parenting Pointers

1. Work through your own attitudes about death and dying.

2. Share your own thoughts and fears about your immortality.

3. Welcome each day as a gift and share that with your children.

DEFIANCE, DISOBEDIENCE, AND REBELLIOUSNESS

"My child refuses to cooperate with anything I ask of her. She is what you would call a strong-willed child—defiant, disobedient, and rebellious. I have tried every punishment *in the book and nothing works. Some have suggested she has an oppositional defiant disorder and needs to be on medication. This seems too extreme to me, but at this point, I just don't know what to do."*

Understanding Your Child, Yourself, and the Situation

You and your child are in a power struggle that can easily turn to revenge. The more you try to force your will or give in to your child's demands, the more she will defy you and the more deeply discouraged you will both become. Defiant, disobedient, and rebellious children are gifts sent to parents who need to practice inviting cooperation instead of practicing power over others, or being too lenient.

Suggestions

1. The first thing to do is to look at your own behavior. Defiance, disobedience, and rebellion is often a direct response to parents who are excessively controlling or overly protective.

2. If your child is an arguer, she may have someone nearby who gives her arguing practice. If it's you, practice letting your child have the last word. (This is harder than you think. Try it.)

3. Get into your child's world and make some guesses to learn what is behind the defiance. For example: "Could it be that

you are angry because you think I boss you around too much?" "Could it be that you feel hurt because the baby gets so much attention?" You can usually guess what is going on in your child's life that may be provoking defiance. Your child will feel validated and understood when you guess correctly. If you guess incorrectly, try again.

4. Let your child take the lead whenever possible by offering limited choices. For instance, ask your child, "Do you think you are ready to cross the street by yourself, or would you like me to hold your hand?" "Would you like me to hold on to the back of your bike and help you practice, or can you ride it by yourself?" "When you use the car, are you willing to bring it back with the tank at least half full, or do you want to lose the privilege of using the car?"

5. Some children will push and push until they get a spanking. Then they settle down. They have been trained not to settle down until they are spanked. Instead of spanking, hold the disobedient child firmly on your lap. No matter how much she struggles, do not let go until she settles down. With an older child say, "I'm not going to punish you. I am sorry I have used those methods in the past and wish to change our relationship. I'm not happy with what you are doing, but I love you and would like your help so we can stop fighting with each other and work things out together instead."

6. Instead of telling your child what to do, try asking her what needs to be done. "What do you need to do before you cross the street?" "What was our agreement about what time you will return the car?" This usually invites a child to think and use his or her power to solve the problem instead of defying your direct orders.

7. Let your child know that you need her help and say, "I would appreciate anything you could do to help." This often invites cooperation instead of defiance.

8. Emotional honesty is another help. Remember to use the "I feel _____ because _____ and I wish _____" formula.

Planning Ahead to Prevent Future Problems

1. This is an opportunity for you to learn how to invite cooperation. Pay attention to how much talking you are doing. Are you barking orders, nagging, and scolding? Your child may be "parent-deaf" because you talk more than you act. Talk less and act more if this is the case. Don't say anything unless you mean it, and if you mean it, give the matter your full attention. Say what you mean kindly and firmly then follow through on what you say.

2. For a child who has a pattern of defiance, disobedience, or rebellion, create time for training. (This includes training

BOOSTER THOUGHTS Thirteen-year-old Billy was often called a defiant child by people who spent time with him. He did act like a know-it-all, refusing to listen to anyone. The more others yelled at him, the more he tuned them out and did the opposite.

Billy, his family, and friends went skiing. The ten people in the group spent a lot of time looking for Billy, who took off ahead of everyone and seemed to get "lost" a lot. Everyone was angry with Billy and alternated barking orders at him, threatening him, or whispering behind his back how difficult he was. No one was having any fun.

Billy's older cousin rode up the lift with him and said, "Billy, there's something I want you to think about as you ride up the lift. I'd like your opinion about an idea I have, but I don't want you to tell me what you think until we get to the top of the hill. I was thinking that it might work best, since we're such a large group, to suggest that everyone wait at the top of the hill for the entire group before starting down. I'm not sure if this is a good idea, so please give it some thought and let me know your ideas at the top of the lift." The two boys continued up the long lift talking about baseball, school, and friends.

Billy never said a word at the top of the lift, but the rest of the day he waited patiently for the group to assemble before skiing. He stopped more frequently to look back and wait for stragglers. He had a big smile on his face.

Billy's cousin invited cooperation, and Billy felt important because his cousin asked for his opinion instead of telling him what to do or scolding him one more time. Inviting cooperation works wonders with a defiant child.

for yourself in kindness as firmness.) Take your child someplace such as the park. The moment he starts defiant behavior, take him by the hand and take him home, saying, "We will try again tomorrow." If you are with other people and don't want to spoil their fun, take the defiant child to the car. Have a book handy so you will have something to do while you wait for him to say "I'm ready to try again." Let your child know in advance that this is what will happen. Do not minimize the effectiveness of having an opportunity to make a mistake and try again, and again, and again!

3. Give limited choices and ask questions instead of giving lectures. Ask for your child's opinion and input. Really listen to what he tells you.

4. Get your children involved in problem solving during family meetings. Children are seldom defiant, disobedient, or rebellious when they have been respectfully included in the decision-making process.

5. Many times children become defiant and disobedient because they feel conditionally loved. Make sure your children know you love them unconditionally—and that you know you can find solutions to problems that are respectful to everyone.

6. Choose your battles and let things go that aren't that important. Ask yourself if you will remember or care a week or month or year from now about the issue that seems so important to you in the moment. It takes a lot of energy to plan ahead and follow through to make real changes, so don't waste your energy on issues that aren't that important.

Life Skills Children Can Learn

Children can learn that cooperation works better than arguing when everyone is treated respectfully. They can learn that parents mean what they say, but also allow and respect appropriate choices.

Parenting Pointers

1. Children prefer to cooperate and do what's in their own best interest, but if you treat them disrespectfully, they are willing to suffer great personal pain to show you that you can't boss them around.

2. If you wait and watch before jumping in and controlling, kids will usually do the right thing. If they make a mistake, it's okay to help them correct it or ask how they might do it differently next time. Often it's enough to ask "Would you like to try again?" instead of becoming controlling or punitive.

3. Many children are very independent. Instead of seeing your child as defiant, can you think of the child as assertive and self-confident? Maybe this child needs a bit more room and is feeling suffocated by your hovering.

DEMANDING

"My three-year-old son wanted his milk in a special glass instead of the one I gave him. My nine-year-old thinks it is my job to drive him everywhere. My teenage daughter insists that I type her school papers at midnight. I want to help my kids out, but I wonder if I am spoiling them and teaching them to be demanding and to expect special service from others. On the other hand, if I don't respect their requests, am I damaging their self-esteem by teaching them that their desires are not important?"

Understanding Your Child, Yourself, and the Situation

This is an excellent question that could be asked by all parents who are interested in developing healthy self-esteem in their children. One of the major causes of low self-esteem in a child is not being listened to, taken seriously, and affirmed. However some children become demanding because parents do too much for them, so children develop the expectation that their demands will always be met. It is important to understand that fine line between pampering and becoming a slave to every demand, and discounting children's wishes by negating their importance.

Empowered children have opinions and want to be involved in decision making. Demanding children want everything their way. They are often referred to as "difficult children." Punishment does not help these children, nor does giving in. All kind and firm suggestions help parents avoid power struggles and use methods that teach children important life skills such as cooperation and problem solving.

Suggestions

1. It isn't your job to drop everything and give in to your children's demands. Do not feel guilty when you respect yourself and your needs by saying, "I'm sorry, but I have other plans." You are doing yourself and your child a favor.

It is not respectful to children to teach them that it works to be forgetful, thoughtless, and demanding.

2. Help your child fulfill her own desires by giving her whatever training she requires to learn to meet her own needs, that is, put glasses in a reachable place so she can get one and pour her own milk, create car pools for driving, set deadlines for when you're willing to type a paper, and stick to them.

3. Ask what and how questions to help your child figure out what she can do to solve a problem.

4. Offer a limited choice: "Can you get another glass of milk by yourself, or would you like my help?" "Would you like to ride your bike to the game or call Justin's mom to see if she can take you? I'll be happy to do pickup." "If you'd like me to type your paper, I'll be happy to if I get it by nine P.M. Otherwise you are welcome to use my computer to type it yourself."

5. Discuss the principle of give and take at a family meeting and work on plans that allow for it. "I'm willing to contribute my time and car to help you with transportation. What are you willing to do to help me?" "I can type papers if you take the boys to soccer practice and pick them up." "I can drive and pick up for practice if you do my dishes tonight." Be ready with sug-

gestions about where you would appreciate some help.

6. Include calendar time at every family meeting so upcoming transportation, homework help, etc., can be planned in advance.

7. Find solutions other than taking total responsibility yourself. If your kids are using you as a chauffeur, create car pools with other parents, encourage children to ride their bikes when appropriate, check bus schedules, etc.

8. Help your children help themselves by keeping them company while they learn new skills such as calling other parents and friends to plan alternate transportation, practice pouring their own milk, learning how to type a paper, etc. Don't expect your children to do this alone or think it is your job to do this for your child. Work together as a team. It takes a little extra time, but your children will learn a sense of responsibility for planning ahead.

9. With older children simply say, "Sounds like a reasonable request to me, and I'll bet you can figure out a way to get what you want." Then let them do it, instead of feeling it is your job to do it for them.

10. When your child asks you to do something he or she can easily do, smile and say, "Good try!" Then let your child do the task without your help.

Planning Ahead to Prevent Future Problems

1. When your child is a preschooler, create solutions to recurring problems. For example, if he always demands a special cup, set up a place in a low cupboard for his dishes and a low shelf on the refrigerator with milk and juice in small pitchers, so he can help himself.

2. Take time for training—teach children to clean up spills and to wash their dishes before returning them to the cupboard. Give enough information so that children understand the needs of the situation. For example, milk needs to be cleaned up so it won't sour and smell bad and so we can enjoy a clean kitchen.

3. It is difficult for children to associate time and the inconvenience of others with things they want. They need your help to make this connection and plan for it. Be very clear when you will be available to help your child. For example, if your child demands you do laundry at the last minute, tell your child you will be happy to wash clothes that are in the hamper on your laundry day. All other clothes will have to wait, or, if age appropriate, you will be happy to show your child how to use the washer.

4. Have faith in your child and verbalize encouragement: I have faith in you. You can do it. You are a good problem solver.

5. As soon as your children reach the age of four, family meetings provide an

BOOSTER THOUGHTS Twelve-year-old Janet loved ballet and decided she would like to take classes five days a week. Janet's mother was excited that her daughter wanted to continue with ballet and proud of how well she was doing. However she worked full-time and knew that she wouldn't be able to get away from work to drive five days a week. Mom told Janet she would have to find a car pool arrangement for the days she couldn't pick her up.

Janet objected that no one lived near her. Mom helped Janet check out the bus schedule and figure out how to take the bus to class. Janet was not happy about having to carry all her dance gear to school and lug it on the bus along with homework, transfer downtown, and wait forever for the bus.

Mom explained that she wasn't trying to make Janet suffer, but really couldn't leave work to take her so she needed to think about how important dance was to her. Janet ended up taking the bus. While it was very difficult, she decided the sacrifice was worth it. Years later she realized she had acquired skills and self-confidence that came in handy when she decided to travel around the world.

⊚

Clark took over the household chores for his wife when she was laid up recovering from surgery. He was amazed at how much time it took to do all the work and frustrated that he rarely had a minute to himself. His children constantly needed his help. He tried his best to accommodate everyone's needs as cheerfully as he could, but his patience was wearing thin.

What bothered him most was when he was ready to leave and his children were running around at the last minute doing things they should have done sooner and making him wait. He talked to the kids about this and they promised to do better, but nothing changed. One day he lost it and said, "That's it! You are both grounded for the weekend for making us late today."

His children begged and pleaded for him to relent, but Clark held firm. His oldest was especially

excellent opportunity for them to learn cooperation skills.

Life Skills Children Can Learn

Children can learn that it is okay to want what they want, but it is not okay to demand special service from others. They feel better about themselves when they learn to be self-reliant and respectful to others. Children also learn how to plan ahead to get their needs met and to handle the disappointment of not always getting what they want.

panicked as he had made an important commitment to be at his friend's birthday party overnight for the weekend, but no matter how much he argued, his father would not change his mind.

The boy called his grandmother complaining about the injustice of the situation. She asked how this came about and he told her the story, minimizing the fact that he and his younger brother were constantly late.

"Dustin," Grandmother said, "your father is angry and hurt because you are treating him disrespectfully and I think he is grounding you to get even."

"How am I being disrespectful, Grandma? It's his job to take care of us and drive us places. We're not old enough to drive."

"Honey, your father is doing you a favor. He doesn't owe it to you to drive you around. He is trying to do something nice for you and your brother, and he probably feels disrespected because you are taking advantage of him by keeping him waiting and treating him disrespectfully by not thanking him or doing nice things for him in return for the favor."

"Maybe I should say I'm sorry, Grandma. What do you think?"

"I think it would help if you really mean it and if you figure out how to show your dad you want to change instead of just making promises. You might tell your dad you realized you made a mistake and plan to make it better and ask if he would consider putting off your 'grounding' for one more weekend so you can keep your commitment to your friend."

"I'll give it a try. And thanks, Grandma."

Dustin really had no idea he wasn't entitled to the rides and was making unreasonable demands. His talk with his grandmother helped him understand the bigger picture so he could begin to make improvements with his father.

Parenting Pointers

1. Some parents give in to the demands of their children in the name of love, but that is an unloving thing to do for yourself and for your child. You are teaching your children that love means getting others to take care of their demands.

2. It's okay to draw a line about the amount of driving and help you are willing to provide. Sometimes parents overdo meeting their children's needs at the expense of their own.

DEPRESSED

"My child seems so depressed all the time. Is this a physical or emotional problem?"

Understanding Your Child, Yourself, and the Situation

Everyone feels depressed at one time or another. There is a difference between feeling depressed from time to time and consistently acting in a depressed fashion. When children are depressed, it may be a sign of something disturbing happening in their lives. They may be being abused or molested or neglected by a parent who is addicted to alcohol or drugs. It is important to keep your perspective and look for the pattern. If depression is a recurring

BOOSTER THOUGHTS Two children in the same family displayed depression quite differently. The eight-year-old girl was threatening to kill herself by mixing various concoctions together and then threatening to eat them. Her family came in for counseling and in the course of the session, she admitted that she liked it when her parents noticed her, and that they were very attentive when she threatened suicide. The counselor suggested that perhaps her parents could each spend fifteen minutes a day doing something fun with her as a way for her to get attention.

She loved the idea. After a week of special time, her depression in the form of "suicidal" tendencies disappeared.

Her ten-year-old brother, on the other hand, seemed sullen and angry all the time. His depression was anger turned inward. When the counselor asked him to describe a typical day, it involved six or more hours of watching television by himself. The counselor expressed concern to the parents that his television viewing was addictive and harmful and that he needed some help creating other ways to spend his time. When his parents agreed to limit the time their son spent watching television, he said he didn't know what else to do. His family, the boy, and the counselor brainstormed a list of other activities he could do instead of watching television.

The first week the boy just watched the blank television screen. The next week he would walk over, look at the list, and then sit down with his head in his hands. By the third week he realized his parents weren't going to weaken on the television limitation rule, so he tried out some of the activities on the list. It took him over six weeks to shake his depression, smile, and enjoy other ways of amusing himself.

◎

symptom, get professional help for your-self and your child from someone who practices drug-free therapy. Stay away from therapists and doctors who treat depression in children with antidepres-sants. Your child's feelings are an impor-tant indicator of something serious and putting a drug Band-Aid on them won't get to the deeper issues. Some children have learned that acting depressed is a way to get special service or extra attention.

Suggestions

1. Be curious. Ask your child open-ended questions about what is going on, such as "Is there something happening that you are feeling bad about? Can you tell

Twelve-year-old Mitchell couldn't sleep. He started to go downhill in school and refused to eat. He generally seemed gloomy and grumpy all day. His mother worried about him and took him to the family doctor, who listened to the symptoms and immediately wrote a prescription for antidepres-sants for Mitchell. No one took the time to find out what was bothering him. Instead they looked for a cause, made a diagnosis, and came up with a treatment.

One day Mitchell was spending the night at his father's house. (His parent's were in the process of getting a divorce and had been in an acrimonious battle for more than two years.) He and his dad were watching TV together when Mitchell asked, "Dad, are you planning to marry someone else and leave us with Mom?"

"Mitchell," Dad responded, "what are you talking about? You sound pretty worried. What brought this on? You know I love you and would never leave you kids. Mom and I won't be living together anymore, but you'll always be part of my life and we'll always find ways to be together. I thought you knew this."

"Well, Dad, Mom said that you had a new girlfriend who doesn't like kids and that she'd probably tell you we couldn't come over and make you move far away. I didn't think it was true, but then I overheard you on the phone the other day talking to someone about relocating to another state."

Dad put his arms around Mitchell and said, "No wonder you've been worried. If you ever feel this way again, please check things out with me right away. The conversation you overheard was me complaining to my friend. I wasn't serious. You know how when you are mad you sometimes say things you don't really mean? That was what you heard . . . me exaggerating. I'm here to stay, Mitch, and if there are ever any big changes in the future, you and I will discuss them at length before any-thing happens. I love you."

me about it?" "I see a big gloomy face. Anything I can do to help?"

2. Sometimes you can get information from younger children by asking silly questions or guessing how they feel, such as: "Are you angry because your teddy bear won't play with you?" "I bet I know why you're sad—because I forgot to tickle you today." "You're feeling unhappy because I spent more time with your sister than with you, and you wish I would play with you more."

3. Stay open. Don't assume you know why your child is unhappy. Parents often assume that children are unhappy for the same reasons they might feel bad. Where there has been a divorce or death, parents might think that is causing their child to be unhappy, but when they ask the child what is bothering her, they may find out that she wishes she had a friend to play with or money to buy a special outfit instead.

4. Be aware that often what is called depression is a feeling cocktail including hurt, anger, upset, resentment, fear, hopelessness, and more. Don't oversimplify feelings by giving them a popular label that may be inaccurate.

Planning Ahead to Prevent Future Problems

1. Keep the lines of communication open with your children. Let them know they can tell you how they feel without your making fun of them or telling them they shouldn't feel the way they do.

2. Anger turned inward creates depression. Children may be angry about things they don't realize it is okay to be angry about. Look for ways you may be over-controlling, overly protective, or having overly high expectations for your children. These situations may create unconscious, hidden anger.

3. A common trigger for feelings of depression in children is the belief that they can't live up to the expectations of their parents, so why try. It is very depressing to feel conditionally loved. Make sure your child knows you love her no matter what.

4. Be sure you are not taking sides in your children's fights or labeling a child as a troublemaker or bad child. Children may end up feeling hopeless and helpless if they think they are unloved and have no one who will take their side.

5. Don't make threats you don't mean. Children can get scared and take you literally if you say things like "You kids are making me so angry, I'm going to pack my bag and run away from home." Your children need to know that they are secure, and threats made in the heat of anger can cause a lot of harm if your kids take you seriously.

Life Skills Children Can Learn

Children can learn that they can tell adults what is troubling them and that there is someone for them to talk to. They don't have to figure everything out themselves or carry secrets around. They can learn appropriate ways to express anger so it isn't transformed into depression (see Angry or Aggressive Child).

Parenting Pointers

1. Don't try to talk children out of their feelings or think you know how they really feel better than they do.

2. It's okay for children to be unhappy and depressed at times. If you let them have their feelings, they will probably cycle out of their moods quickly. If you try to make them happy when they aren't, they may stay upset to show you that you aren't in charge of their feelings.

DIFFERENT PARENTING STYLES

"My boyfriend thinks I'm too soft with my kids. He says they are becoming spoiled brats and need a firmer hand. I think he's too strict. We're thinking of getting married, and I'm having second thoughts because I'm not sure whether we can parent the children together."

Understanding Your Child, Yourself, and the Situation

Where did we ever get the crazy notion that co-parenting means both parents have to think and act exactly alike with the children? If there is mutual respect in a relationship, then both parents respect themselves as well as the other and know that it is okay to agree to disagree. Children have no trouble learning that Dad does things one way and Mom another. This is not confusing to children. What is damaging is when parents try to overcompensate for the other parent instead of being themselves, or when they allow children to manipulate the parents against each other and run the family. Once parents learn to value their differences and work with them, there can be joy and shared responsibility in co-parenting. When we speak of co-parenting, the ideas work for blended families, divorced families, families where several generations are helping parent the children, and families with two parents living together.

It is rare that both parents agree on everything. Throw in the second and third marriages, and you'd be hard-pressed to find matching pictures on parenting. Here's the good news—children learn very quickly who thinks what, who will let them get away with such and such, and who to go to when they have certain needs. Your job is to learn to respect each others' differences and build on the strengths.

Suggestions

1. Get out of right/wrong thinking and appreciate differences. Look at what each parent contributes to the family and focus on strengths. Agree to disagree. Let the other parent know that, while you may not like the way he or she does something, you are willing to respect his or her relationship with the children. If one parent has gotten involved disciplining a child, stay out of it unless there is abuse. If you don't agree with what is going on, talk together when the children aren't around and you're not stressed.

2. If you think the children are playing the two of you against each other, suggest that you will let the child know what you think after you've spoken to your partner. If the children need a decision, let them know that they need two yeses (one from each parent) before they can proceed.

3. Don't try to overcompensate for another parent by going in the opposite direction and become too strict (to make up for the other's "wishy-washy" style) or too lenient (to make up for the other's "mean old strict" style). Your children can learn to handle different parenting styles.

4. Model your parenting skills and trust that the less experienced parent may learn from you through observation instead of lectures and nagging.

5. If you think your partner is feeling discouraged, be generous with your hugs and kind words like, "That was a tough one. I bet you're feeling really upset right now. Want to talk about it?"

6. Don't bad-mouth the other parent in front of the children or ask them to carry messages from one parent to the other. Don't complain to the children about the other parent and expect them to help you work out your relationship with your mate or ex-mate.

7. If your children tattle about the other parent, suggest they put their complaint on the agenda for the family meeting or let them know you will go with them while they tell the other parent their concern. Don't try to fix things for the kids without them being part of the solution.

Planning Ahead to Prevent Future Problems

1. Before having children, discuss the baggage you bring with you about parenting roles and responsibilities. Attend parenting classes together and learn and discuss methods that may be new to both of you.

2. Hold regular family meetings where the family discusses issues until all agree on a solution to try out for a week. Allow the plan to go for a week, collecting observations and information about how well it is working. Bring up your comments at the next family meeting.

3. If you believe a parent is being abusive to the children, let that parent know that you will not tolerate abuse and if necessary, you will call the proper authorities for help.

4. Talk with the children and let them know that you realize one parent may be very permissive or too strict. Ask the kids what they can do to empower themselves in such situations. Or just notice how skilled children are at dealing with different parents in different ways.

Life Skills Children Can Learn

Children can learn that differences can be assets instead of liabilities. They learn that there is not a right or wrong way to do things. They also learn to watch human behavior and look for solutions to get their needs met.

Parenting Pointers

1. If your partner's parenting is too different from yours, be clear on what your

BOOSTER THOUGHTS Lurene was the middle child in her family. She was used to being the negotiator and peacemaker, and often found herself "in the middle" trying to work things out between two opposing forces. Once she had children, she was constantly trying to protect her children from their father, who had a temper and yelled when he got really angry. It didn't take long for the children to learn how to work this system. When Lurene wasn't around, they got along fine with their father, but the minute she came home, the kids complained, tattled, and begged her to undo agreements they had made with Dad. The more Lurene tried to "protect" the kids, the angrier her husband became, and the more he yelled.

One day Lurene overheard her children talking about how they were going to get out of doing their chores. "When Dad says it's time to do the dishes, I'll start to cry and say I always have to do the dishes and it's not fair. Then you complain that Dad makes us do all the work around here. I bet Mom will start an argument with Dad and we can go play video games, and then Mom will do the dishes for us." Lurene didn't know whether to cry, yell, or grin. She decided to bide her time.

That evening when the kids pulled their "stunt," Lurene smiled sweetly and said, "I'm sure you can work this out with Dad. I'm off to read my book. Come show me what you did in school when you've finished the dishes." She walked off hardly able to hold back her laughter while the kids stared after her dumbfounded.

boundaries are and respect your right to refuse to see your children being abused or you being constantly criticized.

2. Think about what your children are learning about conflict resolution from your couple relationship. If you practice manipulation and disrespect with one another, your children will learn that. If you practice shared decision making, joint problem solving, and win/win conflict resolution, your children will learn that.

3. If there is violence of any kind in the family—such as physical abuse, sexual abuse, or substance abuse—call for help. These situations can't be solved alone. Most communities have groups and programs to assist families with these problems so that you don't have to feel alone or walk around carrying secrets that damage everyone's self-esteem.

DIVORCE

"I want to get a divorce, but I'm so afraid it will hurt my children. Should I stay in my marriage for the sake of the children?"

Understanding Your Child, Yourself, and the Situation

Many circumstances in life can be hurtful for children, including divorce. There is evidence, however, that a bad marriage is actually more difficult and hurtful for children than divorce. There are many things parents can do to reduce the pain of divorce for children.

Suggestions

1. Encourage children to express their feelings and show understanding. Verbalize that you understand that the change is painful for all of you, and express confidence that you will all be able to handle it effectively with time.

2. Do not fight over the children. Share time as equally as possible. Children want to love and respect both parents. It is easier for children to love four parents (if you remarry) than it is for them to have to choose between their two natural parents.

3. Do not say degrading things about one another in front of the children. You will probably experience a lot of hurt yourself. It may be tempting to seek revenge through the children. Be aware of how much this hurts your children and avoid the temptation.

4. Encourage your children to love and respect each of you. Let them know they are not being disloyal to you by loving their other parent too.

5. Children benefit when the parent who does not have custody of the children maintains contact with the children on a consistent basis that the children can count on.

6. Do not try to be the "good" parent. Often the parent who does not have custody fights for the children's loyalty by providing special treats and outings every time they are together. This makes it difficult for children who need order and daily routines. It eventually becomes difficult for the "good" parent also, since children will learn to expect special treats all the time.

7. Whenever possible, invite all parents to special occasions. Children who can look out in an audience and see all of their parents cheering for them suffer less than kids who try to figure out how to split themselves in half for the parents.

Planning Ahead to Prevent Future Problems

1. Children often wrongly assume something they did caused the divorce. Reassure them verbally that the divorce is not their fault.

2. Maintain routines the child experiences regularly. A parenting class and support group can be helpful at this time.

3. Get children involved in family meetings where feelings can be shared and solutions to problems can be found together.

4. Seek outside help. Because of the pain and trauma you are experiencing yourself in going through a divorce, it may be very difficult to be objective enough to accomplish these guidelines without support.

5. If at all possible, take time before introducing and adding new partners to the children's lives.

6. Allow them to take their time forming relationships with new partners. They may not warm up as quickly as you'd like, and that's normal. Don't try to force them to like your new partner.

7. Spend time with your children away from your new partner.

8. Don't expect your children to fill all your needs, especially those that another adult should fill. Your children are not your therapist, no matter how old they are, and there are some things you should not discuss with them.

9. Inform school people, friends, and other support folks what is going on so that they can watch for opportunities to comfort, console, and listen to the kids whose parents are divorcing.

Life Skills Children Can Learn

Children learn they can handle whatever circumstances life presents with courage and optimism. They can see the opportunity to learn and grow from experiences instead of seeing problems as failures.

Parenting Pointers

1. Studies on children of divorce have shown that when parents handled divorce effectively, their children did

better socially, academically, and emotionally one year after the divorce than they had been doing before the divorce.

2. Your attitude will greatly influence your child's attitude. If you feel guilty, the children will sense that a tragedy is taking place and will act accordingly. If you accept the fact that you are doing the best you can under the circumstances, and are moving toward success instead of failure, children will sense this and act accordingly.

3. Don't expect instant adjustment to a divorce situation. Adjusting to divorce is a process.

BOOSTER THOUGHTS In their book *For the Sake of the Children*,[2] Kris Kline and Dr. Stephen Pew point out that the anger and resentment that often accompany divorce don't dissolve when the papers are signed. More often than not the bitterness lingers on, sometimes for many years. Unfortunately this can cause tremendous harm to the children, who still love both parents.

In many cases, the custodial parent uses the children as a sounding board for his or her anger toward the other parent. In other cases, mentioning the absentee parent becomes taboo, thus making the love a child feels for that parent almost illicit.

In this wise and practical book, the authors offer effective ways to break the pattern of behavior that leads to further pain. They asked children if they had any recommendations for divorcing parents that, if followed, might make the process of divorce less painful for other children going through it. Here are some of the suggestions they received:

"Try not to talk about each other in a negative way in front of your kids. Keep your problems between yourselves."

"Even though you're going to be apart, make an effort to get along, I mean, like anybody else; if you needed to get along with somebody at work or whatever. You know, just for the child, so the child can have both parents around. Just make an effort to get along."

"It isn't fair when your mom says that if you love her you won't love your dad, or you have to love her more than you love your dad."

"Allow the children to like the other parent. Make it okay to like the other parent. And if you don't like them, so what? Grin and bear it."

If one strong theme consistently emerged from conversations with young people, it was a desire to be allowed to love both parents equally without having to take sides.

DOCTORS, DENTISTS, AND HAIRCUTS

"Whenever I take my child to the doctor or dentist or to get a haircut, I want to hide in shame and hope that no one knows this child belongs to me. He screams, wiggles, and refuses to walk in the door unless dragged. Is this normal behavior?"

Understanding Your Child, Yourself, and the Situation

It is only natural for a child to fear the unknown. And once a child has visited a doctor or dentist, if there was pain attached to the visit, then it makes sense that your child wouldn't be looking forward to future visits. You know your child has to receive the proper care, yet you don't like to see him suffer. You can't protect your child from doing what is necessary, but there are things you can do to make the visits less painful and difficult for everyone concerned.

Suggestions

1. Make the visit as much of an adventure as possible. Couple it with a trip to the store or the bakery or the park saying, "First we'll go to the dentist and then we'll go to the bookstore." Or "After we finish getting your hair cut, we can stop at the bakery and get a loaf of your favorite bread to make grilled cheese sandwiches for lunch."

2. Explain to your child that the shot really does pinch, but it's quick, and that it helps keep him safe for the future.

3. It's okay to tell your child that you understand he wishes he didn't have to get his hair cut or his teeth cleaned, but that isn't one of the choices. Be firm and kind and do what is needed.

4. Allow your child to cry and provide comfort for his feelings. It's okay not to enjoy getting a shot or a cavity filled. Once the visit is over, your child might want to talk about his feelings, but most likely, it will all be forgotten. Don't extend the ordeal by feeling sorry for your child.

5. Bring your camera and take pictures. Put the pictures in a special album for your child so you can often talk about the occasion and how he felt about it.

6. If you have a chronically ill child who needs a lot of medical care, make the visits as matter of fact as possible. Write the visits on a family calendar so your child can prepare mentally in advance. Learn to follow through with medication, and whenever possible, teach your child to administer the medicine while you watch.

7. Let Grandma or Grandpa take the child for the visit if you are feeling too squeamish.

Planning Ahead to Prevent Future Problems

1. Choose doctors, dentists, and other caregivers who specialize in working with children and understand their special needs. They will have special child-friendly equipment as well as techniques that can make the visit better.

2. Adjust your attitude. A parent of a diabetic child decided she'd never let her child's illness stop her from doing activities with him.

BOOSTER THOUGHTS Mom took two-year-old Brian for his first haircut. Because Brian was scared, she had him sit on her lap and the hairdresser put the cape over both of them. Brian still wiggled and turned his head a lot. The hairdresser cut snips of hair that were available and Brian ended up with a less than perfect haircut. Brian loved the sucker the hairdresser gave him.

The next trip for a haircut, Brian sat on Mom's lap and held very still. He ended up with a very cute haircut and another sucker. The next time he told his mom he could sit in the booster chair by himself and that he wanted two suckers—before the haircut. With one sucker in each hand, he took turns licking them while getting his hair cut, but got a little frustrated with the pieces of hair that got in his mouth. Now Brian looks forward to haircuts and the sucker—after the haircut.

At diabetes camp, children are taught to give themselves their own injections in the abdomen. Everyone is afraid, but the camp staff make a game of it. They bring all the kids together—the ones who have diabetes and the ones who don't and who want to get in on some of the "fun." The parents are also included. Then the staff asks, "How many people have never given themselves an injection in the stomach?" All hands go up. Then they ask, "Who's the bravest person here?" Once again all the kids raise their hands. Then the nurse looks for a volunteer. A lot of the boys raise their hands, and one is chosen.

On the day that Marti's nine-year-old grandson volunteered, she was so proud as she watched him. First he observed as the nurse stood in front of the group and gave herself a saline solution injection in the stomach, saying, "This doesn't hurt. It just takes courage." Justin pushed the syringe into his belly and said, "She's right. It doesn't hurt at all." Pretty soon all the kids and parents and staff were giving themselves injections in their bellies as everyone hooted and laughed in relief.

3. One of the most difficult situations is when a child has to have medication as a matter of life or death, such as diabetes shots. Be sure you don't make this a power struggle. Focus on solutions that involve your child so she is motivated to take care of herself.

4. If you have a difficult time letting go and are creating power struggles over necessary medication such as diabetes shots, get help. This might mean getting your child involved with a mentor who is able to avoid power struggles, or a child support group where kids share the solutions that have worked for them.

5. Tell your child that it is your job as a parent to keep her safe.

6. Work on dental hygiene in between visits to eliminate cavities and plaque.

7. Practice healthy living and eating to minimize trips to the doctor.

8. Practice ahead of time using role-play and pretend so your child knows what to expect and how to behave. Use words like "Here's what we do at the dentist's office," or "When Molly cuts your hair, you can sit so still she doesn't even see your nose wrinkle or your eyes move."

Life Skills Children Can Learn

There are times when discomfort in the moment is necessary to prevent worse problems in the future. Your child can learn that he can handle the tough stuff.

Parenting Pointers

1. Don't avoid doing what is necessary for your child's well-being because you don't like going to the doctor or dentist or getting a haircut.

2. Remember that children pick up the energy of your attitude. If you feel fear, it is likely that their fear will increase. If you feel calm and matter of fact, that will be reassuring. You calmness may not eliminate a child's fear entirely, but it will help.

DRUG ABUSE

"Our family has a history of drug abuse. What can I do to protect my children so they won't become addicts? And what do I do if my child does start abusing drugs?"

Understanding Your Child, Yourself, and the Situation

If your life has been affected by drug abuse, you know what it's like to live in a nightmare. Addicts will lie, cheat, and steal to protect their use. They make promises they never keep, while codependent members of the family keep hoping this time it will be different. There are many discouraging patterns and behaviors that are part of chemically dependent relationships, so it is only natural that you would want to protect your children. To break the cycle of the addict and the codependent feeding on each other, you'll find that encouragement—the process of building courage—can help you break abusive cycles for yourself and others. This does not mean you can use encouragement to change another person. You can use encouragement to change yourself or to provide an environment where others may be inspired to examine their behavior because they know they will not be judged. Contrary to the popular opinion that addicts are born, not made, *it is not what happens to us, but what we decide about it, that determines the course of our lives.* What can be more encouraging than knowing that you and others in your family can make new decisions!

Suggestions

1. Make sure that your children get information about chemical dependency from an educated source. Use the Web for up-to-the-minute information about drugs and their effects. You'll find many different opinions, which makes for good discussions with your children. Telling kids that if they even try drugs they'll become an addict (or other such threats) is a way of losing your credibility. When kids get accurate information, especially teens, it helps them consider the choices they are making and what the possible consequences of their choices might be.

2. Don't sugarcoat things. Tell it like it is. If you have an adult addict in your house, use words like *alcoholic, drug addict, codependent, blackout,* etc. Accept the *reality of what is* instead of living in denial by acting as though people and situations will fulfill your dreams. Giving kids information about what has been going on is a relief to them. They can see that the family has a problem, and that *they* are not the problem and are not responsible for fixing it.

3. Understand feelings, accept feelings, and practice emotional honesty. If you have a feeling or a belief, it is important to share it as your opinion, but not as the only way to look at things.

4. Decide what you will do instead of trying to get others to do what you want them to do. A good first step is to go to Al-Anon to see how you might be enabling an addict. This is not about blame, but about helping you to decide what you will do instead of trying futilely to control what someone else does.

5. Understand that not all kids who get into drug use become addicted. Addiction occurs when a chemical becomes their primary relationship and appears to be the sole way of solving all problems. When your kids exhibit problem use or chemical dependency, you need

help from counselors, treatment programs, and/or recovery groups.

Planning Ahead to Prevent Future Problems

1. You cannot stop your kids from trying drugs, or even from abusing them, if that is what they decide they want to do. What you can do is practice honesty, equip your kids with accurate information about drugs, keep the doors of communication open by letting your kids know your love for them is unconditional, and remain nonjudgmental by creating a relationship where your kids feel safe to talk to you and get your input about their choices without having to fear punishment or judgment.

2. When you abstain from judgments, your kids know that if they get into an abusive situation with their own experimentation, you will be there with honesty, with love, and support, that is empowering instead of enabling.

3. Question media messages. Discuss TV commercials and other advertising with children to bring to their conscious awareness how they are being bombarded with "do drugs" messages, including prescription drugs to modify or "fix" feelings.

4. Don't be afraid to talk about your own drug use/abuse with your children. It won't encourage them to use drugs, but it will help them know that you have struggled too.

5. Don't try to rationalize with an addict, and don't listen to promises. When a person is on drugs they cannot be rational. Think of yourself as talking to a drug, not a person, and get professional help. You may have to face the hard truth that your child needs to be in a recovery program to get better and cannot do so in either your home or the community.

Life Skills Children Can Learn

Children can learn that they don't have to hide their feelings or participate in "family secrets." They can learn that their nonaddicted parent will be supportive and nonjudgmental, and will provide them with information to deal with an alcoholic parent. Children can learn that their parents will get them professional help if they get into trouble with drug abuse.

Parenting Pointers

1. Drug abuse is a family affair. No one escapes; each person simply suffers in a different way. In families where someone is abusing drugs or alcohol, the focus is either on the drug or on the person using the drug. Parenting in such families is inconsistent, unpredictable, and sometime abusive. Individual family members feel isolated and lonely, and

are unable to define boundaries and set respectful limits. Get involved in support groups to help break this vicious pattern.

2. It is amazing how much misinformation and lack of information people have about dependence and codependence. Groups such as Al-Anon offer the kind of information and support that can help you give up dysfunctional patterns and learn healthy patterns of relating that promote healing and growing.

3. When drug use becomes a regular or daily pattern, and kids are trying to change their feelings and solve their problems with chemicals, drug use is no longer social or experimental. It's become a way of life. These young people need professional help to break their addictive pattern, whether it's an in-patient treatment program, twelve-step program, or counseling.

EATING AND MEALTIME HASSLES

"My kids' table manners are atrocious. They get up and down during the meal, grab food across the table, and complain about my cooking. One of my kids is always on a diet and another one will only eat hot dogs. I thought mealtimes were supposed to be a pleasant family event?"

Understanding Your Child, Yourself, and the Situation

You are correct. Mealtime should nourish both the body and the soul. Too many families forget this and turn mealtime into a nightmare of corrections, nagging, threats, fighting, and individual grandstanding—if they even have a mealtime. Many families take the kids out for fast food, or everyone eats at a different time of day. In some families, the kitchen is open all day with

family members grabbing snacks whenever they feel hungry. While some children seem to survive on an unhealthy diet, there is an epidemic of overweight children and adults. Quite often, instead of providing healthy choices and trusting your kids to eat when they are hungry and stop when they are not, you inadvertently interfere in this natural process. Without knowing it, you could be planting the seeds for eating disorders. We have several suggestions to make mealtime a place where your family can have a positive experience together, eat healthy foods, and enjoy each other's company. It starts with you.

Suggestions

1. At least once a day, sit down as a family and eat a meal together. Do not eat in front of the television. Adults should sit down and eat with the kids—at a table. Occasionally set the table with flowers, candles, or place mats, or eat in the dining room to create a special experience for the family.

2. If kids know it's okay to choose what they will or won't eat, they are less apt to complain. Don't try to force your child to eat anything. Do not insist on children eating everything on their plates or tasting every food. Don't give your child a lot of undue attention if they refuse to eat something.

3. It is normal for young children to play with their food, spill their milk, and drop food on the floor. Behavior appropriate for their ages is not misbehavior. Clean up spills, let kids finger paint in their food, and let the dog eat what drops or put a plastic sheet under your young child. Teach your children to help you clean up the mess.

4. Let your kids serve themselves and do not discuss what they eat or don't eat. Simply clear their plates at the end of the meal (fifteen to twenty minutes is plenty of time).

5. If kids complain about your cooking, tell them it's okay not to eat what they don't like, but it hurts the chef when people complain. With a young child,

when he says, "I don't like this," remove his plate and say, "Okay, you don't have to eat it." That usually ends the complaining very quickly.

6. Some families allow children to make themselves a sandwich or tortilla with cheese if they don't like the meal. This is better than cooking special dishes for each child.

7. If you think your children's behavior has become too obnoxious, you might try deciding what you will do instead of trying to control your children. Pick up your plate and go to another room to eat.

8. Don't panic when your child says she is going on a diet. Wait and watch to see what really happens. She may say one thing and do another.

9. Don't perpetuate secrets. Let your child know that you saw her make herself throw up (or any other unhealthy behavior that you have seen). Ask what steps she will take about her eating problem and what help she needs from you.

10. If dysfunctional eating patterns, such as anorexia nervosa (self-starvation) or bulimia (binging and purging) persist, get information from an eating disorder clinic, a dietician, or therapist about possibilities for help. This is particularly important if there is any history of addiction within the family since there can be a correlation between family history and eating disorders.

11. If your child decides to become a vegetarian or try out any other health-conscious new way of eating, ask your child how you can be supportive. Don't make fun of your child or insist he or she eat the way you do, or treat the new habit as an eating disorder. Many vegetarians made the decision to change their eating as very young children. If you are a vegetarian and your child insists on eating meat, the same advice applies. Do not force your way of eating on your children.

Planning Ahead to Prevent Future Problems

1. Schedule your meals. (But allow snacking on healthy things—don't make children wait until they are overly hungry to eat.) Stress that mealtime is a time to share stories about the day, visit with each other, and share the good feelings of being together as a family.

2. When children complain about the food, it may be time to involve them in choosing what they eat, at least one night a week. Let each child cook dinner one night a week. Even small kids can tear lettuce leaves, open a can of beans, and make a simple salad.

3. Plan with kids what they can do to contribute. Talk about the different jobs

that need to be done, such as setting the table, cooking dinner, washing the dishes, and feeding the pets.

4. Do not bring junk foods into the house. Of course children won't eat regular meals when they have filled up on snacks or junk foods. Especially avoid products that contain sugar. Sugar can really mess up the body's natural craving for good foods.

5. Provide healthy snacks. It is fine if your children don't eat because they have filled up on cheese, carrot sticks, or other healthy snacks. Who said good food should be eaten only at mealtimes?

6. Practice good table manners at a time other than mealtime, or choose one night a week to practice. Make it fun. Exaggerate.

7. During a family meeting, get the whole family involved in planning ways to make mealtime enjoyable for everyone.

8. Look at your own attitudes about weight, food, and eating patterns and what they may be suggesting to your children. Are you saying things like "Finish everything on your plate," and then later getting upset because your child is overweight? Do you tell your kids they can't eat between meals, which may encourage them to binge at mealtimes? Are there other ways you are unconsciously trying to control your child's food intake?

Life Skills Children Can Learn

Children can learn that they are not going to get in trouble at the table, so they don't have to sidetrack their parents with bad manners. The table *is* a fun place to be, and there are many positive ways to get attention by joining in and being part of the family. Children can learn that they can develop a taste for foods on their own schedule. They can learn that they will not be pressured to eat what they don't want, nor will be they be given special service. Children can learn that respect is a two-way street.

Parenting Pointers

1. You can help your child learn to listen to his or her feelings and body wisdom instead of training the child to be an overeater to please you or a picky eater to defeat you. Think of how many overweight adults were members of the Clean Plate Club as children and have completely lost touch with the meaning of the word *hungry.*

2. If you see mealtime as a time to make kids eat and to lecture about manners, the kids will probably pay you back with bad manners. If your attitude is that meals are one of the special times that families can share together, the kids probably reflect that thinking.

3. At different stages of development, your children's bodies may not fit the national ideal, so be patient with them and with yourself. When all else fails,

BOOSTER THOUGHTS One of our toddlers participated in a university preschool program where they put all kinds of foods on the lunch table and allowed kids to eat what they wanted. Sometimes he would eat cake first, and sometimes he would eat broccoli first. The main thesis of this program was that children would naturally choose foods that would balance out to good nutrition (over time) when they were allowed to choose from a variety of nutritious foods—without anyone making a fuss.

◎

One mother thought it was her job to control what her daughter ate. If her daughter didn't eat her oatmeal for breakfast, Mom would give it to her for lunch. If she didn't eat the oatmeal for lunch, Mom would give it to her for dinner. Of course her daughter refused to eat it. The daughter became sick. A doctor discovered she was developing rickets. It was more important for the daughter to win the power struggle than to eat.

When the doctor learned what was happening, he said, "Please put good food on the table, and then leave your daughter alone." When the mother did this, her daughter started eating better. Not perfect, but better.

◎

The first time I sat down to eat a meal with my new stepchildren and their grandparents, I was dismayed at the number of comments that were made about the youngest's eating habits. He was coaxed to try this, that, and another thing, he was labeled the family's picky eater, I was told that he doesn't eat vegetables or fruit, etc. Of course he was a picky eater, getting tons of negative attention and also engaging in a power contest at every meal.

trust your sense of what is normal for your children.

4. Encourage regular exercise. Turn off the television and kick the kids off the couch if necessary.

5. We have talked to people who were raised during the Depression. They say picky eating was never a problem. Parents didn't make a fuss when a child didn't want to eat because there often wasn't enough to go around. When children didn't get any "mileage" out of being a picky eater, they ate what was available or went hungry.

ELECTRONICS: TV, VIDEO GAMES, IPODS, COMPUTERS, ETC. (*SEE ALSO* CELL PHONES)

"My children would play video games or watch television all day if I let them—except for the time they want to spend with an iPod glued to their ears. They spend hours on the computer sending instant messages to as many as twenty-six people at a time, they can type out text messages on their cell phones with two thumbs faster than I can type with all ten fingers. Are their brains getting fried? Are their attention spans going to be nonexistent? And what about their morals and social skills? I worry about what they might be finding when they surf the Internet. It is difficult to tear them away from their electronic gadgets to have dinner with social interaction. I know I should limit their use of electronics, but I don't know how to win this battle."

Understanding Your Child, Yourself, and the Needs of the Situation

Welcome to genM—the multitasking generation. Electronics are here to stay. Our guess is that there will be more electronic gadgets invented before this book goes to press. Television, video games, DVD players, iPods, cell phones, computers, and the Internet—they aren't the bad guys, but they can become a real problem when what stops happening when everyone is plugged into electronic equipment (often many at the same time). Have you and your family stopped having meals together? Have you stopped having face-to-face discussions, family meetings, playing games together, talking while driving in the car? Electronics can be entertaining, informative, and help children develop many transferable skills when used with awareness. However overuse can create

serious problems. Eliminate the "battle" by deciding what you will do, being kind and firm, and getting children involved in creating healthy guidelines for the use of electronic equipment.

Suggestions

1. Give young children limited choices. "You can watch either one show or two; you choose." "You can play a video game for half an hour or you can watch half an hour of TV." "You can watch TV for thirty minutes before dinner or after dinner." "You can spend two hours a day on screen time.

You decide on a schedule of your choice, and I'll check to see if it works for me too."

2. Don't allow TVs in your children's rooms. Sit with your children and watch with them instead of just censoring a show you don't like. Talk to your kids about what they are watching, what they like about it, and what they are deciding about it. Turn the TV off when there is violence.

3. Discuss commercials with your children and explore with them what advertising is all about.

4. Decide what you will do and what you won't do. If you don't want your children to spend too much time watching TV or spending time on computer games, don't buy them. If they have to work to earn the money to pay for these things, they will be doing something besides watching screens.

BOOSTER THOUGHTS Following is a small taste of statistics on the television-viewing habits of children. (We could fill reams of paper by quoting all the research on all kinds of screen time. We'll stick to this and we think the point will be made for all such electronics.)

- American children ages two to seventeen watch television, on average, almost twenty-five hours per week, or three and a half hours a day. Almost one in five watch more than thirty-five hours of TV each week. Twenty percent of two- to seven-year-olds, 46 percent of eight- to twelve-year-olds, and 56 percent of thirteen- to seventeen-year-olds have TVs in their bedrooms. Children spend more time watching television than any other activity except sleeping.[4]

- In a national education study, students reported spending four times as many hours each week watching television as doing homework.[5]

- Some kinds of programming artificially manipulate the brain into paying attention by violating its natural defense mechanisms with frequent visual and auditory changes. Multitasking may condition the brain in some individuals to an overexcited state, making it difficult to focus when they want to.

- Some television and other electronics may have a hypnotic, and possibly neurologically addictive, affect on the brain by changing the frequency of its electrical impulses in ways that block normal mental processing.

Planning Ahead to Prevent Future Problems

1. Notice your own behavior. If you watch TV or use other electronics excessively, you will not be able to convince your children that too much isn't good for them. On the other hand, if you live a balanced life you will have a firm foundation to teach your children to do the same.

2. There may be shows on television that you don't want your children viewing, so it is up to you to create guidelines for use of the TV. As your children get older, they need to be part of this planning process. You need to create guidelines on all screen time and use of other electronics until your children are old enough to be involved in helping to create the guidelines.

⊚

The Jensen family includes Mom, Dad, and five sons. When the boys were very young Mom and Dad decided that they would have only one TV in the house (small enough to cover up when not in use) and that they would bring it out only when there was something they really wanted to watch. As the boys got older, they recognized the benefits of a computer, and the skills that could be formed by playing a few video games. So they purchased one computer for the family room where they could always be aware of what was happening. Everyone in the family (including Mom and Dad) had to negotiate for time on the computer. They couldn't purchase a video game until Mom or Dad reviewed the contents to make sure it didn't include violence or sex. When the boys wanted iPods, they first had to come up with a plan for how they would use them a reasonable amount of time, and how they would earn the money to pay for them. They decided to purchase three cell phones on a family plan, and each family member (except Dad) made a case for when they needed to take the cell phone when he or she left the house. They decided text messaging did not make sense for "community" phones. All this required planning, negotiating, respect for each other, and cooperation. The result was a balanced use of time regarding electronic equipment.

3. Use the family meeting to discuss the use of electronics. Use the newspaper or *TV Guide* to sit with your children and help them plan ahead about the shows they want to watch during the week. Decide together on the amount of time that is "balanced" for the use of other electronic equipment. If you have TiVo, you can program what shows your kids would like to watch and set up a viewing time when you are around.

4. Help the kids make a list of activities they enjoy so that when they are bored they can find something else to do instead of flipping on the TV or turning on their video games (see Boredom).

5. Talk with the kids about the addictive qualities of TV and video games, so they know why you are concerned and want to limit their viewing and playing.

6. Let the children know they need to set up a rotation for sharing video games or picking channels to watch. If they fight over this, either turn off the equipment and let them know they can try again later or you take over the choosing until they have come up with a system for sharing that they all can live with.

7. Try a day of the week or a month when no one in the family watches TV or uses other electronic equipment and see what the family can learn from the experience.

8. Remember that any activity can become addictive besides electronics (see Drug Abuse), so don't overact. Know the difference between an interest and an addiction.

Life Skills Children Can Learn

Children learn how to plan ahead and think through using TV, video games, and other electronic equipment instead of getting into habits of indiscriminate use. Children develop nonabusing habits that can help them when they are dealing with other potential substances of abuse.

Parenting Pointers

1. Turn the TV and other electronic equipment off during meals and talk with your children instead.

2. Don't expect children to follow electronic equipment use agreements when you aren't at home to monitor them. If you think they are badly abusing their agreements, disconnect the TV and confiscate other equipment until they are ready to follow their commitments.

FAIRNESS AND JEALOUSY

"My oldest is always complaining that his sister gets more than he does and is treated better. He says I'm not being fair. I try to make everything even, but he still thinks I love his sister more and that she is spoiled and he is deprived."

Understanding Your Child, Yourself, and the Situation

Many parents bring issues of fairness with them from their own growing up. We call these justice issues. Our justice issues can get passed on to our children and create problems if we are unaware of them. The more a parent tries to be fair, the more children make an issue of fairness. Fairness is a very personal, selective idea—what is fair to one person may seem unfair to another. It is normal for children to compare themselves with their siblings or feel jealous. This doesn't mean that the parent's job is to fix everything or try to control the family so a child never feels these feelings.

Suggestions

1. When children say, "It's not fair," listen to their feelings and validate them. Avoid the temptation to do more. Just feeling validated can be enough. Tell your children, "You're feeling jealous and hurt because you think someone is getting more than you. You wish you were being treated the same." Children will let you know if that's not what they're upset about.

2. Encourage a deeper level of sharing by asking curiosity questions: Can you tell me more about that? Can you give me some other examples of when you thought things weren't fair? Is there anything else that is bothering you? Anything else? This last question can be repeated until the child says no. Again it is often enough just to be listened to thoroughly.

3. Use a sense of humor. For instance, if your child says, "He gets to stay up later and that's not fair," you could say, "Of course he gets to stay up later. That's because he has more freckles than you do." Then give your child a big hug. Another response is, "Good try! Now off to bed. See you in the morning."

4. Let children tell you why they think things are unfair and how they would fix things to make them fair. Suggest that they pretend they have a magic wand that can make everything fair. If they waved the wand, how would things change? You may or may not wish to act on their ideas.

5. Ask your child, "If you were the parent, what would you do about this situation?" and listen carefully to the ideas.

6. Explain your rationale for the decisions you have made without feeling you have to justify them.

7. Put the problem on a family meeting agenda and let the kids decide how to make things fair. Some ideas might include letting the kids serve themselves, letting one kid divide the items and the other choose first, or having the kids pick a number or a hand held behind the back. Let the kids brainstorm for a solution they can all live with. (See the Booster Thought below for an example.)

Planning Ahead to Prevent Future Problems

1. Hold regular family meetings so the kids can place items important to them on the agenda. At the meeting, ask your children if they just want to complain or if they would like to have the family do some problem solving. Either would be fine.

BOOSTER THOUGHTS Three kids, ages five, seven, and eight, were always fighting over who got to sit next to the windows in the backseat of the van. No matter how many times their father explained to them why it was fair for them to take turns, there were always hurt feelings and complaints from the one who had to sit in the middle. One day, in exasperation, the father said, "I have faith in the three of you to come up with a plan you can all live with for sitting next to the windows without fighting. Please work out a plan when I'm not around. I don't want to know what it is, either. Just let me know when you are ready to share the windows without fighting, and we'll all try again."

A few days later, the three children came to their father and said, "We have a plan for the backseat, and we're ready to try again." Their father said fine and watched as they got in and buckled their seat belts in the seat of their choice. For weeks the children, as if by magic, took turns based on some kind of mysterious system that the father never figured out.

One day the kids started bickering over the windows again, and their father said, "Your plan for sharing seems almost perfect, but it still has a few kinks in it. Work them out and let me know when you're ready for me to start driving." Then Dad sat in the car reading his magazine. Within two minutes the problem was worked out, and from that day on, the seat changing operated without a hitch.

Too often as grown-ups we think we are the only ones who can make things fair, but until fairness fits our children's sense of justice, which may be very different from our own, the complaining and fighting persist. Have faith in your kids to work out many of the problems that you think only a parent can handle.

2. Explore your own justice issues. Think of things you thought were unfair when you were a kid and see if you are teaching your children to hold the same opinions. Ask yourself if that is what you want to do.

3. If you have a "fair button" you might want to get rid of it. Children know how to push your "buttons."

Life Skills Children Can Learn

Children can learn that equal doesn't mean the same and that it is more important to understand differences than to accept one person's notion of what is fair. They also can learn problem-solving skills, and a variety of ways to make choices and decisions when there are differences of opinion.

Parenting Pointers

1. It's more important to try to understand why your children think the way they do and what their issues are than to try to rectify the situation or prevent injustices from happening.

2. "It's not fair" ceases to be an expression that manipulates parents to fix things when it is met with either curiosity or turning the problem back to the children. One father stopped complaints about unfairness simply by saying, "I don't do fair."

FEARS (CHILDREN)

"My child has nightmares and complains about monsters in his room. He seems so fragile compared to other children his age. He's afraid to leave my side. This doesn't seem normal to me."

Understanding Your Child, Yourself, and the Situation

"A bruised knee can mend, but bruised courage lasts a lifetime."[6] Sometimes children have fears because we don't help them deal with the unknown by showing them how to do things in small steps. Most children have some fears, but they become bigger when others make fun of them, call them babies, or tell them that it's not okay to be scared or to cry, or label them as "overly sensitive." Fears also get bigger when parents feel sorry for children and try to overprotect them. Then children don't develop the confidence that they can handle some discomfort.

Fear is usually about the unknown (which is why a fear of the dark is common

and usually passes). However at other times children have good reason (such as bullies or sexual abuse) to be afraid. It's your job to know when to protect your children and when to help them without overprotecting them.

Suggestions

1. Don't laugh at, minimize, judge, or discount your children's fears. Contrarily don't overindulge or overprotect or try to explain away your child's fears.

2. Listen when your children tell you what they are afraid of. Validate their feelings, such as saying, "You're afraid of dogs because they might bite you, and you wish the dog would go away and leave you alone." Sometimes just having their feelings validated is enough to lessen the fear.

3. Help your children find ways to handle situations when they are afraid. Help them explore several possibilities so they feel they have some choices. You might ask, "What would help you the most right now—a flashlight, a teddy bear, a night-light?" Telling them not to be afraid isn't helpful; looking for solutions is.

4. Don't be manipulated by your children's fears. Offer comfort, but don't give them special service or try to fix their feelings for them. It is important for children to learn that they can handle

their fears, even though it is uncomfortable. Help them problem solve (as above) so they learn they can handle their fears themselves. Letting children sleep with you when they are afraid is a subtle way of saying "You can't handle this. Let me fix it for you."

5. Encourage your children to deal with difficult situations in small steps. If they are afraid of the dark, put a nightlight in their room. If they don't think they can sleep in their own rooms, fill their hands with your kisses and tell them every time they miss you to open their hands and take out a kiss. If they think there are monsters in the closet or under the bed, do a search with them before bedtime and let them sleep with a flashlight.

6. Listen carefully. Are your children trying to tell you that someone is hurting them or that you are doing something that is frightening them? Take what they say seriously.

7. Sometimes children's fears are irrational and they can't explain them. They may need your support and reassurance until the fear goes away.

Planning Ahead to Prevent Future Problems

1. There are many wonderful children's books dealing with fears that you can

read with your children so they can see they aren't alone.

2. If there is a scary show on television or a scary movie, discuss ahead of time with your child whether it is a good idea for him to see it. If you both agree he is ready to watch, discuss how you can be supportive (see Booster Thoughts).

3. Don't lay your fears on your children. If your children decide they are ready to try something, work with them in small steps to make it safe and then let go instead of stopping them from doing things you are afraid of yourself. If you're too afraid, arrange for a friend or relative to do the activity with your child.

4. It's okay to share your fears, but don't expect your children to have the same ones you do. Telling your children about a fear that you conquered may be comforting to them. It will assure them that fears are normal.

5. Ask your children if they would be willing to try out scary things two or three times before deciding against them.

6. Don't push your children into doing things they are afraid of such as swimming or riding a horse. Some parents insist that their children do these things in spite of their fears and create lifetime fears in their children, as well as a strong feeling of inadequacy.

BOOSTER THOUGHTS Ten-year-old Lisa decided she wanted to watch *Halloween III*, an extremely scary movie. Her parents said they thought the movie was too scary, but she insisted on watching it. No one in her family wanted to watch the movie with her, so Lisa decided she would watch it by herself. Her parents said they would be in the next room, and if she got scared, she could come in for reassurance.

Lisa's mother made her a bowl of popcorn, and her father helped her carry in her stuffed animals and special quilt. He turned on all the lights at Lisa's request and left the room as the movie began.

About ten minutes later, Lisa came into the living room and said, "I don't think I'm really in the mood to watch that movie tonight. Maybe I'll watch it another time."

Some children do what they really don't want to do so they can win the power struggle with their parents. Lisa's parents supported her to learn for herself how much she could handle.

7. Turn off the TV and stop immersing your kids in the news which is filled with violence and natural disasters. Too much TV has been the trigger for many children's fears, and rightly so.

Life Skills Children Can Learn

Children can learn that it's okay to feel fear, but they don't have to be immobilized by it. There is someone who will take them seriously and help them deal with their fears so they aren't so overwhelming. They learn they can trust their parents to protect them from dangers they can't handle by themselves.

Parenting Pointers

1. If your children are afraid to leave your side, spend time with them, but also create situations where they can be away from you for short times. Many a preschool teacher has had to pull clinging, screaming children off their parents' legs. Minutes later, with the parents gone, the children have settled in and are happily playing with the other children.

2. Don't force your children into situations that are overwhelming to them just so they will be brave. Some children learn by jumping into the pool, and others watch from the sidelines for a summer before they put their faces in the water. Respect their differences and have faith.

FEARS (PARENTS)

"We live in such a dangerous world. I worry every day about my child being kidnapped or molested or shot in a drive-by shooting or even at school. How can I possibly protect my child from so much danger?"

Understanding Your Child, Yourself, and the Situation

While it's true that the world has changed, one of the biggest changes is that we hear more about the problems than we used to because of excessive media coverage. Danger has always been present, and what parent hasn't worried about a child's safety? No parent wants to outlive a child, or live with the awful uncertainty that follows a disappearance. But it would be unfair to children to hold them so tightly that they suffocate or wither because of your fears. It takes courage to raise children and to develop the understanding to know the difference between what is in your control and what is not.

Suggestions

1. Your job is to empower your children and teach them to care for themselves. Work every day on building skills and courage in children.

2. Strengthen your courage muscles by letting children do for themselves those

things that they feel ready to do. Be a coach and a cheerleader. Stay at a safe distance to help when needed, but give your children the space to try and make the kind of mistakes they can learn from without suffering too much. When you watch your children before you jump in, you may be amazed at their ability to handle many situations.

3. Teach your children to understand that all people aren't nice and that some people can do things to hurt children. Know who your children are playing with and whose house they are spending time at. Think up a family password—if anyone comes up to the children at school or anywhere else and says, "Your mom and dad told me to pick you up," they can ask the person for the password. If they don't have it, they should run away and get help.

4. Check the Internet to find out if a child abuser has taken up residence in your neighborhood. Make sure your children understand exactly how to stay safe by discussing the fact that there is a child molester in the neighborhood. Show them his or her picture and how important it is to avoid any contact. It is a good idea to have your children walk in pairs or groups.

Planning Ahead to Prevent Future Problems

1. Work in your schools and neighborhoods to develop safe practices and community activities that stress the positive. Get to know your neighbors and your children's teachers. Be involved.

2. Take a look at what you are reading and watching on TV. So many books for today's parents are suggesting you overprotect your children and make you feel guilty if you don't. Make it a policy to learn as much as you can about empowerment so that you can avoid codependence.

3. Take a parenting class and listen to the stories other parents tell so that you can discover that you aren't alone and that your fears are natural. That doesn't mean that you should act on your fears, but it does help to have them acknowledged and validated.

4. Talk to parents who are older than you and ask them to remind you of how they grew up. It wasn't too long ago that children were working to help their families at a very young age, taking buses and walking to school by themselves, and helping out on the farm. We're not suggesting we can go backward, but it helps to have a sense of history to put your fears in perspective.

5. Take small steps with your children to help you build confidence. When your children feel ready to try something, you can observe from a short distance to see if they really are ready.

BOOSTER THOUGHTS Grandma Lynnie and two-year-old Zachy love to ride the BART trains in San Francisco. If Grandma gets too close to the yellow line, Zachy stands in front of her and moves her back a few steps to keep her safe. That's his job, and he takes it very seriously.

◎

Stan was raised by a mother who constantly expressed her fears. "Be careful riding your bike so you don't fall and break your teeth." "You're too little to ride that pony." "Be careful when you are swimming so you don't drown." "Don't ever touch a toilet seat, and wash your hands to make sure you don't have germs." Stan heard a constant barrage of fears. As a grown man, Stan has many phobias. He is afraid to sit in a movie or any auditorium unless he has an end seat near the back. He is terrified of flying. The one time he flew, he had to have oxygen before the plane even took off. He hasn't been on an airplane since, and misses many special family events. When he got his doctorate degree he got the night sweats because he was afraid he would have to sit in the middle of a row—and finally decided to just receive his degree in the mail.

Remember that children are always making decisions. Be careful that you don't create opportunities for them to develop beliefs and fears that will cripple them for life.

6. Watch out for expressing too much worry around your children. They may go in an opposite direction and become daredevils and extremists just to prove you wrong. Many children don't want to hear what you are worried about, as it saps their own self-confidence. Tell your worries to a friend instead.

Life Skills Children Can Learn

Children can learn that their parents have confidence in them to solve problems, be strong, be assertive, and be capable. They can also learn that their parents' fears are simply that. They are feelings, not facts.

Parenting Pointers

1. It's okay to feel afraid, but it's not okay to turn your child into a basket case because you're one.

2. Just because you did crazy things as a kid doesn't mean your child will follow in your footsteps or have the same results and experiences if they do.

3. Be careful you don't create a self-fulfilling prophecy by putting too much negative energy into your world.

FIGHTING (FRIENDS)

"My child seems to fight a lot with her friends. How can I help her?"

Understanding Your Child, Yourself, and the Situation

As parents, it is painful to watch your children suffer hurt, rejection, and isolation when they fight with their friends. However this seems to be a part of the growing-up experience. Even though children seem to suffer terribly when they fight, they usually get over the pain much more quickly than adults do. It is a mistake for you to think you should protect your children from experiencing problems in life. Instead of playing the rescuer, help your children more by being the observer, listener, coach, and cheerleader. In this way children learn they can deal with life experiences in productive ways—or that they can simply deal with the pain, and that it goes away when they get on with their lives.

Please note that we are talking about normal life experiences—not pain inflicted by abnormal experiences or safety issues such as sexual abuse, gangs, bullies, or racism. There is a difference between friends fighting and your children becoming victimized and powerless. If the latter is occurring, you need to take a very active role in getting outside help and/or helping children cope with a situation that may be beyond their ability to manage safely.

Suggestions

1. Be empathetic and listen without trying to rescue your child or solve the problem.

2. Show faith in your child. "Honey, I know this hurts, but I know that you can deal with it somehow."

3. Offer support. "Let me know if you need a sounding board or if you want any suggestions. My suggestions will be just brainstorm ideas. You can decide if any would work for you."

4. Don't treat your child like a victim or she will learn to think of herself as a victim.

5. When your child doesn't want to see or play with a friend, support her in that decision and don't push her to make up. If your child decides to cut off a relationship with a friend, trust her. She may have very good reasons why she doesn't want to play with that friend anymore (see Friends [Choosing]).

6. If you have more than one child, don't expect friends to like playing with all your children. It is important that each child be allowed to make and maintain separate friendships and play uninterrupted by siblings if that is his or her preference.

Planning Ahead to Prevent Future Problems

1. Share information about accountability without blame. "When we look at what

we might have done to create a situation, we have the power to change our part if we want to. Knowing that you and your friend are both responsible for what happened, can you think of what you might have done to create the problem?"

2. Share your own stories of childhood fights—what happened and how you felt.

3. While tucking your children in bed at night, ask about their saddest and happiest times of the day. They will know they can share their experiences—both happy and sad—with you.

Life Skills Children Can Learn

Children can learn that they have the courage and confidence to deal with painful experiences in life. They can take responsibility for their part in creating the pain and can choose to make changes. It is nice to have someone who can listen without rescuing or blaming them. In the case of safety issues, children will learn that you are there to make sure they have the help they need.

Parenting Pointers

1. Accept that fights among friends are normal and view them as a necessary part of your child's experiences. Know that the conflict will pass, usually in less

BOOSTER THOUGHTS Melissa and Janey were best friends all through elementary school. When they went to middle school, Corrine joined them, bringing with her a group of girls who were very popular. Corrine thought it was fun to pick on one girl at a time in the group, ostracizing her and making sure that everyone "hated" her. This is behavior that's not unusual for this age, but it's still unacceptable. Janey told her mom what was going on and said that she didn't like it, but if she didn't go along, she wouldn't have any friends. Janey's mom suggested that it might not be long before Janey was the one they picked on, because at some point, everyone would have a turn. She encouraged Janey to get involved in activities outside of school where she made another group of friends.

Sure enough, the day arrived when Janey became the scapegoat and was excluded from the group of friends. Even Melissa refused to have anything to do with her. Janey was brokenhearted, but she was also relieved that she had another group of friends to hang out with, thanks to her mother's encouragement.

time than you think. Children almost always finish a fight much quicker if adults stay uninvolved.

2. Remember that children, like adults, often need a sounding board more than they need solutions imposed on them.

3. Keep in mind that there is a difference between normal fighting and safety issues or violence against a person, and adjust your role appropriately.

FIGHTING (SIBLINGS) (*SEE ALSO* SIBLING RIVALRY)

"What should I do when my children fight with each other?"

Understanding Your Child, Yourself, and the Situation

Most siblings fight. Most parents inadvertently interfere in ways that increase competition and the need to fight. When parents interfere, they may stop the fight for the moment, and then feel frustrated because the kids are fighting again two minutes later. To really be effective in helping siblings handle the real issues, it helps to deal with the belief behind the behavior as well as the behavior (see Booster Thoughts). Are kids symbolically fighting for their place in the family, because they think they have to win to be significant? Do

they feel hurt and want to hurt back? Do they feel they are being treated unfairly and that fighting is the only way to gain justice? Is fighting the only way to solve problems in your family? Are the kids fighting to show you that you can't make them stop? Fights can be reduced significantly when you help children change their mistaken beliefs about belonging and significance and teach them alternatives to fighting.

Suggestions

1. Do not take sides. This reinforces the belief about the need to compete. Treat children exactly the same—as demonstrated in many of the following suggestions.

2. Say, "You can both go to separate rooms until you are ready to stop fighting." This can serve as a cooling-off period when fights get out of hand. Tell them they can come out and try again when they are ready.

3. Give both of them a choice. "You can either stop fighting or go outside to fight. If you choose to fight, I don't want to listen to it."

4. When a baby is involved, pick up the baby first and say to the baby, in front of the older child, "You'll need to go to your room until you are ready to stop fighting." Then take the older child by the hand and repeat the same message. It may seem ridiculous to put

an innocent baby in her room for fighting. However it's important to treat children the same, so you don't train one to be a victim and the other to be a bully (see Parenting Pointers).

5. It can be comforting to kids if you let them fight while you sit quietly nearby, trusting that they can work it out without involving you. (This is a tough one because it is hard for parents to avoid getting hooked.) Some parents are even able to put their arms around both kids and say, "You know you love each other. How about saying 'I love you' and move on?"

6. If kids are fighting over a toy, remove the toy and let the kids know they can have it back when they are ready to play with it instead of fight over it.

7. Sometimes kids' fights are a way to play with one another. Think of them as cute little bear cubs and let them tussle as long as neither is in any danger.

BOOSTER THOUGHTS When his children were fighting, their father would stick his thumb in front of them and say, "I'm a reporter for CBN. Who would like to be the first to speak into my microphone and give me your version of what is happening here?" Sometimes his children would just laugh, and sometimes they would each take a turn telling their version. When they told their versions of the fight, the father would turn to an imaginary audience and say, "Well folks. You heard it here first. Tune in tomorrow to see how these brilliant children solve this problem."

◎

Four-year-old Becky was feeling dethroned by the birth of a baby brother, and was experiencing confusion about her feelings for the baby. Sometimes she loved him, and other times she wished he had never been born because Mom and Dad spent so much time with him. She didn't know how to get attention for herself, except to act like the baby.

One evening when the baby was asleep, Becky's mom sat down at the kitchen table with her daughter and said, "Honey, I would like to tell you a story about our family." She had found four candles of varying lengths. "These candles represent our family." She picked up one long candle and said, "This is the mommy candle. This one is for me." She lit the candle as she said, "This flame represents my love." She picked up another long candle and said, "This candle is the daddy candle."

8. Put all the fighters on a couch and tell them they have to stay there until they give one another permission to get off the couch and try again. This distracts them to work on cooperation instead of fighting.

9. Send those with the conflict to a room with the instructions that they can come out as soon as they have worked out a solution.

10. Leave the room. Believe it or not, a major reason kids fight is to get you involved. Kids want you to take their side by blaming and punishing the other child. Then they can feel important.

11. Interrupt the fight to ask if one of the participants would be willing to put the problem on the family meeting agenda to work on a solution.

12. If real danger is imminent (such as a child about to throw a rock at another child), keep your mouth shut and act. Move quickly to stop the rock throwing. Then use any of the other approaches.

She used the flame from the mommy candle to light the daddy candle and said, "When I married your daddy, I gave him all my love—and I still have all my love left." Mom placed the daddy candle in a candleholder. She then picked up a smaller candle and said, "This candle is for you." She lit the smaller candle with the flame from her candle and said, "When you were born, I gave you all my love. And look. Daddy still has all my love and I still have all my love left." Mom put that candle in a candleholder next to the daddy candle. Then she picked up the smallest candle and, while lighting it from the mommy candle, said, "This is a candle for your baby brother. When he was born I gave him all my love. And look—you still have all my love, Daddy has all my love, and I still have all my love left because that is the way love is. You can give it to everyone you love and still have all your love left. Now look at all the light we have in our family with all this love."

Mom gave Becky a hug and said, "Does this help you understand that I love you just as much as I love your baby brother?"

Becky said, "Yes, and I can love lots of people just the same."

What happens to us is never as important as the beliefs we create about what happens to us. Our behavior is based on those beliefs, and the behavior and beliefs are directly related to the primary goal of all people—to feel that we belong and are important. Mom had learned to deal with the belief behind Becky's misbehavior and from then on it was much less of a problem.

13. Use a sense of humor and play Pig Pile. When you see your kids fighting, wrestle them to the floor and say, "Pig Pile." This is an invitation for everyone to playfully climb on the pile and see who can end up on top. This can become a fondly remembered family tradition.

Planning Ahead to Prevent Future Problems

1. Have a discussion on fighting during a family meeting. Ask the children to share their ideas on why kids fight and on alternatives to fighting. Family meetings give them a great model for focusing on solutions.

2. When tucking kids in bed at night, after they have had a chance to share their saddest and happiest moments of the day, ask, "Would this be a good time to talk about what is going on when you fight with your brother and to work on some solutions?" Then listen to the child's point of view before working together on some possible solutions.

3. Never compare children. You may think you are encouraging improvement by saying, "I know you can do as well as your sister." Instead you are creating discouragement and competition.

4. Talk about all of these suggestions during a family meeting and ask kids which one they would like you to use when they are fighting.

5. Use the candle story to show that love for one child doesn't diminish the love for another (see Booster Thoughts on pages 132–133).

Life Skills Children Can Learn

Children can learn that there are other ways to solve problems besides fighting. They have belonging and significance in the family without having to fight for their place.

Parenting Pointers

1. Be careful to treat older and younger fighters the same. Otherwise it is easy for the younger to believe "The way to be special around here is to get my brother into trouble." Soon she will be provoking fights in ways you do not see. By always blaming the oldest, "You should know better! You are older!" it is easy for him to believe that "I'm not as special as my younger sister, but I can get even." This is how victims and bullies are created.

2. Create an atmosphere of cooperation through valuing differences, encouraging individuality, involving children in solutions, and treating them with dignity and respect. Fighting is greatly reduced in an atmosphere of cooperation.

FOUL LANGUAGE/ SWEARING

"My boys use foul language all the time with each other. I can hardly stand being around them. My husband and I don't talk that way and we've told them to stop. They stop for a minute and then start right up again. Help, please!"

Understanding Your Child, Yourself, and the Situation

Swearing and the use of foul language have become very commonplace in so many arenas of life—the media and with adults—that it is very important to teach children the difference between respectful and disrespectful behavior. You may use foul language without even noticing, and your children could be copying something they don't even understand but mimic because they "feel" the impact. If you are overly sensitive to the use of foul language, your kids might use it for shock value. If you spend time at the playground, you may notice that your children aren't alone in the use of foul language. Regardless, if it offends you to listen to foul language, you'll need to tackle this issue.

Suggestions

1. Let your kids know that you don't like to listen to foul language and ask for their help. Suggest that they either find other words to use or confine their use to times when you don't have to hear it.

2. If they persist, ask them to go elsewhere or you'll leave the area until they are done.

3. Let the kids know that the language, though fun to use, may be inappropriate for the situation because it is disrespectful. They need to know that some people are very offended by foul language and that they could miss out on some great opportunities if they don't learn to tell the difference.

4. With preschoolers say, "Let's say _____ instead." If you can give some choices that sound interesting, like drats, dagnabit, bummer, fiddle de dee, or Mickey Mouse, your chances are excellent that they will do as you ask. One family had fun saying, "Oh, halitosis!"

5. Sometimes simply ignoring the language makes it go away before it becomes a habit.

6. If the swearing comes from frustration or anger or some other obvious feeling,

say, "You seem to be really frustrated right now. Want to talk about it?"

7. Let your child know that you respect his right to his feelings and you'd appreciate it if he'd respect your right to hear them without foul language.

Planning Ahead to Prevent Future Problems

1. Whether dealing with children who swear to copy their playmates and startle the adults around them, or with children who use foul language to test their power, respond calmly instead of reacting with horror and you can usually confine this phase to a brief interlude.

2. Use family meetings as a way to discuss swearing in an open and nonjudgmental way. Teach the possibility of showing their intelligence by finding more impressive ways to express themselves.

3. Ask your child if she knows what the word means. If not, give the meaning and ask if that is what your child meant to convey. Teach that the use of certain words border on sexual harassment or racial defamation.

4. If family members want to cut down on foul language, start the quarter jar. Every time someone uses foul language, he has to put a quarter in the jar. When the jar has enough money for pizza, order one and enjoy an evening with the kids.

Life Skills Children Can Learn

Children can learn awareness of the effects their behavior has on others. They can learn acceptable and respectful ways to express themselves.

Parenting Pointers

1. Be aware of the impact of television, movies, and the computer. Monitor the exposure your children have to the media (especially when they are young), and engage them in discussions about the dif-

BOOSTER THOUGHTS Mrs. Stone became very concerned when her teenager started to swear at home. She decided to count the number of times he used improper language around her. She then told him how many times he used certain words and told him she would continue to count them. She shared, "I have found that he is more conscious of his use of swear words and they have decreased in the past week. I think that it was a matter of unawareness rather than disrespect here at our home."

ference between respectful and disrespectful behavior that is portrayed in the media (especially as they get older).

2. Don't expect anything to work after just one try. Try again, and again.

3. Remember and remind your kids that they can feel what they feel, but they have many choices as to how they act out their feelings. It is more acceptable to say, "I'm really angry with you," than to use the F word.

FRIENDS (CHOOSING)

"I have one child who complains that she doesn't have any friends. Another child keeps choosing friends I don't like. How do I help my children make friends with children I approve of?"

Understanding Your Child, Yourself, and the Situation

We often forget to honor the different styles and personalities of our children and try to make them all fit one mold. This tendency can be most blatant when it comes to the secret dream of most parents—to have popular children. Some children are quiet and passive, some are active and assertive, some choose conventional lifestyles, and some choose unique lifestyles. The following suggestions focus on meeting the true needs of the situation—to help your children honor the uniqueness of each individual and feel comfortable with who they are.

Suggestions

1. Allow your children to choose their own friends, but help your kids have contact with others their age by signing them up for after-school activities and driving them to sleepovers and playdates. When your kids are young, arrange playdates for them at your house too.

2. If your child chooses a friend you don't like, invite that person into your home often and hope that the love and values you practice will be beneficial to him or her.

3. If you are afraid a friend you don't approve of will have a negative influence on your child, focus on being a positive influence through a good relationship with your child. It is okay to express your concerns as long as you are sharing ideas and not giving orders.

4. When your child has a fight with a friend, listen empathetically, but do not interfere. Have faith in your child to handle the fight (see Fighting [Friends]).

5. Don't worry about whether your child has the right number of friends. Some prefer just one best friend; some like to be part of a large group of friends.

6. If your child complains that he or she has no friends, practice your listening

skills. Try rephrasing your child's complaint using feeling words, such as "You're pretty upset right now because you don't think you have any friends. Did something happen today between you and your friends at school?" Often children will catastrophize and speak in absolutes, when what they are really trying to say is that they are having a problem with one of their friends. Be a good listener to help your child think through the situation out loud.

Planning Ahead to Prevent Future Problems

1. Help children who have difficulty making friends by exposing them to many opportunities, such as trips to the park, Scouts or other youth groups, and church groups.

2. Do not expect your children to enjoy the children of your friends or insist that they play together if your kids don't enjoy their company. Find time to spend with your friends without subjecting your children to feeling stuck having to play with kids they don't like or with whom they don't have anything in common.

3. Go along with your child's wishes about clothing styles so he/she won't be embarrassed about not fitting in.

4. Make your home a place where kids love to come because they experience unconditional love, safe and respectful rules, and plenty of fun, child-oriented activities.

5. If you have issues about having enough friends yourself, don't worry about your child having the same problem or project your experience onto your child. Be careful not to put your judgments about friendships on to your children. You may think friends are forever while your child may enjoy moving in and out of different groups of friends. Be a good observer and see how your child handles friendships.

6. Children don't like to bring friends home when one or more of their parents is chemically dependent, because they are embarrassed and fear what they might walk into with their friend. If someone in your family suffers from chemical dependence, get help, because your children will be missing out on a lot if they are afraid to bring friends home.

Life Skills Children Can Learn

Children can learn that their parents are their best friends because they love them

> **BOOSTER THOUGHTS** Peers don't make children what they are. Children choose their peer group as a reflection of where they are at the time. Drop a skater into a high school, and he'll find the other skaters by noontime. The same is true for cheerleaders, jocks, and brains. (And even as adults, when we go to a party, we tend to seek out people who have similar interests and avoid those who don't.)
>
> Sometimes teens think their lives are over if they don't have a friend. Often we overemphasize the importance of having friends, so that children who choose to be alone feel uncomfortable with that choice, because they "should have friends," rather than learning to be a friend to themselves.

unconditionally, value their uniqueness, and have faith in them to choose friends that are right for them. Their friends can feel safe around their parents because they offer guidance without lectures and judgments.

Parenting Pointers

1. If your child is consistently choosing friends of whom you do not approve, look at your relationship with your child. Are you being too controlling and inviting her to prove you can't control everything? Is your child feeling hurt by your criticism and lack of faith in her and trying to hurt back by choosing friends you don't like?

2. Have faith in your children and honor who they are. Try to make the people your children choose as friends welcome at your home, even if they are not the friends you would choose.

3. Your children may be making decisions about friends based on how you treat your friends. Are you acting how you would like your children to act?

THE "GOOD CHILD"

"I attended a parenting lecture and the presenter said that 'good' children can be as discouraged as 'problem' children. What does that mean?"

Understanding Your Child, Yourself, and the Situation

Placing too much emphasis on children being consistently good has some potential dangers. It is easy for these children to create the belief that they aren't worthwhile unless they are always good. Children who get too much validation for being good cannot handle the slightest mistake without feeling like they are failures. They may lie or avoid activities to cover up their imperfections. The extreme danger of this belief can be suicide by a person who truly believes that they don't deserve to live anymore because they have made a mistake and are no longer perfect.

The purpose of the good behavior is more important than the behavior. Is the child being good to win approval or because he sees the value of being good for self-fulfillment and because it is helpful to others?

Suggestions

1. Don't compare your kids or say, "Why can't you be good like your brother?" Doing this is a double-edged sword. It makes the other children feel less than the "good" child and it puts pressure on the "good" child to please you.

2. Notice progress and effort instead of results. Use encouragement instead of praise or rewards and punishment. "You worked hard at that," or "You seem to have a real interest in that," are much more empowering than "What a good boy," or "I'm going to give you a new bike if you get all As."

3. Notice if you blame or pick on one child excessively. Behind most "problem" children are "good" children trying to look or be good so you'll notice how "bad" their siblings are.

Planning Ahead to Prevent Future Problems

1. Consistently emphasize and mean that mistakes are wonderful opportunities to learn. "Try again" is the magic phrase that lets children know it's okay to make a mistake and then learn from it. Create a mealtime ritual of having everyone take turns sharing a mistake and what they learned from it.

BOOSTER THOUGHTS If I could eliminate forever four phrases from our language in the interest of healthy people, it would be "good boy," "bad boy," "good girl," and "bad girl," and all their related derivatives. Keep what people do separate from who they are so that a bad act doesn't make a person bad nor a good act make a person good. This is an important key to healthy self-esteem.[7]

2. Instead of praising your child for being good, joke with him that he might not be taking enough risks so he can learn from mistakes and failure.

3. Anyone can fall down, but it takes courage to pick yourself up and try again. Make sure your children get this message.

4. Don't let your kids get away with avoiding new activities. Tell them they can decide to quit after three to four times. By doing this you head off the person who won't take risks in case he or she can't be the best.

Life Skills Children Can Learn

Children can learn that they don't have to be "good" all the time, that they don't have to hide their mistakes, and that it's really great to be a learner and try something new.

Parenting Pointers

1. Children need to learn that they have your unconditional love no matter what. That way they don't have to worry about disappointing you.

2. It may be easier to live with a good child, but that doesn't mean it's healthy for the child. If you have a "good" child, ease up slowly and talk to your child about the potential dangers of trying to be perfect.

GRANDPARENTS

"My parents and I don't agree on how to raise my kids. They think it's okay to spoil the kids when the children visit them, but they want me to be stricter and spank the children when they misbehave at our home. I find it really awkward to spend time with them when the kids are around."

Understanding Your Child, Yourself, and the Situation

For many people, being a grandparent is the highlight of their life. They adore their grandkids and love spending time with them. That said, they also come with their own thoughts about how to parent, and it wouldn't be unusual for those thoughts to be different from yours. It's really okay that you don't agree, but it's not okay to treat each other disrespectfully. Most people feel really lucky to have grown up with grandparents and felt unconditionally loved by them. That's why it is important that you figure out how to make sure your kids get the best from their grandparents and you don't suffer in the process.

Suggestions

1. Lovingly and firmly tell your parents that you value their opinions, but you might decide to do things differently at your house, and you'd like their support on that. You are willing to hear what they have to say, but you expect them to

listen to your ideas too, without an argument.

2. Ask your folks if they would be willing to follow your routines when the grandkids are with them, especially when they are babies. Tell them that you realize that they may have fed their kids cereals at one month of age, but you prefer that your child not start on solids until later, etc.

3. When you bring the kids to visit, bring food and diapers, etc., so your parents can use what you prefer instead of having to go out and buy supplies.

4. When the kids are older, trust that they can have a special relationship with their grandparents that is different from what they do at your house. If the kids say that Grandma or Grandpa let them stay up later or eat junk food, don't interfere, but make it clear that's not how it works at your place.

5. Don't be afraid to ask your parents to help out with the kids. Ask for what you want and trust them to say yes or no based on their schedules.

6. For some grandparents, it's difficult to visit with more than one child at a time.

BOOSTER THOUGHTS Grandma Bea takes her grandkids to cello lessons, diabetes camp, and piano lessons. Grandma Jean has a basement filled with toys, TVs, VCRs, video games, and sleeping bags for sleepovers. Grandpa Ted has a workshop with tools that the grandkids can use with his guidance. Grandpa Bart has a camper that he uses to take each grandkid camping once or twice a year. Grandma Lonnie takes the kids to art museums and Grandpa George takes the grandkids for train rides. Grandma Mary loves to shop and buys the cutest clothes for all her grandkids. Grandpa Ken takes the entire family to Disneyland. Grandma Dora plays poker with the kids and lets them win, and Grandma Connie teaches the grandkids how to bake. Grandpa Lou buys the kids chocolate-covered donuts and hugs them when they feel sad. Grandma Lee takes every Thursday off from work to spend with her grandson and gives him her undivided attention for the whole day. Many grandparents set up college funds or are available for babysitting at a moment's notice. These grandparents are giving their grandchildren the message that they are special and unconditionally loved—a huge boost to their sense of self-worth that will make a difference in their lives. The memories never end.

Honor that and help set up special times for each grandchild.

7. If your parents live with you or are helping you raise your children, keep the roles clear. You're the parent and they are the grandparents. Sometimes it takes a lot of people to help kids grow up, so it can't hurt to have a houseful of adults who love them and treat them firmly and kindly.

Planning Ahead to Prevent Future Problems

1. Be clear with the grandparents on which issues are nonnegotiable. If they want to take your child in a car, they must have proper car seats or borrow yours. If the kids are going to nap or spend the night, it would help if they had portable cribs available. Help them pick out age-appropriate toys.

2. You may want to spend time with the grandparents either at their house or yours until they feel comfortable with your children. Yes, they raised kids, but it's been a while, and they may appreciate you showing them how you do things.

3. If your parents are willing, set up a grandparent day of the week or month so your kids know when they will have time with Grandma and Grandpa.

4. As your parents get frailer, make sure that your children find time in their lives to help out by visiting or taking Grandma and Grandpa shopping or to the doctor, or just for a ride.

Life Skills Children Can Learn

Kids can learn that they are part of a larger group of folks who love them and have a lot to teach them. Every grandparent has different gifts for their grandchildren, and children can learn that they are important and special and deserve to be loved unconditionally.

Parenting Pointers

1. If you have an attitude of gratitude with the grandparents, your children will experience many positives and you'll get some breaks for yourself.

2. Think about who each grandparent is and what he or she has to offer. That way you can figure out how each grandparent can have a special relationship with your children.

HABITS

"Our daughter is constantly clearing her throat, and it drives me crazy. I told her I'd let her know when she was making that noise, so she'd be aware of it and stop. That isn't working."

Understanding Your Child, Yourself, and the Situation

If you try not to think about elephants, what happens? You think about elephants.

The same applies to irritating habits. The more we remind, mention, nag, and suggest, the worse the habit gets. Throat clearing, nose picking, and other habits that may be annoying to adults usually start off quite innocently and then gather force as your child is reminded a thousand times not to do that. Some parents worry that their children are reacting to stress and often give more attention. The more attention children get concerning their habit, however, the more they persist. Kids don't plan bad habits to keep adults busy with them, but they are willing to play that game when adults start it.

Suggestions

1. Ignore the habit and let children decide if or when they want to stop. Leave the room if that helps you ignore it.

2. Let children know you understand that they may not be able to help it that they make a particular noise or have a particular habit. Also tell them that it's hard for you to be around when they do that, and if you feel bothered, you'll go somewhere else for a while.

3. If your children are concerned about a habit and want your help to deal with it, reassure them that you love them just the way they are. If you have a suggestion, share it with them. Some nail biters stop when they keep their nails filed and polished. Kids who carry blankets around will often let their parents put them in a special place for certain times of the day until they want to use them again. Kids who pick their noses may be willing to substitute a Kleenex for a finger, especially if they get their own little packet of tissues to use.

4. Encourage your children to express their feelings while you simply listen as an indirect way of dealing with stress that may be contributing to the habit.

Planning Ahead to Prevent Future Problems

1. Throat clearing and other noise-making habits might be related to a physical condition. It would be helpful to have a general physical for your child without drawing attention just to the throat.

2. If children bite their nails or engage in other habits that annoy you, do not refer to them as problems or nag about the behaviors. If you can think of these habits as cute and adorable, the habits will probably take care of themselves in time.

3. Let your child know that there are some behaviors that are private and best done away from other people because others may feel uncomfortable (see Masturbation).

4. If you are creating stress in your child by making excessive and unreasonable demands for high performance in school, music, or sports, stop.

5. Realize that children can experience stress that has nothing to do with you, so don't take their behavior personally. Try to find out what is bothering them through discussion, games, role-play, and by asking questions. The best questions are the ones that seem silly. Your child will set you straight and tell you what is really going on when you ask a really "stupid" question. For instance, if your child is handling stress with nail biting, you could ask, "I wonder if you bite your nails because you are trying to sharpen your teeth?" Most children will look at you like you are weird and tell you the real reason they bite their nails.

Life Skills Children Can Learn

Children can learn that they are not bad or neurotic. They have some special habits that they can choose to handle differently when other people do not pressure them. They can realize that while other people may not like their behavior, only they can decide to change.

Parenting Pointers

1. Children want to know they belong and are special. You can give them that message by loving them for who they are and spending time with them—or they can feel special because they get so much attention through nagging, scolding, or

BOOSTER THOUGHTS Four-year-old Betsy loved to spit. Every time someone said, "Hello, Betsy," she would pucker up and get ready to spray the person with a cloud of saliva. Her parents were embarrassed and couldn't understand how she started such a "bad" habit. They were both very respectful people and didn't understand where Betsy learned to do such a "naughty and disgusting" thing. All their efforts to get Betsy to stop fell on deaf ears.

One day they visited a friend of the family, and when Betsy puckered up to spit, the friend smiled broadly and said, "Betsy, I bet you love to spit. Let's both go in the bathroom and spit into the toilet. I think it's fun to do too."

Betsy's parents watched in a mixture of shame and amazement as Betsy took her friend by the hand and the two disappeared into the bathroom. After a few minutes, they returned and Betsy stopped spitting. What Betsy's parents realized is that they had been creating a power struggle by trying to control Betsy's behavior. Now they had an option and could tell Betsy, "Spitting is okay as long as you do it in the toilet." It didn't take long for Betsy to give up her "habit."

trying to control one of their habits. Kids will take attention in either form, but they may decide they are unlovable and don't belong when they get negative attention. Often they get caught up in a vicious cycle of seeking attention in increasingly negative ways.

2. Bugging children about sucking their thumbs by telling them they will have to wear braces or that they will ruin their mouths does more damage to their spirits than their mouths. Unconditional love and faith in them to manage their lives reduces their stress and increases the chances that they may make different choices.

HITTING AND SPANKING

"I have tried everything I can think of to get my child to stop hitting her little brother. Sometimes she hits me. This really makes me angry. Punishment doesn't seem to work. I have spanked her and made her say she is sorry, but the next day she is hitting again."

Understanding Your Child, Yourself, and the Situation

How are we ever going to teach our children it is not okay to hurt others when we keep hurting them? We are reminded of a cartoon depicting a mother spanking her child while saying, "I'll teach you not to hit someone smaller than you." When children hit, it could be that their feelings are hurt. (Children can feel hurt or frustrated just because they can't get what they want—now!) You probably feel hurt and frustrated too, because you want your child to treat others respectfully and may even worry that your child's behavior is a reflection on you as a parent. Perhaps you are overreacting and treating your child disrespectfully out of shame and embarrassment, trying to prove to the other adults around that you won't let your child get away with this behavior.

Most likely your child simply doesn't have the words or skills to get her needs met and lashes out (hits) because she doesn't know what else to do. Toddlers are short on both language and social skills, and when they play together they can easily become frustrated. When they lack the ability to express what's wrong in words, hitting and other types of aggression sometimes result. It is developmentally normal for toddlers to hit. It is the parent's job to supervise and handle toddlers kindly and firmly until they are ready to learn more effective ways to communicate. Kids will grow out of it if they get help (skills training) instead of a model of violence (hitting back).

Suggestions

1. Take the child by the hand and say, "It is not okay to hit people. I'm sorry you are

feeling hurt and upset. You can talk about it or you can hit this pillow, but people aren't for hitting."

2. Help the child deal with the anger (see Angry or Aggressive Child).

3. With children under the age of four, try giving them a hug before removing them from the situation. This models a loving method while showing them that hitting is not okay. Hugging does not reinforce the misbehavior.

4. You never really know at what age a child begins to understand language. For that reason, use words such as "Hitting hurts people. Let's find something else you can do," even if you think your child can't understand.

5. Show children what they can do instead of telling them what not to do. If you have a child who has a pattern of hitting, supervise closely. Every time she starts to hit, gently catch her hand and say, "Touch nicely," while showing her how to touch nicely.

6. When your preschooler hits you, decide what you will do instead of trying to control your child. Let her know that every time she hits you, you will put her down and leave the room until she is ready to treat you respectfully. After you have told her this once, follow through without any words. Leave immediately.

7. Later you might tell your child, "That really hurts" or "That hurts my feelings.

If I have done something to hurt your feelings, I would like to know about it so I can apologize. When you are ready, an apology would help me feel better." Do not demand or force an apology.

Planning Ahead to Prevent Future Problems

1. When children are preverbal, take time for training without expecting that the training will "take hold" until they get older. (Lots of supervision is the main parenting tool for preverbal children—along with distraction and redirection.) Help her practice touching family members or animals softly. Show your child how to be gentle and say, "Pat, pat," or "People are for hugging, not hitting" (see Booster Thoughts on page 149). This does not eliminate the need for supervision until she is old enough to understand.

2. Teach verbal children that feelings are different from actions. Feelings are never bad. They are just feelings. Tell your child that what he feels is okay, but it's still not okay to hit others, even if he is angry. He can tell someone, "I'm angry because _____ and I wish _____." Help children brainstorm ways to deal with feelings that are respectful to themselves and others. One possibility is to tell people what he doesn't like. Another possibility is for him to leave the scene if he is being treated disrespectfully.

3. Get your child involved in creating a Positive Time-Out area. Teach her that sometimes we need time to calm down until we feel better before doing anything. Don't send her to time-out, but let her know that she can choose her special time-out area any time she thinks it will help her feel better. Sometimes when she doesn't want to use her special time-out area, ask her if you can use it until you feel better—or create your own and model using it to feel better.

4. Find ways to encourage your children with unconditional love and by teaching skills that help them feel capable and confident.

5. Show that hitting is unacceptable by never hitting your child. If you make a mistake and hit your child, use the Three R's of Recovery to apologize so your child knows hitting is not acceptable for you either (see Part 1, page 21).

6. Look around and see if there are ways you are hurting your child without realizing it. Are you sending your child to his or her room frequently, scolding and criticizing regularly, singling out the child when a problem occurs? If so your child may be feeling really hurt and upset and the hitting is a way to strike back at the world. Be more encouraging and positive and stop the hurtful behaviors and see if you don't notice a change in the hitting behavior.

Life Skills Children Can Learn

Children can learn that it is not okay to hurt others. Their feelings are not bad and they are not bad people, and they can get help to find actions that are respectful to themselves and to others. They can learn that what they do doesn't define who they are. They are not a bad child because they hit, but the behavior is unacceptable.

Parenting Pointers

1. Be aware of the discouraged belief behind the misbehavior. A child who hits usually is operating from the mistaken goal of revenge with the belief "I don't feel like I belong and am important and that hurts, so I want to hurt back." Children will feel encouraged when you respect their feelings and help them act appropriately.

2. Many people use the biblical admonition "spare the rod and spoil the child" as an excuse for spanking. Biblical

BOOSTER THOUGHTS Grandma had the opportunity to take care of her eighteen-month-old granddaughter for a week while her parents were on vacation. Sage was developing a habit of hitting when she felt frustrated (or it seemed, just for the fun of it). She would hit her grandma and the dog—sometimes for no apparent reason at all. Grandma watched closely for the hitting to start and would gently grab Sage's hand and say, "Touch nicely," while guiding her hand to gently stroke her grandma's cheek or the dog. Soon Sage would start to hit, but would first look at her grandma who would say, "Touch nicely." Sage would grin and touch nicely. Within a few days, Sage was touching nicely instead of hitting. (It is much more effective to show children what they can do instead of telling them what not to do.)

◎

He: There are times when it is necessary to spank my children to teach them important lessons. For example, I spank my two-year-old to teach her not to run into the street.

She: After you have spanked your two-year-old to teach her not to run in the street, will you let her play unsupervised by a busy street?

He: Well, no.

She: Why not? If the spanking teaches her not to run into the street, why can't she play unsupervised by the street? How many times would you need to spank her before you would feel she has learned the lesson well enough?

He: Well, I wouldn't let her play unsupervised near a busy street until she was six or seven years old.

She: I rest my case. Parents have the responsibility to supervise young children in dangerous situations until children are old enough to handle that situation. All the spanking in the world won't teach a child until he or she is developmentally ready. Meanwhile you can gently teach. When you take your children to the park, invite them to look up the street and down the street to see if cars are coming and tell you when it is safe to cross the street. Still, you won't let them go to the park alone until they are six or seven.

Studies show that approximately 85 percent of all parents of children under twelve years old resort to spanking when frustrated, yet only 8 to 10 percent believe that it is dignified or effective. Sixty-five percent say that they would prefer to teach through positive methods to improve behavior, but they don't know how. This book shows you how.

scholars tell us the rod was never used to hit the sheep. The rod was a symbol of authority or leadership, and the staff or crook was used to gently prod and guide. Our children definitely need gentle guidance and prodding, but they do not need to be beaten, struck, or humiliated.

3. Don't hit your child to show an onlooker that you are a good parent and not going to allow your child to get away with something. Your relationship with your child is much too important for that.

HOMEWORK

"Every night there's a battle over homework at our house. Our son is behind at school and his teacher says if he doesn't start catching up on his homework he may have to stay back a grade. How can we get him to do his homework?"

Understanding Your Child, Yourself, and the Situation

The more you make homework your job, the less your children make it theirs. Kids who think homework is more important to their parents than it is to them don't take the responsibility on themselves. Out of fear and frustration, adults will keep trying what isn't working in spite of overwhelming proof that their methods are failing. If

forcing kids to do homework was effective, we would not have so many discouraged kids dropping out of high school or so many kids who feel their worth depends on their success or failure (who then go through life as approval junkies looking for someone to please). If it worked, we would not have so many kids who resist being told what to do in order to salvage some sense of themselves. If it worked, we would not have so many parents who feel discouraged, guilty, and like failures if they can't accomplish what the teachers can't accomplish.

Suggestions

1. Much of what you can do to be effective requires advance planning. Read the "Planning Ahead to Prevent Future Problems" section first.

2. If the teacher sends you a note or calls, ask the child if homework is a problem for him, and if so, what he intends to do about it. Put him on the phone with the teacher instead of thinking you have to handle the problem, or ask the teacher

to set up a conference for all of you (teacher, parent[s], and child).

3. When your child waits until the last minute to accomplish an assignment, listen empathetically, but do not rescue. Allow him to experience the consequences of his choices—which may be to fail.

4. Avoid the temptation to say, "Looks like you should have started when I suggested it," or "Too bad you didn't take advantage of my consultation period" (see Planning Ahead 3). Lectures of this kind are very disrespectful. They require the assumption that your child is stupid and didn't understand the conditions you set forth. Your child will learn much more from kind and firm follow-through than from lectures.

5. Another possibility when your child complains about being late is to listen empathetically. You might say, "This must be very upsetting for you." Again avoid the temptation to lecture or to rescue. You might add, "I wonder what happened." Your child may or may not tell you his excuses. Whatever he says, keep listening empathetically.

6. You can also do joint problem solving with your child. Listen to and understand the child's issues as well as express your own, and then brainstorm together until you find a solution that works for you both. Do not ask for progress reports from the teacher unless you and your child have agreed to this in advance as a way of solving the problem. If your child thinks this will help, by all means, support him or her by asking for progress reports, but only under these circumstances.

7. Use emotional honesty to tell your children what you think, feel, and want, without demanding that they think, feel, or want the same. This may sound like "Education is important to me, and I feel scared when it doesn't seem important to you. I really hope you will explore the value of good study habits. If you want my help, please let me know."

Planning Ahead to Prevent Future Problems

1. It is appropriate to set up a routine at your home with a time of day set aside for quiet work without the TV or radio going and when everyone is involved in some form of learning. (Your child may or may not choose to do homework at this time, but it is still important to create the space for contemplation.) Involve

your child in making choices about this time, such as where he wants to sit while doing his homework.

2. Before you jump in with any solutions, sit back and watch to see what your child does about homework for at least a week. Then sit down with your child and tell him or her what you noticed, what you wish, and what you will do to help. For example, "I noticed that you didn't start working on your homework until bedtime each night this last week. I wish you would start earlier in the day. I'd be happy to help you look at your schedule to see when a better time would be, or even sit down and read my book or work on the computer while you do your homework, if you'd like some company. I'm also available to help between 6:30 and 8:30 P.M., but after that, it's too late for me to focus." Involve your child in planning the time of day that is best for him to do his homework, and where he wants to do it, such as at a desk in his room or at the dining room table.

3. Tell your children you will no longer nag or remind them about schoolwork and then follow through by keeping your mouth shut. Let them experience the consequence at school of what happens if their work is undone. Call the teachers and let them know that you are doing this because you feel that school is your children's job (see Overprotection, No-Rescue Contract, page 192).

4. Let your children know you are willing to help if they ask, but only if you can help without taking over or getting into a battle—and only during times you have scheduled in advance. For example, you might say, "I'm available for homework consultation on Tuesdays and Thursdays from 7:00 to 8:00 P.M.

5. Schedule special needs in advance, like trips to the library or to buy materials. Let your children know it is their responsibility to inform you ahead of time about their needs.

6. Do not compare your children. Rather than motivating slower children, this discourages them.

7. Some kids will never like school and are better suited for more individualized programs. Do not buy into the myth that the only way to be successful is to get a college degree. Also know that some children are late bloomers. They may drop out of school and then decide later that they want a college degree. Let children know that they are not failures if they don't do well in school, and that someday they might be motivated to try again.

8. Allow for different styles of learning. Some children study with the radio and television on; others need complete silence. Some kids don't have to study at all and have a knack for understanding the material. Be aware that your child may need extra help. Most will not do well in every subject—don't expect him

to. If the work is too hard for you to help, get a tutor or friend to help.

9. Find ways to support your children's schools and the educational process without interfering in their school-work—volunteer at school if you have time, take classes, join the PTA, and read books.

Life Skills Children Can Learn

Children can learn that they can think for themselves and take responsibility for the consequences of their choices, and that their parents support them when they take responsibility to ask for their help. They can discover that mistakes are wonderful opportunities to learn, know how to solve

---

BOOSTER THOUGHTS Sixteen-year-old Frank had to attend summer school one year because of deficiencies in credits toward graduation. His parents didn't shame him or rush around doing makeup work for him. Instead they planned a nice summer and proceeded without him. Partway through the summer, they discussed what Frank thought about the value of being prepared and doing his homework on time in the future. He said, "I don't like it that I had to miss so much this summer. I don't want that to happen again, so I plan to keep up next year."

Since that summer, Frank has stuck to his plan. His parents never mention homework to him except to ask if he needs help so he knows they are interested.

◎

Although this may sound strange, several parents of preteens found a solution to getting home-work **done** by offering to do their children's homework for them. One father explained how it worked. "I told my daughter that I noticed she never did any of her homework and that I was con-cerned about it and was willing to volunteer to do her homework for her. She looked at me as if I were crazy, and then grinned and said, 'Sure. No problem.' I told her that she needed to sit me down each day at 5:30 to go over the assignments with me and show me what I was supposed to do, and then sit and keep me company if I had any questions. On the first night, we did this and I did most of the work and had very few questions. The next night, I had to ask her regularly where certain information might be found, or if her teacher had explained how to do a certain math computation so that I could complete the work properly. Before she knew it, she was doing most of the work herself, and I was helping in places where I could clearly see she didn't have the concepts. And we were having fun."

problems, feel good about themselves, and have the courage and confidence to handle situations that life presents.

Parenting Pointers

1. Watch out—it's easy to take responsibility for your child's work and then live under the illusion that the child is being responsible because the work gets done.

2. Show faith in your children to learn great things through failure instead of shaming, punishing, or humiliating them for it.

3. Remind yourself that your child isn't stupid—just not interested or discouraged and hopeless. This same child probably never needs a reminder to do what he loves or is good at.

INTERRUPTING/ PESTY BEHAVIOR

"I can't get on the phone or talk to a visiting friend without constant interruptions from my three-year-old. I have told her a hundred times not to interrupt me, but she still does."

Understanding Your Child, Yourself, and the Situation

Children often come to the mistaken conclusion that their belonging and significance are threatened when their parents focus on something or someone else. It helps to understand that this is normal and to deal with the threat in respectful ways instead of increasing the threat through anger or punishment. The more the child demands, the more parents—and teachers—give them attention, be it positive or negative. In fact children who are pests often receive too *much* attention—not too little. No amount of attention can fill the hole for children who believe they do not belong unless they have constant attention.

The longer this problem persists, the harder it is to retrain yourself and your child. Therefore it is extremely important to start early, in infancy, setting your limits of attention giving and sticking to them. You also need to give your kids opportunities to find belonging through cooperation and contribution. When you respect yourself as well as the kids, you'll know it's okay to have time to yourself and that your children can figure out how to entertain themselves. They won't die from lack of attention.

Suggestions

1. When a friend comes over, say to your child, "I would like to spend five minutes with you without any interruptions from my friend. Then I would like some uninterrupted time with my friend. You first, then my friend." (Let your friend know in advance what you would like to do and why—to help

your child feel loved and to learn to respect your time too.)

2. For ages two to five, say, "Would you like to get a book or toy and sit next to me while I'm on the phone?" For ages five to eight, say, "I want some time on the phone or with my friend. What ideas do you have to keep yourself busy for ten to fifteen minutes so you won't need to interrupt me?"

3. Tell your child, "It is a problem for me when I'm interrupted while talking on the phone or visiting with a friend. Would you be willing to write this problem on the family meeting agenda for me, or should I?"

4. If your child has been waiting all day to play with you, when you come home from work ignore the chores and spend fifteen minutes having fun with her or ask her to work with you.

5. Spend time with your spouse and other adults while your children are around. This lets them know that they will get some of your time, but not all of it. If they interrupt, move to another room where you can put a door between you and them or ask them to play somewhere else.

6. Let your children know that you hear them interrupting but you choose not to respond when you are busy doing other things. One way to do this is to use a nonverbal response such as putting your hand on their shoulder while ignoring their demands. This lets them know you care about them even though you won't respond to constant demands.

Planning Ahead to Prevent Future Problems

1. If your child is being a pest, plan special time with him/her where he/she has you all alone. When she bugs you, say, "This isn't our time to play. I'm looking forward to our special time at 2:00."

2. Set up places where your children can play safely and entertain themselves. Let your children know that you still love them when you are busy with a friend or another child, but it is not time for you to be with them. Try setting a timer for the amount of time you need to spend uninterrupted. If they can't handle that, ask them to play in their rooms and try again later.

3. Let your children know when you are available for certain activities, such as "I'm free from 7:00 to 9:00 to help with homework." "I will be happy to make library runs on Monday and Thursday after school." "I'd like to read the paper first and then spend time hearing about your day." Then act like you mean it. Keep control of your schedule.

4. Wait until small children are sleeping to make phone calls. For ages three to four, let your child help you put some favorite

toys in a box. Label this the "phone box." Plan ahead with your child to keep herself busy with the phone box while you are on the phone.

5. Have a junk drawer near the phone. There are all kinds of interesting throw-away things you can put in a junk drawer. Let your child explore the junk drawer when you are on the phone.

BOOSTER THOUGHTS During one of our Teaching Parenting the Positive Discipline Way workshops, we were doing a role-play on effective ways to help children with the mistaken goal of "undue attention." The group who planned the role-play chose the behavior of interrupting while Mom was on the phone. In scene one, the person playing Mom portrayed ineffective ways to handle this situation. She scolded the person role-playing her three-year-old daughter. In the second scene, Mom portrayed an effective method as follows: Mom said "excuse me" to the person she was talking to on the phone. Then she took her watch off her wrist and handed it to her daughter, saying, "Honey, please take my watch and tell me when the second hand (she showed her which one) goes all the way around and reaches the twelve at the top two times." Then she started talking again. Her little girl watched the wristwatch intently. When her mother hung up the phone, her little girl said, "Mommy, Mommy, you had more time."

This role-play portrayed an excellent way to redirect the child and to show her how to get attention in a helpful way. Another participant had an equally effective but different method. She put her finger to her lips, lovingly patted her child, and kept talking. First the child tried interrupting more. Then he stomped his foot and shook his fist. Then he found a toy and started to play.

In the classroom, teachers have found that an agreed upon nonverbal reminder works wonders. One teacher had an agreement that whenever one of the kids talked out of turn, she'd hold up a finger. She never got past three fingers before he stopped interrupting and waited his turn.

6. Discuss the problem at a family meeting and get everyone's ideas on how to solve the problem.

Life Skills Children Can Learn

Children can learn that they are loved and important even when they aren't the focus of attention. They can take care of themselves while respecting their parents' desires to pay attention to other people or things. They can experience the concept of give and take. They can entertain themselves. They will feel better when satisfaction comes from within instead of having to constantly seek attention from others.

Parenting Pointers

1. Since this problem requires so much concentration and commitment on your part, make sure you have a plan and then follow it consistently until your child learns that you have a right to uninterrupted time.

2. Anytime you have a recurring problem, you will be most effective if you deal with the belief behind the behavior (help the child feel belonging and significance) and take time for training.

3. You do a real service to your children if you help them correct their mistaken notion that they count only when they are the center of attention. If you do this while your children are growing up, you can save them years of rejection and isolation as adults.

LISTENING

"My child doesn't listen to me. When I ask her to do things, she ignores me until I get angry and yell or threaten. Lectures don't seem to help. It would be easier to do things myself, but I know that wouldn't teach her responsibility."

Understanding Your Child, Yourself, and the Situation

Many parents unintentionally teach their children to be "parent deaf." This disease strikes many children early in life—especially when parents scream, yell, or lecture them while they are trying to explore their worlds and develop their sense of autonomy. Don't worry, it's not terminal. Hope is in sight if you learn to act more and talk less. If your child doesn't hear anything you say, or if you find yourself repeating things over and over, she may already have tuned you out. Instead of looking for the causes of this problem or deciding it's just a stage, it is better to look at your behavior for what you may unconsciously be doing to create the problem.

Suggestions

1. If you want your kids to listen more, it is important to use fewer words. Say what you mean as succinctly as possible and then follow through with actions.

2. Use one word to communicate what needs to be done: "Lawn." "Dishes."

"Bathroom." "Laundry." Be sure you have eye contact and a firm and loving expression on your face. Or if one word won't work, you can use ten words or less. "It's time to learn to do your own laundry." "Call if you plan to stay at your friend's late." Or you can even use nonverbal signals: point at what needs to be done. Smile, but don't say a word.

3. Use your sense of humor: "Here comes the tickle monster to get children who don't listen!"

4. Use emotional honesty. "I feel upset because you spend time on everything but homework, and I wish it was more of a priority for you." (Be sure this doesn't sound like whining—just a statement of fact.)

5. Use action. Take the child by the hand and lead her, kindly and firmly, to the task that needs to be done.

6. Writing a note may get your child's attention better than talking.

7. Children listen carefully when you whisper so they have to listen to hear you. Try it.

8. Ask children to summarize or paraphrase what they are hearing you say to teach listening skills. (See Won't Talk to Me for more information on how to listen to your child.)

9. Give your child a choice that requires his help and attention. "What is the first thing we should do now?" "Do

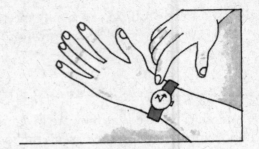

you want to leave in five minutes or ten minutes?"

Planning Ahead to Prevent Future Problems

1. If you are screaming, yelling, or lecturing, stop. All of these methods are disrespectful and encourage "parent deafness." In self-defense, children usually rebel—actively by being disrespectful to you, or passively by tuning you out.

2. Children know when you mean it and when you don't. Don't say anything unless you mean it and can say it respectfully. Then follow through with dignity and respect—and usually without words.

3. Model respectful listening. Children will listen to you when they feel that you listen to them. We often wonder why children don't listen without realizing we don't give them an example of what real listening is about. Explain to your children that conversation is an art of give and take, back and forth, and not an attempt to make someone do what you want.

4. Invite listening by asking curiosity questions instead of lecturing.

5. Ask if your kids are willing to listen before you give them information. "I have some important information about that. Would you like to hear it?" They feel respected because they have a choice. If they agree to listen, they usually will. If they don't agree, and you lecture anyway, you might as well be talking to the wall.

6. Have regular family meetings where all members, including parents, listen to each other in an atmosphere of mutual

BOOSTER THOUGHTS In Janet's family, every time Mom opened her mouth to speak most of the family members either walked away, rolled their eyes, or started reading the paper. Mom had trained everyone to tune her out by going on and on and on about what she wanted and how she thought and felt. After attending a workshop on communication skills, she realized that she had to work on saying less if she wanted to be heard.

Mom said, "I sure go on and on when I talk to you guys." (Twelve words, but an improvement from before.) No one spoke, because they were used to Mom saying another paragraph or two. Mom just waited quietly.

Janet said, "Were you talking to us?" "Yes." (One word.)

"What do you want?" asked Janet, feeling quite confused and uncomfortable.

"To let you know I'm practicing saying less." (Eight words.)

"About what, Mom?"

"About everything, Janet, and I'd like your help." (Eight words.)

Now Janet felt more at home. Mom was going to give her the "nobody ever helps me" lecture and Janet already had that memorized, so she didn't need to pay attention. After zoning out for a few moments, Janet realized no one was talking. She was shocked. Janet said, "Mom, what are you talking about? What kind of help do you want?"

"If I go on and on, tell me to stop." (Ten words.)

"Sure, Mom, whatever you say."

It's easy to see that if Mom really works on this, she'll learn to be clearer before she starts talking. She'll also get a lot more attention from her family. And most of all, she'll create opportunities to experience the real joy of conversation, which is the give and take, back and forth, that comes when people are truly engaged in the discussion.

respect—where blame is out and problem solving and listening are in.

7. Be respectful when you make requests. Don't expect children to do something "right now" when you are interrupting something they are doing. Ask, "Will it work for you to do this during commercials or right after the show?"

Life Skills Children Can Learn

Children can learn that they are part of a family where people treat each other with respect. They can learn cooperation instead of rebelling against parental control. They can learn respectful listening skills because they are modeled by their parents.

Parenting Pointers

1. Screaming, yelling, and lecturing are usually based on reaction instead of thoughtful action. It helps to have skills (knowing what else to do) before you can break the screaming habit. Following the suggestions will give you the skills you need.

2. Don't expect children to remember what they are supposed to do after one encounter. (They remember things that are high on their priority list, but it takes continuous training to help children learn social interest and cooperation for things that are not high on their priority list.)

LYING OR FABRICATING

"I don't know how to get my child to stop lying. We have tried very hard to teach high moral standards. The more I punish him, the more he lies. I'm really worried."

Understanding Your Child, Yourself, and the Situation

We have searched and searched and can't find a single adult who never told a lie as a child. Actually we can't find many adults who never lie now. Isn't it interesting how upset parents get when children have not mastered a virtue they have not mastered themselves? We do not make this point to justify lying, but to show that children who lie are not defective or immoral. We need to deal with the reasons children lie before we can help them give up their need to lie. Usually children lie for the same reasons adults do—they feel trapped, are scared of punishment or rejection, feel threatened, or just think lying will make things easier for everyone. Often lying is a sign of low self-esteem. People think they need to make themselves look better because they don't know they are good enough as they are.

Fabrication is a normal part of early childhood as fantasy and reality tend to merge. Enjoy it and become part of the story whenever possible—you may end up with a creative child.

Suggestions

1. Stop asking setup questions that invite lying. A setup question is one to which you already know the answer: "Did you clean your room?" Instead say, "I notice you didn't clean your room. Would you like to work on a plan for cleaning it?" Focus on solutions instead of blame. "What would we do about getting the chores done" instead of "Did you do your chores?"

2. A slight variation of saying what you notice when what your child is saying sounds more like fabrication than lying is to say what you think. "That sounds like a good story. You have such a good imagination. Tell me more about it."

3. Be honest yourself. Say, "That doesn't sound like the truth to me. Most of us don't tell the truth when we are feeling trapped, scared, or threatened in some way. I wonder how I might be making you feel that it isn't safe to tell the truth? Why don't we take some time off right now? Later I'll be available if you would like to share with me what is going on for you."

4. Deal with the problem. Suppose your child tells you he hasn't eaten when you know he has. Why would he say he hasn't eaten? Is he still hungry? If he is still hungry, what does it matter if he has eaten or not? Work with him on a solution to deal with his hunger. Does he just want some attention? Deal with his need for attention by working together to find some time you can spend with each other. Does he just want to tell a story? Let him tell a story. Identify it for what it is: "That sounds like a good story. Tell me more."

5. Another possibility is to ignore the lie and help your child explore cause and effect through "curiosity" questions. When he says he hasn't eaten all day, ask, "What happened? Anything else? How do you feel about it? What ideas do you have to solve the problem?" These questions can be effective only if you are truly curious about the child's point of view. Do not use these questions to catch him in a lie. If at any time you think it is a fabrication, go back to suggestion 2.

6. Respect your children's privacy when they don't want to share with you. This eliminates their need to lie to protect their privacy.

7. Remember that sometimes a fabrication is a harmless story. It might be fun to explore the story as much as you can and even help your child write a story about it.

Planning Ahead to Prevent Future Problems

1. Help children believe that mistakes are opportunities to learn so they won't

believe they are bad and need to cover up their mistakes.

2. Let children know they are unconditionally loved. Many children lie because they are afraid the truth will disappoint their parents.

3. Show appreciation. "Thank you for telling me the truth. I know that was difficult. I admire the way you are willing to face the consequences, and I know you can handle them and learn from them."

4. Stop trying to control children. Many children lie so they can find out who they are and do what they want to do. At the same time, they are trying to please their parents by making them think they are doing what they are supposed to do while they are doing what they want to do.

BOOSTER THOUGHTS As a four-year-old, Harold was afraid of the dark. His three-year-old sister used to tease him about it and put him down. One night they were staying in a place where they had to cross an outside porch to get to a toilet. The wind was blowing, and the night seemed quite frightening to Harold. Finally his fear of wetting himself overcame his fear of the "journey" to the toilet, so he set out for the other end of the porch. Halfway across the porch he stepped into the light from a streetlight and was startled by his own large, "powerful" shadow.

In Harold's childish mind it dawned on him that if he were large and powerful like his shadow, he would always feel secure. From that point on a lifelong pattern developed where Harold tried to appear bigger than life in order to feel secure and accepted. When people became annoyed by his fabrications he would feel more insecure and develop another fabrication. Finally someone looked beyond the fabrications to see what they meant to Harold and helped him see that he is much better than any shadow—no matter how large.

Remember the octopus, when threatened, releases an ink cloud bigger than it is to hide and escape behind. A skunk believes that the bigger stink it can create, the safer it will be. So fabricators have some company in the animal kingdom.

5. Most stories, even made-up ones, have an element of truth. Look for the deeper meanings and talk to your child if you think there is a problem.

Life Skills Children Can Learn

Children can learn that it is safe to tell the truth in their family. Even when they forget that, they are reminded with gentleness and love. They can learn that their parents care about their fears and mistaken beliefs and will help them overcome them.

Parenting Pointers

1. Most of us would lie to protect ourselves from punishment or disapproval. Parents who punish, judge, or lecture increase the chances that their children will lie as a defense mechanism. All of the above suggestions are designed to create a nonthreatening environment where children can feel safe to tell the truth.

2. Many children lie to protect themselves from judgment and criticism because they believe it when adults say they are bad. Of course they want to avoid this kind of pain.

3. Remember that who your child is now is not who your child will be forever. If your child tells a lie, don't overreact to the behavior by calling her a liar. She is not a liar, but a person who has told a lie. There is a huge difference.

4. Focus on building closeness and trust in the relationship instead of on the behavior problem. This is usually the quickest way to diminish the behavior that you find objectionable.

MANIPULATION

"My child is very manipulative and isn't above lying or sneaking around to get what she wants. She doesn't seem to care about what others think or want. What really worries me is that she has started manipulating her friends and teachers."

Understanding Your Child, Yourself, and the Situation

Manipulation is a learned behavior. Many parents don't realize how they teach manipulation "in the name of love." They do this when they think they are doing their children a favor by giving in to their demands for one more story, or buying a toy in response to pleading or a temper tantrum. Children would not use manipulative behavior if it was not effective. When parents give in to manipulation time after time, it doesn't take long for children to adopt the belief that "I belong only when I get my own way" or "Love means getting other people to do what I want."

Some children may try manipulation because they feel powerless and don't know how else to get their needs met—or they may feel hurt and try manipulation as a revenge tactic. Other children who use manipulation may be discouraged because they haven't learned that they are capable of dealing with disappointment or they haven't learned to work for win/win solutions with other people. Discouraged children need the kind of encouragement that teaches the many respective alternatives to manipulation.

Suggestions

1. Sometimes children manipulate because they know that if they plead with their parents long enough or throw a temper tantrum, a no will turn into a yes. Stop allowing manipulation to work and your children will stop attempting to manipulate you. Don't say no unless you mean it, and then kindly and firmly stick to your decision. A "hugging no" can be very effective.

2. When you are feeling manipulated, give your child a hug and say, "Let's take time to calm down." This may be enough to avoid manipulation. Or try putting your hand on her shoulder as you avoid the manipulation attempts, to show that you care but won't be manipulated. After teaching children that it is okay to ask directly for what they want, without playing games, reply to manipulation by saying, "I'll wait for a respectful request."

3. Call it what it is. "Sounds to me as though you are trying to manipulate by (begging, throwing a tantrum, demanding attention, lying). I have allowed that to work in the past. Now I have faith that we can find a win/win solution. Any ideas?"

4. When your child pleads for one more bedtime story, don't say a word. Give your child a kiss and leave the room. If she comes pleading after you, kindly and firmly (with lips closed) take her by the hand and return her to her bed as many times as it takes. Or if your child pleads for a toy at the store, ask, "Do you have enough money saved from your allowance?" If the child says, "No," say, "Lets go home and figure out how long it will take for you to save for this toy" (see Allowance).

5. When children tell you that your spouse said they could do something if you say they can, say, "Mom (or Dad) and I will discuss this in private and then give you an answer." Then take the time to get together with your spouse so children don't learn to play one against the other.

You can also let your children know that they need two yes votes (one from each parent) before a decision can be made.

Planning Ahead to Prevent Future Problems

1. At a family meeting, mention that you are aware of manipulating behavior and that you would like to brainstorm other ways for people to get their needs met or to find respectful solutions.

2. Apologize for your part in teaching manipulation skills. You might say, "I made a mistake. I thought I was showing love for you when I let you have your own way. I was not teaching you that I have faith in you to handle disappointment, or to create a plan to get what you need, or to find solutions that are respectful to everyone. It may not be easy for us to change, but it will be more loving for both of us."

3. If you think your child is manipulating because she is hurt and wants to hurt back, ask her what she is upset about. If she doesn't know or can't say, guess. For example, "Could it be that you feel the baby is getting more attention than you get?" "Could it be that you feel other people boss you around too much and this is your way to feel powerful?" "Could it be that you feel hurt that your mother (or father) and I got a divorce and you need more reassurance that we love you?"

4. If you notice a child manipulating her sibling or friend, do not intervene during the conflict. Later ask the sibling or friend if he would like some help in figuring out how to deal with the manipulator.

5. Get your children to help you create bedtime and morning routine charts (see Routines in Part 1), and then let the chart be the boss. When children try to manipulate, ask, "What is next on our routine chart?"

6. Are you too quick to say no or "We'll talk about this later"? Sometimes children become manipulative because they get nowhere when they try to deal honestly and openly with a parent.

Life Skills Children Can Learn

Children can learn that their needs and feelings are important and that parents will help them figure out how to get their needs met without manipulating. They can learn that sometimes they can't have what they want, and that they can deal with the disappointment. They can also learn that they can't manipulate their way out of important routines, such as going to bed at appropriate times.

Parenting Pointers

1. Sometimes the best approach is to mind your own business and stay out of your child's relationships with others. They

BOOSTER THOUGHTS Ten-year-old Brett told his father, Sam, "Mom said I can stay overnight at Skip's house and that I don't have to play in my baseball game tomorrow morning."

Sam was enraged and said, "You'll be at that game, and I don't care what your mother said."

Later that day, Brett's mom, Helen, said to Sam, "Why did you tell Brett he can't stay at Skip's house?"

Sam asked, "Why did you give Brett permission to miss his baseball game?"

Helen was dumbfounded. "Sam, why would I say a thing like that? I thought we stressed how important it was to be at all the games if the kids decided to play ball."

"Well, I thought so too," replied Sam.

"I think someone is taking advantage of us, and it's time we stopped Brett in his tracks. Let's tell Brett that he has to get two yeses before he can do what he is asking. If you think he's making up stories, bring him to me while he asks for the second yes."

Sam smiled. "I like that idea. I think these games should stop."

Later that day Brett approached his father and said, "Mom said I can go to the store by myself. See you later, Dad."

"Wait a minute, son. Let's go check that out. It's okay with me if you go to the store by yourself, but let's go see what Mom says together."

"But, Dad, Mom always lets me go to the store."

"Great. Then this won't be any problem at all."

Brett looked sheepish, as he reluctantly followed his dad.

"Helen, Brett says it's okay with you if he goes to the store. It's okay with me too."

"Excuse me," exclaimed Helen. "I just told Brett that he has to clean his room before he can go anywhere. When he's done with his room, it's okay with me for him to go to the store if it's also okay with you."

Brett grinned and said, "That's what I meant, Dad." He ran up the stairs to begin cleaning his room, while Helen and Sam chuckled quietly.

will figure out what is going on and deal with it, or they will be willing to give in to a child for reasons of their own.

2. Are you setting an example of manipulating to get your way? If so, be more direct about your own needs. Ask for

what you want and be willing to take no for an answer. Your children will see your behavior and manipulation will stop being a way to solve problems.

MASTURBATION

"This is so embarrassing. My three-year-old plays with herself while she is watching TV. She doesn't seem to mind that everyone can see what she is doing. How do I get her to stop?"

Understanding Your Child, Yourself, and the Situation

Parents think it is so cute when their babies discover their toes and their fingers. However many think their children may be sexual deviants when they discover their genitals. Some form of masturbation (often children are merely exploring their genitals) is normal for children from six months to six years of age. Most children lose interest in their genitals between the ages of six to ten. Somewhere around the age of eleven interest returns and throughout adolescence most children experiment with masturbation.

Suggestions

1. For ages two to six, ignore it and most likely interest will pass just like interest in other body parts will decline. Making an issue of masturbation could make it worse. If you tell your kids it is bad to play with their toes, they will probably become fixated on their toes.

2. If ignoring is too hard for you (the messages you received as a child may be difficult to overcome), offer a choice. "I'd like you to turn off the TV and go to your room for privacy or stop fondling your genitals while you are around other people." Children usually prefer company at this age, so stopping will be the better choice.

3. Another possibility is to teach social appropriateness. When your child plays with herself in public, say, "It is not appropriate to fondle your private parts in public."

4. Don't tell your children hair will grow on the palms of their hands if they touch themselves in "dirty ways."

5. Usually children aged six to ten are not interested in masturbation, so don't create problems that don't exist by making threats or using scare techniques. If you have strong religious views on this subject, remember that guilt, shame, and scare tactics are more likely to produce negative long-term results than positive. You will do better with openness and honesty. Use "I feel because and I wish" statements to share your thoughts and feelings (see Develop a Feeling Vocabulary in Part 1, page 10).

6. For ages ten to eighteen, allow your kids to have privacy in their own rooms. Do not go into their rooms at night to see if they are sleeping with their hands outside the covers.

7. Teach children to use the washer and dryer and let them be in charge of washing their own sheets and making their own beds.

Planning Ahead to Prevent Future Problems

1. Make sure there isn't a problem such as lack of cleanliness, which can create irritation and itchiness.

2. Help your child develop interesting activities. Masturbation often takes place when children are bored.

3. If you are worried that your child's interest in masturbation seems excessive after reading this section, you may wish to consult a therapist. In some cases, excessive masturbation may be a sign of possible sexual abuse.

Life Skills Children Can Learn

Children can learn that they have the right to figure out what is best for them sexually as long as they are not hurting anyone else. They are not bad or evil for normal exploration of their bodies.

BOOSTER THOUGHTS We would like to quote Dr. Fritz Redlich of Yale University on this subject. He gives, in his book *The Inside Story—Psychiatry and Everyday Life*,[8] the following possible arguments for ignoring this activity when it does occur.

"First, there is no danger that your child will suffer physical harm from a limited amount of masturbation. The old wive's tales about its causing blindness, insanity, bad complexion . . . have been scientifically disproved. Secondly, there is some danger that an emotionally charged parental forbidding of the child's touching himself may result in such repression of the child's sexual urge that when grown up he may not be able to function normally in this respect. Thirdly, there is comparable danger that the child may develop terrible self-loathing and lack of confidence when he finds he cannot (when half-asleep) completely keep himself from doing what he has been so forcefully told is unnatural and vile. If we have never frightened our child about masturbation, he may feel free to tell us when and if little school friends make physical advances (which little school friends sometimes do), thus enabling us to protect him."

Parenting Pointers

1. Avoid overconcern.

2. Research shows that 98 percent of men admit that they masturbate. Experts believe the other 2 percent are lying.

3. Trying to force your religious or moral convictions on your children may create open rebellion or sneakiness. It is not helpful to teach children that they are bad for doing something that is normal human behavior.

MATERIALISM

"I'm concerned about my children's materialism. They can't seem to live without brand-name clothes, sunglasses, expensive cars, and more junk food than my family could ever afford when I was growing up."

Understanding Your Child, Yourself, and the Situation

Our children live in a consumer age in which the media portrays a world of new, exciting, wonderful—and usually expensive—things. It is easy for children to get the idea that they are deprived if they don't have these things. Parents often give their children too much because of the mistaken notion that their children should not have to do without—and because they are materialistic themselves. Parents often fall for their child's argument, "All my friends have it," and give in to peer pressure of their own, not wanting to be different from other parents. You deprive children of the opportunity to learn essential skills when you provide things for them that they could earn (or at least partially earn) for themselves.

Suggestions

1. If you can afford it, don't say, "I can't afford it." Be truthful. Say, "I'm not willing to spend my money that way. When you earn your own money, you can decide how you want to spend it."

2. Don't accept promises—require that the work or savings be accomplished before obtaining the desired item. This will teach patience and deferred gratification.

3. Children should not be allowed open choices. For ages three to five, choose two pairs of shoes that fit your budget and practicality and give your child a choice of which she would like. For children ages five to eight, tell them what

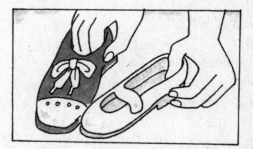

their budget is. "Let's go to the store and you can choose a pair of shoes within your budget."

4. Ask, "What is it that you need?" and "How is that different from what you want?" (The child may need new shoes but want an expensive name brand.) For children ages eight to twelve, say, "I'm willing to provide the best quality for the most reasonable price for items you need. If you want something more than that, then I need to know what you will do to contribute to the difference." (Some ideas are: working more on Saturday, saving his allowance, or taking a paper route.)

5. For children ages twelve to sixteen, teach budgeting through regular discussions with your children concerning their present and future needs. Provide an agreed-upon clothing budget (see Allowance). Allow children to learn from their mistakes by being nonjudgmental and not rescuing them.

6. For children ages sixteen to eighteen, start the weaning process. Discuss what you have been providing and your desire to provide less now that they are capable of doing more.

Planning Ahead to Prevent Future Problems

1. Help children develop an attitude of gratitude. Allow time during family meetings or at dinnertime for family members to share things for which they are grateful.

2. Avoid the temptation to give your children everything they want. This may lead to them thinking that love means getting material things from others.

3. Help older children plan for the future by discussing their needs for such things as cars, gas, dating, and savings and what they can do to meet these needs. For young children, it might be saving for the ice cream truck or a desired toy. Then leave it up to them as much as possible. (Resist your urge to rescue.)

4. When children make mistakes, ask, "What happened? What choices or decisions on your part led to what happened? What do you think you'll do next time?"

5. Encourage your children to serve others unselfishly through charitable work such as providing child care, helping the homeless, buying toys at holiday time for needy children, and visiting nursing homes.

6. Watch for examples in life, the media, and books where service to others held a higher value than materialism. Emphasize these stories through personal appreciation and discussion with your children.

7. Resist parent peer pressure by ignoring the question, "How will I look in the eyes of other parents?" Ask yourself instead "How can I best teach my children the life skills they need?"

BOOSTER THOUGHTS We foster materialism by teaching kids they can have just about anything they want if they hassle us enough. We do this by setting limits we don't respect and threatening children with things that we don't deliver. We often say things we don't mean like "I can't afford it." But what does "I can't afford it" mean to children who have never had to do without and have found that most of the things that they want come without a struggle?

When a child says she wants a new bicycle, and her father says he can't afford it, she wonders, "What on earth could Daddy be saying to me?" She reflects on her experience and remembers, "The last three times Daddy said that he couldn't afford it, I hassled him until I got what I wanted. So he must mean that I haven't hassled him enough for him to make this a priority."

Father says, "I can't afford it."

And she says, "Hassle, hassle."

He reassures her, "No, dear, I really can't afford it this time."

And she says, "Hassle, hassle, hassle."

Finally he says, "Look, the only way I can consider it is on my credit card, and it is full."

She thinks, "Now we're making progress. He's considering ways to get it for me. I'm very close." So she continues to hassle.

Father's last weapon is to say, "If I get this for you, you have to give up your allowance for three years."

She thinks to herself, "Well, last time I 'gave it up for two years' and still haven't gone without a nickel for one day in my life, so that's no big deal."

She proceeds with hassle, hassle, hassle, and finally Father gives in.

What is her perception of how you get what she wants? Wish for it, hassle for it long enough, and she can even overcome "I can't afford it."[9]

8. Watch TV and read ads with your children and discuss how advertisers work to create desire for things we don't really need.

9. Don't be afraid to live simply. Your children will learn a lot from what you do, and not just from what you say.

Life Skills Children Can Learn

Children can learn to understand the difference between wants and needs and have confidence in their ability to fulfill some of those wants and needs through their own efforts (sometimes with help from their parents). Children can learn that happiness and fulfillment don't come from how much you buy or own.

Parenting Pointers

1. Throughout history, parents have tried to make abundant for their children that which was least abundant for them as they grew up. When they succeed, they generally end up criticizing their children for not appreciating "all the things we provide for you." Appreciation comes from hard work, not from handouts.

2. Children learn their values by watching what you do more than by listening to what you say. If you live a materialistic lifestyle, don't be too surprised if your children follow suit.

MORNING HASSLES

"By the time my kids leave for school every morning my nerves are frazzled and I'm practically in tears from fighting with them to get ready. Then when they're finally out the door, I'm faced with a big mess to clean up and a rush to get myself off to work. How do I get my kids to cooperate and get themselves ready in the morning?"

Understanding Your Child, Yourself, and the Situation

The family atmosphere is established by the parents, and the tone for the day is set in the morning. Many children and parents start each day with a struggle because, as we have said many times, children continue to do what works. Too often it works for children to ignore their parents nagging and lectures and allow their parents to do everything for them. The following suggestions will help you invite cooperation from your children that will help everyone feel better so the day goes more smoothly for everyone.

Suggestions

1. By now you may know that one of our favorite parenting tools is getting children involved in creating routines (see Planning Ahead 1 below). Instead of nagging or lecturing, let the routine be the "boss." Simply ask, "What is next on your routine chart?"

2. Set a deadline for morning chores. In many families, the deadline is breakfast. You can establish a nonverbal reminder to show that a child still has unfinished work. Turning his empty plate upside down (as a nonverbal reminder that has been discussed in advance) at the breakfast table works well.

3. Spend your time taking care of your chores and getting ready yourself. Do not nag or remind the kids about what they need to do. Let them experience the consequences of forgetting. If a child comes to the table with unfinished duties, turn her plate upside down and

let her finish her work before she joins the rest of the family for breakfast. If children miss the bus, let them walk. (One mother followed along in her car to make sure her child was safe while she allowed him practice taking care of himself by walking when he missed the bus.) If they forget homework or lunches, allow them to experience the consequences from their teachers or being hungry (which is unlikely because other kids will share their lunches).

4. If it is difficult for you to refrain from nagging, take a long shower while your children get ready for school.

5. Establish an agreement that the television doesn't go on in the morning until the chores are done. If your children are watching television and their work is incomplete, simply turn off the set.

Planning Ahead to Prevent Future Problems

1. Create a morning routine chart. Sit down with your children at a time when you feel calm and help them brainstorm a list of things they need to do to be ready for school each day. Help them make a chart that will help them remember the things on their list. (See Establish Routines, page 17, for creative ways to make charts.) The chart should be used as a reminder and not as a way to reward children for doing what needs to be done.

2. Get alarm clocks for the kids as soon as they start school and teach them how to use them.

3. Children learn responsibility and contribution when they include a small job that helps the family as part of their list: setting the table, making toast, pouring juice, scrambling eggs, or starting a load of wash.

4. Let your kids decide how much time they need to accomplish everything on their lists and then figure out the time they need to set on their alarm clocks. Allow them to learn from mistakes.

5. Take time for training and have fun by role-playing how the morning will go from the time the alarm goes off.

6. Avoid rescuing kids who need a little time to learn that they can be responsible. Contact their teachers and explain your plan for helping your kids learn to be responsible for getting themselves up and off to school in the mornings. Ask the teachers if they would be willing to allow the kids to experience the consequences of being late to school. It usually takes one or two tardies to change a slow morning person's habits. They might have to stay in at recess or after school to make up the work they miss.

7. As part of your children's bedtime routine, include preparation for the

BOOSTER THOUGHTS Six-year-old Gibson created a routine chart in the form of a big clock depicting one hour in the morning (6:30 to 7:30) by using a paper plate to trace a large circle on a poster board. Then he made a list of all the things he had to do to get ready for school and figured out how much time he needed for each task. His father took pictures of him doing each task which Gibson pasted on the clock next to the time it would take. At the top of the clock he wrote 6:30 and pasted a picture of him waking up. Going clockwise, he wrote 6:34 because he decided he could get dressed in four minutes, and pasted a picture of himself getting dressed next to this time. Next to 6:36 he pasted a picture of him making his bed (two minutes). Between 6:36 and 6:46 was a picture of him eating breakfast (10 minutes). Next to 6:48 was a picture of him brushing his teeth. Between 6:48 and 6:53 was a picture of him making his own lunch. Gibson was delighted to discover that he then had from 6:53 to 7:25 (32 minutes) to play with his toys. (Before he made this routine chart, it seemed as though the whole morning was spent with him trying to play with his toys between each morning task and listening to his dad nag him to hurry up and do his morning tasks.) He got his dad to take several pictures of him playing with different toys to paste around more than half of his one-hour clock. The picture next to 7:25 showed him putting on his coat and backpack to leave for school. Gibson loved following his morning routine chart—and Dad thought he had gone to No Nag Heaven.

morning, such as deciding what they want to wear (with young children, lay out the clothes on the floor next to the bed in the shape of a person) and putting their homework by the front door. Many morning hassles can be prevented by evening preparation.

8. Don't forget to discuss morning hassles during a family meeting, and ask everyone to brainstorm for ideas to make mornings a positive experience.

Life Skills Children Can Learn

Children can learn how to plan their time and contribute to the family. They can learn that they have control over their time and can feel as rushed or calm as they choose. They are capable and do not have to be babied to get things done.

Parenting Pointers

1. Don't do for children what they can do for themselves. Empower your children

by teaching them skills instead of being a slave to them.

2. Some parents sleep in while their children get ready. Instead of seeing this as neglectful, we notice that the children are often very responsible. If this plan works for you, be sure to find special times to spend with your children later in the day.

MOVING

"We have to move to another state. My eight-year-old is devastated. Will he survive?"

Understanding Your Child, Yourself, and the Situation

Moving can be very stressful, but it can also be an opportunity to strengthen your family by working together, planning together, and encouraging each other. Moving is a significant change for children—but they do survive. It can be difficult to give up familiar places and people, meet new people, and get used to new places. Showing an appropriate amount of empathy along with the following suggestions will help you and your children experience a more joyful relocation.

You may also be dealing with your own loss and therefore have a more difficult time as you try to help your child. The grieving process for a move can be similar to that of a loss through death. Understand this and allow the process to take its course. On the other hand, there are families that move regularly and the children think of this as life, are quite used to it, and don't see it as a disadvantage. It is best not to make assumptions. Moving could be hard for you and easy for your child or vice versa, so make sure you check how a family member feels and don't assume that you know.

Suggestions

1. Share your grief and your excitement. Also share your plans to deal with your grief. This models for your children that it is okay to feel sad and excited.

2. Take time to be aware of your children's feelings and to listen and help them process their feelings. Just listening is often enough.

3. Avoid getting so focused on the move that you neglect your children. The more you involve them, the less neglected they will feel.

4. Include your children in the packing and allow them to take their important treasures. This is not a time to argue with them about things they want to keep. Save spring housecleaning for another time.

5. Purchase home magazines so each child can clip ideas for decorating his or her new room.

6. When you arrive at the new destination, help your children explore the new area. Take them to the library to get library cards. Go for bike rides to explore the neighborhood. Find the closest parks and recreation to see if special classes are offered. Visit the Chamber of Commerce to learn about special features of the new area. Take your children to the closest shopping center and movies. (It won't be long before they will have friends and your teenagers won't want to be seen in these areas with you.)

Planning Ahead to Prevent Future Problems

1. During a family meeting, have a brainstorming session where everyone can contribute suggestions for making relocation easier.

2. Help your children decide on ways to stay connected to the old location. These plans provide a bridge until children make new friends and lose some interest in their former home. Plant a memorial tree, plan return visits and put them on the calendar, give friends ten self-addressed, stamped envelopes to encourage writing, plan a small phone budget, let your children have their own e-mail address, or encourage each child to make a scrapbook including pictures of their home, favorite places, and friends.

3. Discuss your children's former experiences with change, such as beginning a new year at school, making a new

BOOSTER THOUGHTS Jocelyn is a pack rat. She can't seem to throw anything away, even though she hates all the piles in her home and the overloaded shelves and closets. One day she decided to talk to her counselor about this problem so she could look for ways to make some changes. Her counselor asked her to think back to any time when she was a child. Immediately Jocelyn remembered when her family moved across the country after her father had lost his job. Her mother did all the packing, including throwing out every bit of memorabilia Jocelyn had saved over the years. No one asked her what she wanted to save or allowed her to participate in packing. The lightbulb went off for Jocelyn. "Wow," she said, "I guess I'm making sure that no one takes my treasures ever again. I never realized that my behavior now is connected to something that happened so long ago. I guess I could clean house now, because this time I'm in charge of what I keep and what I toss."

friend, or going someplace new for vacation. Emphasize what was gained through the experience. Then explore what they may gain through moving.

4. If possible, include your children in looking for a new house or apartment.

Life Skills Children Can Learn

Children can learn that it is okay to feel sad about loss and change. They can also learn that working together and planning together helps them through transition periods and strengthens their family.

Parenting Pointers

1. Avoid being overly responsible for the child's struggle and feelings. Show acceptance and understanding but avoid rescuing him.

2. Share with your children some of the transitions you have experienced where you faced fear and uncertainty at first but ended up growing and learning. Make it a personal sharing rather than a lecture.

3. Avoid bribes and blackmail as ways to resolve conflict so that you demonstrate acceptance and cooperation rather than manipulation.

4. Family meetings, rituals, and traditions provide structures that help with transitions while strengthening your family.

NAPS (*SEE ALSO BEDTIME HASSLES*)

"My child refuses to take a nap, but she gets so tired and cranky by 5:00 that everyone is miserable. Sometimes she falls asleep by 5:30 or so and then wakes up raring to go around 8:00. Then bedtime becomes a nightmare. How do I get her to take a nap when I know she needs one?"

Understanding Your Child, Yourself, and the Situation

Children resist sleep, not because they don't need it, but because they don't want to miss out on anything as they explore their exciting world. It is important to treat their need for autonomy with dignity and respect while helping them learn to make choices and follow rules that make life more enjoyable for themselves and others. You have the right to quiet time, and it is okay to expect your children to entertain themselves for a while. Start by calling it "quiet time" instead of nap time. Your child may or may not fall asleep. You could schedule a one-hour rest after lunch as an opportunity for you to have time to yourself and for your kids to play quietly in their rooms. Do not insist that children sleep during quiet times, but ask that they respect other people's need for space.

Suggestions

1. Don't tell your child she is tired (even though you think she is). Admit another truth—that *you* are tired and need a break.

2. Tell your child she doesn't have to sleep, but that she has to stay in her bed or special quiet-time place (see Planning Ahead 4) for one hour doing something quiet such as looking at books or listening to soft music.

3. Give her a limited choice: "Do you want to start your quiet time at 1:00 or at 1:15?"

4. Follow through with kindness and firmness. Every time your child gets up before quiet time is over, gently take her by the hand and lead her back to her quiet-time place. You may have to repeat this twenty or more times for several days until she knows you mean what you say.

Planning Ahead to Prevent Future Problems

1. Establish a routine and stick to it. Quiet time can be preceded by five minutes of special time to read a story or play a game.

2. Children enjoy routines and should be involved in setting them up. Use questions and limited choices to find out what your child thinks will make quiet time work.

3. While planning a quiet-time routine, be sure it follows quiet activities instead of

BOOSTER THOUGHTS In their *Parents Book of Discipline*,[10] Barbara and David Björklund give the following examples:

One mother we know lets her preschooler take his nap in his older brother's room, as long as he . . . goes to sleep nicely. Another grandmother we know keeps a Mickey Mouse sleeping bag in her closet that belonged to the kids' uncle. They can pick any room in the house for a nap and use the sleeping bag to "camp out" if they go right to sleep. (These kids never nap at home, but always take two- or three-hour naps at Grandma's.)

being scheduled right after activities that are stimulating.

4. Try making quiet time different from bedtime. Allow your child to choose a special quiet-time stuffed animal, a different bed, a different blanket, or a special sleeping bag in a different room.

5. Teach your child to use a simple cassette player. Let her choose from a collection of quiet-time music and start the cassette player him/herself.

Life Skills Children Can Learn

Children can learn that their resistance will be treated with dignity and respect. They can learn that, while they have some choices, they also need to follow routines that are respectful to everyone.

Parenting Pointers

1. All children do not need the same amount of sleep. Some are through with napping by the time they're two or two and a half. Others need naps until they start kindergarten.

2. It does not hurt your child's self-esteem to demonstrate her frustration by "crying it out." It is damaging to self-esteem for a child to develop beliefs that "I'm not capable to handle disappointment." "I don't have to follow any limits." "I can manipulate others to give me my way."

NEGATIVE CHILD

"I am so worried and irritated with my son that I don't know what to do. Nothing is ever right or enough for him. We just had his birthday party, which he planned. He rented a game, had a friend over, and at the end of the party, when I asked if he had a good time, he said, 'Well, sort of.' I would fall over if he ever sounded positive. All he can think of is what he doesn't have or didn't do."

Understanding Yourself, Your Child, and the Situation

Children who never seem satisfied by what they have are difficult to be with and hard to like. If they feel cheated and compare themselves to their friends, insisting all their friends have something they don't, they may be stuck trying to keep up with a standard that doesn't fit your pocketbook or your value system. When your children are unhappy, you may think it is a reflection on you and that you must have done something wrong. You probably want your children to be happy and positive, because it would be nice for them and easier for you and everyone else to live with them, but despite your best efforts things are never quite right. Negative kids often develop their attitudes and behaviors as a way of finding a unique spot in the family, rebelling from controlling parents, or reacting to parents who are always trying to make them happy.

BOOSTER THOUGHTS Ian was convinced that his mother liked his brother more than him and that his brother always got his way. No amount of explaining and coaxing could get him to change his mind. He drew a picture of the family, and his brother had a halo over his head while Ian had horns. His mother was worried about Ian's attitude, but also weary of his constant complaining.

One day she took him out to lunch and said that she had a serious problem and needed his help. To his surprise, she said, "I don't know what to do about your brother. He's such a Goody Two-shoes that he's driving me crazy. I'm sick and tired of his constant volunteering to help. Any ideas?"

Ian's jaw hung down to the table as he sat in shock. Finally he said, "I don't know what you can do, because he makes me mad too. I thought he was your favorite."

"Well, Ian, I guess we'll have to give this more thought. Thanks for listening to me. Now what should we have for dessert?"

When they went home, Ian seemed lighter. It didn't completely change his negativity, but he had more positive moments and his mother found that he winked at her every time his brother offered to do one more nice thing.

Suggestions

1. Accept your child as he is. It's okay to acknowledge that your child sees the glass half empty or that Oscar the Grouch is going to get a run for his money. Don't say this to your child; just accept it. Also ask others (siblings, relatives, and other parents) to avoid labeling your child. Don't compare your kids to one another.

2. Don't ask questions like "Did you have a good time?" or "Are you happy?" of a child who has negative tendencies unless you like having rain on your parade. Instead try humor: "On a scale of one to ten, how bad was your day?" or "Show me with your hands how much you hate your new outfit."

3. Tell your child that you are willing to hear about the disappointments but would also like to hear about the positives.

4. When your child complains, listen without talking or trying to fix anything. It may not be beneficial to be negative if there isn't any payoff.

5. Avoid getting hooked. Instead of reacting with your own negativity, model the positive attitude you hope she will learn someday. You can hope for improvement while accepting what is.

6. Don't mimic or be sarcastic. It is not helpful or encouraging to say things such as "Well, here comes the grump."

7. When your child blames everyone else for her problems, listen respectfully and then say, "That's her part. What might your part have been in causing this to happen? Do you want help with problem solving for this situation, or were you simply wanting to tell me how you feel?"

Planning Ahead to Prevent Future Problems

1. Help your child learn how to create success for herself. Show her how to set up a savings account to save for things she wants, create a list of what to do when bored, and make up a gratitude list.

2. Teach your child how to express feelings using the "I feel _____ because _____ and I wish _____" formula (see Part 1).

3. Spend special time each day with your child so that she can get attention by doing something with you other than complaining.

4. Really listen to your child. Perhaps he has a legitimate problem and you aren't taking him seriously.

5. If you have another child who is positive, realize that a lot of what you are dealing with is sibling rivalry. (See Sibling Rivalry for solutions.)

6. Sometimes it helps to agree with your child and jokingly say, "What do you think we should do to that culprit?" Often this is enough for your child to feel your support.

Life Skills Children Can Learn

Children learn that life has ups and downs, that they are able and responsible to make their worlds the way they want them to be. They can learn that the universe doesn't revolve around them.

Parenting Pointers

1. The more you empower instead of fix or scold your child, the happier you all will be.

2. Create your own schedule, get a life, and be clear about what you are willing to do for and with your child. Make sure your child knows that you have important things to do for yourself and others. If this bothers your child, that's okay. Let her have her feelings without trying to fix or change them.

NO! (*SEE ALSO LISTENING AND TERRIBLE TWOS*)

"My toddler is always saying no. It doesn't matter if I ask him to do something nicely or yell, he says no. He even says no when I ask him to pick out a story book. I've heard of the terrible twos, but this is ridiculous."

Understanding Your Child, Yourself, and the Situation

Too often the word *cooperate* means *do what I say!* If your children say no or refuse to do what you want, this doesn't mean they are uncooperative. Sometimes with very young children, "no" is simply a short, direct, fun word to say. They might not even mean no—don't turn it into a power struggle. Or your child may be going through a normal individuation process—taking steps to separate himself as an individual from you or practice having different opinions. Instead of discouraging the autonomy, this is a time to learn more about who your child is. If children are hindered through excessive control or punishment when they try to assert their autonomy, they may develop a sense of doubt and shame about themselves. There is a line, however, between raising a bully and helping your child individuate. The balance comes in learning to nurture and support the individuation process while establishing respectful and safe boundaries so that it does not turn into a power struggle.

Suggestions

1. Ignore the word *no*. When possible simply leave the scene. If action is required, act with your mouth shut. For example, if your child needs to go to bed, take him/her by the hand and lead him/her to the bedroom.

2. Give choices that can't be answered by a yes or no. "Do you want to wear your yellow pajamas or your blue pajamas?" "Do you want a long story or a short story?" Don't ask questions that can be answered by yes or no. Instead use time for, first we _____ and then we _____, or how fast can you climb into your car seat?

3. Give your child power by asking for his/her help and inviting him/her to make decisions. "I need some help cleaning up this mess. Which part do you want to do, and which part do you want me to do?"

4. Diversions work well, whether changing the subject or moving on to a new activity.

5. Listen for feelings and identify them. Say, "You're upset because you can't play outside any longer. You wish you could. I wish you could, too, but it's

time to have dinner. Let's go set the table."

6. Celebrate. "Hooray! You are starting to think for yourself and deciding what is important to you." A two-year-old may not understand what you are saying, but it will help you remember how important it is for your child to establish him/herself as an individual.

Planning Ahead to Prevent Future Problems

1. Learn about age-appropriate behavior so you won't expect your child to do things (or to avoid things) that are not developmentally appropriate. With this knowledge, you will understand the importance of using kind and firm methods that teach life skills and invite cooperation instead of rebellion.

2. Avoid demands and offer choices. "It is time to leave the park and get in the car. Would you like to help by carrying my keys or my purse?" "It is time to go to bed. What is next on your bedtime routine chart?" Give your child many opportunities to make decisions and choices that foster a sense of power and importance instead of rebellion.

3. Watch out for the "no monster." Are you saying no without thinking every time your child asks you a question or makes a request? Do you say "no" every time your toddler touches a forbidden object?

Many parents say no constantly and wonder why children follow their lead. When children are very young, use distraction to show them what they can do instead of saying no. When they are older, find a way to say "yes." For example, when your child says, "I don't want to do what you say," reply with "Yes, I can understand that. How about putting the item on the agenda for the family meeting or telling me your idea of what you think would work better so I can think it over?"

4. Often preschool-age children will say no to everything just because they like the word. If you don't find this cute and adorable, stop asking them questions that can be answered by a yes or no.

5. Never say "bad boy" or "naughty girl." Children may do unacceptable things, but they are not bad people.

6. Don't underestimate how much your child really understands. Talk to your child and explain things and then wait and see if he or she gets the concept. For instance, you could say, "The stereo might break if you play with the knobs. If you want to play music, come get me and we'll turn it on together."

Life Skills Children Can Learn

Children can learn that their parents respect them as individuals and will help them have

> **BOOSTER THOUGHTS** Mrs. Knight was relieved to learn about the individuation process. She had been engaged in a heavy-duty power struggle with her son. She thought it was her duty to make him mind her and do what she told him to do. The more she said, "Yes, you will," the more her son said, "No, I won't."
>
> She started to use humor. The next time he said no, she grabbed him in a big hug and said, "What do you mean, no? I'm going to tickle you until I hear a yes." Soon they were laughing, and the power struggle was forgotten.
>
> Other times, when her son would say no, she would say, "Actually that is what I meant." Then she would sing, "No, no, a thousand times no." Again the power struggle was diffused and she would gently lead him to what needed to be done.

as much autonomy as they can handle. They can learn that parents will not insist on total control, but will invite involvement and be there for support and guidance.

Parenting Pointers

1. Think of your child as cute and adorable as he/she seeks autonomy. This will help you avoid reacting and provoking a power struggle. Remember this process is necessary—children who do not individuate successfully may become adults who are approval junkies.

2. Don't turn the no into a power struggle by taking the word too literally—your child might not even mean no. Some toddlers use the word no for everything, so listen carefully and be sure to put the word in context.

OBEDIENCE

"My child is so disobedient. I'm worried that if I spare the rod I will spoil the child, but the more I punish him to get him to obey, the more disobedient he becomes."

Understanding Your Child, Yourself, and the Situation

It is very important to think about your long-term goals when you think about obedience. Teaching children to be obedient can be dangerous in today's society. Children who learn obedience may become "approval junkies" and be obedient to whomever wants to exercise control over them—first family, then peer groups, gangs, cults, and perhaps autocratic or abusive spouses. Some children refuse to lose their sense of power and become rebellious. Parents who don't know better increase their efforts to force obedience and create a fierce power struggle. It is better to teach children cooperation, problem-solving skills, and respect for themselves and others. Biblical scholars tell us that the rod was not used to hit or punish, but to guide. Children need guidance, not punishment.

Suggestions

1. For ages two to four, use the many parenting tools suggested throughout this book: follow-through; asking curiosity questions; positive time-out; taking time for training; and age-appropriate chores to teach responsibility, cooperation, and the value of making a contribution.

2. For ages four to eighteen, use the above parenting tools plus family meetings and one-on-one joint problem solving to teach problem-solving skills, emotional honesty, and letting go to teach children mutual respect and life skills. Here's the short version of how to do this: ask your child for his wants; tell the child your wants; see if you're close together. If you aren't, make a list of as many ideas as the two of you can come up with and pick one to try out for one week; come back together at the end of the week to compare notes on how the issue is working out.

Planning Ahead to Prevent Future Problems

1. Help your children learn to deal with arbitrary rules they might encounter in the outside world. Teach them to accept what is appropriate and beneficial and to respectfully try to change what is inappropriate and disrespectful. This can be done at dinnertime or through family meeting discussions where you explore the possibilities and consequences of following, defying, or changing rules.

2. Not demanding blind obedience does not mean permissiveness. There are times when it is appropriate to work out solutions together, and there are times when action is more important than discussion. Decide in advance what you will do and follow through with dignity and respect. If your children run into the street, grab their hands and hang on. Say, "I'll let go when you are ready to stay by my side." If they run around at the grocery store, take them to the car and sit quietly until they are ready to try again (remember you have to let them know in advance

BOOSTER THOUGHTS In the "good old days," there were many models of submission. Even Dad obeyed the boss so he wouldn't lose his job and Mom obediently did whatever Dad said—or at least gave the impression she did—because it was the culturally acceptable thing to do. Minority groups also accepted a submissive (obedient) role. Children had many models of submissiveness.

It is difficult now to find models of submissiveness for children. Today minority groups are actively claiming their rights to full equality, dignity, and respect. Most women want a marriage of partnership instead of submissiveness. Many men want a wife who contributes financially instead of someone who needs to be taken care of. Men don't want a second-class role any more than women do, and have formed many groups to assess their roles and assert their rights. As Rudolf Dreikurs pointed out, "When Dad lost control of Mom, they both lost control of the children." Children are simply following the examples all around them. These days teaching kids to be responsible and moral is more important than obedience.

The psychiatrist Rollo May[11] once said, "What America should ultimately do is erect a statue of responsibility in San Francisco Harbor to offset the Statue of Liberty in New York Harbor to remind us constantly that without one we cannot have the other."

what you will do). All of this is done with kindness as well as firmness—no lectures or humiliation added.

Life Skills Children Can Learn

Children can learn self-discipline, responsibility, cooperation, problem solving, and respect for themselves and others.

Parenting Pointers

1. Obedience may have been an important characteristic necessary to survive in society many years ago. To be successful, happy, contributing members of society today, individuals need inner control and the life skills for good character instead of obedience.

2. When parents use punishment and rewards with the intention of teaching children to be obedient, what they actually teach is that children need to be obedient only when the parents are around. It becomes the parents' responsibility to catch kids being good and give them rewards and catch them being bad to punish them. What happens when the parents are not around?

3. Parents are often fooled when they use punishment because the behavior stops for the moment and they think they have achieved obedience. They might be surprised if they check out what the child is really learning. Children usually make one of five decisions when they are punished:

- Resentment: "This is unfair. I can't trust adults."
- Revenge: "They are winning now, but I'll get even."
- Rebellion: "I'll do just the opposite to prove I don't have to do it their way."
- Sneakiness: "I just won't get caught next time."
- Reduced self-esteem: "I am a bad person and can't think for myself. Unless I do as I'm told, I won't be loved or have worth."

OBESITY

"I am constantly hearing about the childhood obesity epidemic. My kids seem to be doing okay so far, but I'm wondering if I need to worry or prepare for this problem in the future."

Understanding Your Child, Yourself, and the Situation

According to our research, 300 million people in the world are obese, even though obesity is one of the ten most preventable health risks according to the World Health Organization. In the United States alone, 9 million kids six years and older are obese. This means that those kids have a large amount of extra body fat, not just a few extra pounds or some baby fat that's still lingering. They are eating more calories than they burn.

You have cause to worry if your kids are at risk. How can you tell? Aside from their weight, ask yourself the following questions: Are they sedentary? Do they eat a lot of fast food or junk food high in fat, sugar, and salt? Do they drink a lot of sodas or other sugary beverages? If so they could be on their way to some serious health problems including extra stress on the joints, bones that break easily, breathing problems, sleep apnea, high blood pressure, high cholesterol, liver disease, and type 2 diabetes. On top of that, they usually suffer social and emotional problems that accompany being overweight.

Obesity isn't a genetic or physical problem as much as it is a lifestyle and health awareness issue. The key factors that can reduce and eliminate childhood obesity are increased physical activity, more healthful eating habits, and improved health education.

Suggestions

1. When your kids beg for soda pop and junk food, just say no. Be kind and firm. Let kids have their feelings, and validate

them. "It must be hard to watch other kids eat junk food when you can't."

2. If you have decided your kids can have junk food once a week (maybe Tuesday) and they want it during another time, ask, "What is our rule on when we can have junk food?" If they keep begging, just listen with your mouth shut.

3. When you have time, respond to pleas for junk food by inviting your child to explore the Internet with you to find information on why you are saying no.

Planning Ahead to Prevent Future Problems

1. Start involving your kids in learning about nutrition and the fat, sugar, and salt content in foods. Read labels and teach your kids to do the same.

2. Subscribe to a magazine or get a cookbook that specializes in healthy eating. Cook with your kids at least once a week, using recipes that are healthy.

3. Take a walk or do a physical activity like biking, hiking, swimming, tossing a ball, or roughhousing every day with your kids, even if it's only ten minutes.

4. Turn off the TV and limit the time spent at the computer.

5. Get involved at your school to influence the school lunch menus or snack choices to more healthy ones.

6. Make portion sizes smaller.

7. Never force kids to eat or be a member of the Clean Plate Club.

8. Don't use food for rewards or punishment.

9. As often as possible, eat meals together, and not in front of the TV. Set the table, serve the food, and engage in conversation about the day, current events, or topics unrelated to how much someone is or isn't eating.

10. Do not buy sodas or sugary drinks. Try keeping pitchers of water with fresh fruit cut up in them in the fridge. You can encourage drinking water by having a pitcher at the table at all meals. Also try making decaffeinated solar tea by throwing three tea bags into a pitcher of water and letting it sit overnight. Juice is almost always very sugary; limit your kids to a small glass once a day.

11. Serve fresh fruit, lean meat, and vegetables. Cut up a tray of fresh vegetables (with your child's help) and put it out when they come home from school and are looking for a snack.

12. If your school's lunches are high in fat, teach your children to make their own lunches. Make lunches in the evening instead of in the morning. Let your kids pick out lunch treats at the grocery store that they can pack in their lunches. Keep the treats low in fat, like pretzels, yogurts, berries, and fruit.

BOOSTER THOUGHTS One mother complained, "My child won't eat anything except potato chips."

The facilitator of her parenting class asked, "Where does she get the potato chips?"

Mom explained, "Well, I buy them because that is all she will eat."

We are sure you can figure out what is wrong with this picture.

☮

The Marker family created a ritual that took place on Sunday afternoons when they sat down together and planned the week's dinner menus. Everyone in the family suggested dinner ideas, which Dad wrote on a large erasable weekly calendar. For example, Sunday night Dad would cook his famous ribs. Monday was pizza takeout. Tuesday Mom signed up to cook chicken, while Junior volunteered to make hot dogs on Wednesday. Jesse said he'd make tuna casserole on Thursday. The family members thought Friday could be "leftovers" day, and Saturday, the family would go out. Once the menus were decided, Mom made a shopping list so that all necessary ingredients would be on hand for the entire week, thus avoiding endless trips to the store or last-minute decisions to order takeout or eat fast food rather than shop for food.

Once the grocery list was completed, Mom called the family together. Each person had a piece of paper and a pen that they used to write down ingredients they wished to collect at the store. Before they left home, someone set a stopwatch to see if they could complete the shopping in an hour.

The family members piled into the car and headed to the store. When they got there, each person grabbed a cart and took off in a different direction. About twenty minutes later, they met at the checkout counter and unloaded the groceries. Then it was home again, where all helped unload the car, put away the groceries, and fold the bags. Breathlessly the family checked the stopwatch to see how well they did. If you are shaking your head in disbelief as you read this scenario because it seems impossible, you couldn't be further from the truth. The Marker family created such a fun-filled event on shopping day that the kids' friends often asked to come along and help. (From Lynn Lott and Riki Intner, *Chores Without Wars*.)

13. Set up a candy day for your kids and limit sugary treats to one day a week.

14. Make time for cooking and eating together instead of purchasing pre-made or packaged foods that contain a lot more fat and calories. Limit eating out to one day a week.

15. Walk instead of drive, use stairs instead of elevators, eat half as much and exercise twice as much.

16. When your kids say they are bored, send them outside to play. Sign your kids up for sports or physical activities. Check your local YMCA or parks and rec programs for low-cost physical activities.

Life Skills Children Can Learn

Children can learn how to have a sense of control over their bodies and the value of healthy eating and an active lifestyle. They can also learn that spending time as a family shopping, cooking, cleaning, exercising, or eating, can be a positive experience. Values are first formed in the family, so kids are learning the value of family time.

Parenting Pointers

1. You have a big influence in your child's health future by how you deal with food and exercise. Think ahead instead of giving in to the short-term feel good of fast food, prepared foods, and a sedentary lifestyle.

2. If you need help, don't hesitate to get involved in a cooking class, a weight-loss program for you or your child, or an exercise group.

3. Avoid treating weight problems with medication. Your doctor may not know any more about nutrition than you do, but there are resources everywhere to help you help your children. Use them.

4. The choices children make can last a lifetime, so it's up to you to take action to reverse an unhealthy trend for your kids.

OVERPROTECTION, SPOILING, AND RESCUING

"I think it's my job to make sure that my child is happy at all times and never suffers in any of the ways I did growing up. My husband says I'm turning our little girl into a cripple by overprotecting her. How can it be wrong to love a child and make sure she is happy?"

Understanding Your Child, Yourself, and the Situation

Tootie Byrd, an inspirational speaker, once said, "There are four stages of development for children: Pick me up, hold me tight, put me down, let me go." While this may be an oversimplification, at some point, your goal as a parent is to raise a child who will be able to function as an adult, who can be independent, and who can contribute to and feel successful in life. You will not end up with a child who grows into a happy, successful adult if you overprotect, spoil, and rescue. Children need opportunities to develop their "disappointment" muscles so they can handle the ups and down of life. The more you attempt to intervene and micromanage, the more your child loses confidence and opportunities to learn from mistakes. Worse yet, your child may become an adult who believes she is entitled and that others must take all responsibility for her health and welfare.

Suggestions

1. Take your lead from your child. Before you jump in, watch to see what your child does first. Keep a safe distance, but keep your lips zipped and your eyes wide open. You may be surprised at how often your child solves a problem without your help. With older children wait awhile and then ask, "Would you like my help?" Even then, don't rescue, but brainstorm ideas they can implement.

2. Know the difference between praise and encouragement. Watch out for good boy, good girl, and instead be specific about what the child does: "Thanks for helping me walk the dog. She really likes the way you hold her leash." Or "I notice that you're the kind of kid who likes to cut your own food."

3. Allow for feelings and learn to identify them, name them, and allow them. If your child is frustrated, it's okay. He won't die from it. Simply say, "You're really frustrated by that puzzle piece and you wish it would go in the way you want it to. Do you think you might want to try turning the piece around to find another way it might fit?" If your child feels hurt after being rejected by a friend, just give her a reassuring hug and have faith that she will survive. (Didn't we all?)

4. Have a house full of small tools, brooms, chairs, stools, etc., so your child can help you work around the house. (See Chores regarding the importance of involving children in the process of contributing.)

5. Give an allowance and when your child runs out of money, don't rescue or buy things for them. Say, "It is upsetting to be short. I feel the same way. And I know Allowance Day feels like its a million miles away, but I know you can make it." (See Allowance for more tips.)

6. Set boundaries for when you're willing to do things for your child and then follow them. It's okay to say that you wash only the clothes in the laundry basket and that you don't deliver forgotten lunches to school.

Planning Ahead to Prevent Future Problems

1. Set up family chore times and expect all your children to participate. Don't feel

sorry for them if they have a paper due or a lot of homework. Expect them to manage their time and do their part or trade with someone. Have faith in your child. When he/she says, "I can't," and you know she can, say, "I'm sure you can handle it." If you don't think she can, say, "We'll forget about it for now, and I'll teach you how tomorrow." (Wait until tomorrow so you aren't buying into the feeling of helplessness today.)

2. Expect give and take at all times. Help children who are helping themselves.

3. Expect your children to try out new activities and give them three to four chances before they decide if they don't want to continue the activity. It's okay to be afraid, but it's not okay not to try.

4. Be careful you don't treat your youngest child as special and think he is incapable

BOOSTER THOUGHTS Mike Brock is a certified Positive Discipline associate, certified counselor, and coauthor of *Seven Strategies for Developing Capable Students*.[12] This appeared in one of his newsletters and we think it could be used by all parents. He calls it the "No-Rescue Contract."

Recognizing that our ultimate responsibility as parents is to provide our children with both roots and wings—roots so they will always know where home is, and wings so they will someday be able to make it on their own—and committed to raising our children as self-reliant young people who will grow to understand that their efforts do have consequences, we hereby pledge to try our best to support them in those efforts by:

- affirming them as capable young people who can dress themselves, do their own homework, pack their own bags, find their own way to their desks, and deal with forgotten homework, supplies, and lunches on their own;

- affirming them as significant young people who are true contributors in our family life, not just objects of our direction or recipients of our rescuing, and who can, with our patient assistance, come up with ideas on their own on how best to do their homework, how best to ensure that their clothes are ready in the morning, and how best to remember to bring all their supplies to school; and

- affirming them as young people of influence who can make decisions on their own, experience the consequences of those decisions, and work with us to grow in an understanding of why their particular efforts yielded the results that they experienced.

just because he looks younger and smaller than other family members. Youngest children often lose out because they are kept as babies in the family.

5. Be willing to suffer now to prevent greater suffering later. Your children's crying and pleading for special service probably hurts you more than them. When you are confident that it is not helpful to your children to pamper them, it will be easier for you to kindly and firmly avoid pampering.

Life Skills Children Can Learn

Children learn that they are strong and capable and that all beginners have a tough time until they've done something more often. They can learn that you are there as their coach and cheerleader, but not their servant or maid. Children learn

As parents, we realize that it is far more important that our children make mistakes from which they can learn than that we always look good. We pledge to work with them in both their successes and "near-successes" so that they can learn from them. We further pledge to support the efforts of the teachers to ensure effective discipline at the school and, in the event of a disciplinary concern, to dialogue with our children in ways that will help them gain a greater understanding of what happened, why it happened that way, and what they can do next time to ensure a better outcome.

As students, we pledge to take responsibility for our behavior and our assignments and to work cooperatively with our teachers and fellow students.

And together, we parents and students pledge to treat each other respectfully at all times, understanding that respect is not something that we need to earn but is, rather, owed to every man, woman, and child unconditionally.

Parent Signature(s) _____

Student Signature _____

Date _____

time management from having the experience of being stressed and accomplishing what is needed. Children exercise their courage muscles instead of their victim muscles.

Parenting Pointers

1. We know you want to be needed, and you always will be, but do give your child the chance to get strong and fly free.

2. It's okay to do favors once your child has shown you that she can accomplish a task without your help.

3. Have faith in your child to learn from mistakes and watch with awe as your child makes corrections based on experience.

PETS

"How do I get my child to keep her promises about taking care of her pets?"

Understanding Your Child, Yourself, and the Situation

All children want pets, and all children soon forget the promises they made to take care of them. It would be hard to find a child who remembers to take care of his or her pets all the time, and it would be hard to find a parent who isn't upset by this. It helps to see the problem as normal and

then use it as an opportunity for the continuing process of teaching responsibility. (The key words are *continuing process*.)

Suggestions

1. Accept the fact that your children won't always remember to take care of their pets. Accept the possibility that you will need to remind your child (this is not a time to allow children to learn from the natural consequences by allowing the pets to go hungry) and do it kindly and firmly. You might even ask your children what kind of reminder will work best for them. They might choose a reminder through charades, a finger pointing to what needs to be done, or asking them what needs to be done. Acceptance is the key to saving yourself from upset and anger.

2. You can also make it your pet and responsibility—and allow your children to share.

3. Keep your expectations realistic. Create a schedule that is easy to check on, such

as "Feed the dog before we sit down to eat." If the dog dish is empty and the dog looks hungry, use follow-through and ask the person whose job it is to feed the dog before dinner.

4. Appreciate the ways children do contribute to having a pet. Don't discount petting, playing with, talking to, and walking the pet.

5. If your child simply cannot take care of their pet, you may want to give a choice. "We can take care of the pet or find a new home for the pet where people will care for it." Follow through even though it is difficult with all the tears. Don't be vindictive. Simply say, "I know this is hard. I will miss our pet, too. Maybe we'll be ready to try again in a few years" (see Booster Thoughts on page 146).

Planning Ahead to Prevent Future Problems

1. Involve the children in discussing the joys and responsibilities that go along with pet ownership before getting the pet. Make lists of responsibilities.

2. If the pet will cost money, let your children earn money and contribute to a pet fund before it is purchased. Let the children contribute (even if it is only ten cents to one dollar) to a fund for food, supplies, and veterinarian bills. This will increase their appreciation for the pet.

3. Discuss problems in weekly family meetings. Get your children involved in solutions and agreements. At the next meeting, discuss solutions that did not work and create new ones.

4. Avoid blame, guilt, and shame and work on solutions on a continuing basis. Accepting that children may always need reminding does not mean to stop using this problem as an opportunity to keep working on solutions.

Life Skills Children Can Learn

Children can learn that even though they aren't consistently responsible, they will be held accountable consistently and with dignity and respect. Opportunity and responsibility go hand in hand.

Parenting Pointers

1. You can save yourself so much grief by accepting the fact that children are normal—not defective or bad—when they shirk responsibility. They have

BOOSTER THOUGHTS[13]

So often what seems to have been a miserable failure is really a big learning experience to share and cherish. My son Noah's first pet, Rose, helped teach him that mistakes are great ways to learn. He also learned that we, his parents, mean what we say—consequences can be counted on.

Noah was only five when he asked for a pet. We were well aware of the need to take time for training, so we researched and conferred and agreed upon a turtle. The pet store informed us that turtles carried diseases and were a bad choice, and wouldn't we like a rat? They love to be held and never bite. All they need is food, water, a clean cage, and lots of love. It was a perfect match. Noah agreed to feed her daily, clean her cage, and play with her each day. He paid two dollars for Rose. We paid thirty dollars for Rose's necessities and the training began. We worked diligently at teaching Noah how to feed Rose and love her. At first we did it together, then Noah did it with us observing. Soon he knew all the steps and was confidently caring for his pet.

Then the novelty wore off. Our family meeting agenda always seemed to have Rose on it. We devised signals and hung pictures to remind Noah to feed her. We broke it all down into small steps again. We reminded and coaxed and discussed. Since this was our first try, we let too much time pass before we stated that consequences would be forthcoming. If Rose was to stay, Noah was to take responsibility for her by the end of one month. He didn't, which meant that Rose was to go to a new home.

Tears flowed. I experienced the pain of following through on a consequence that seemed to be breaking my child's heart. Eventually a friend's twelve-year-old agreed to adopt Rose, and Noah agreed to the adoption.

On the day of Rose's departure, Noah cried, "I'm only a little boy and my life is very busy. I don't have time to take care of her!" We agreed and said that it was okay, that he was too busy and Rose needed to be somewhere where she could get good care. He now knew that it wasn't the right time for him to have a pet.

Noah bounced back quickly. He likes to visit Rose—about every six months or so. He hasn't said he misses her in some time. We all agree that we are not ready for a dog or a bird or even a fish right now, but some other time we could try again.

other priorities in life, but they still need to learn responsibility.

2. If you want a pet, don't use your children as an excuse. Get one and take care of it.

POOR SPORT

"My six-year-old child can't stand to lose. It breaks my heart to see him get so upset. He usually drops out of competitive sports as soon as he starts losing. He will even sometimes cheat to win. I let him beat me when we play games, but I don't know how to protect him from losing when he plays with others. And I don't want him to go through life cheating."

Understanding Your Child, Yourself, and the Situation

We might guess that this child has adopted the belief, "I feel I belong and am important only if I am first or best."[14]

Many children are involved in team sports at a very early age and love learning the skills and playing games. They thrive being part of a team. When there is too much focus by parents or coaches on winning instead of playing, or when children are compared to each other, a lot of the fun goes out of the game and children feel like giving up.

For some children, this could also be a developmental issue. Before the age of eight or nine there are children who are not interested in or fully able to appreciate the meaning and purpose of rules. When five- and six-year-olds play games, it is normal for them to play for fun and make up the rules as they go, although they may be frustrated if everyone else isn't playing by the same rules.

Suggestions

1. Avoid overprotecting your child and allow him to experience disappointment when he loses. Don't lecture or try to talk him out of his feelings. Validate his feelings by saying, "I can see that you are really disappointed that you lost. It's okay to feel like that." This helps him learn that disappointment is a part of life that he can handle.

2. Until he is older, try playing games for fun—without the traditional rules. Have fun making it up as you go. Or play games that don't have winners and losers—everybody wins.

3. As he get older, when you purposefully lose all the time, you give your child the false illusion that he can always win. This sets him up for bigger disappointment when he gets out in the world. When you win some of the time, he can experience losing in a safe environment

because you have faith in his ability to deal with his disappointment.

4. Suggest that your child take a break to calm down if he is taking his loss too hard. When he is calmer, you can ask what and how questions. "What did you enjoy about the game? How did you feel about your participation? How do you think others would feel about playing with you if they always lost? What can you do to enjoy the game whether you lose or win? How would you rate your team's performance?" Asking what and how questions in a friendly manner eliminates the defensiveness created by lectures.

5. Decide what you will do. "I really enjoy being with you, however it isn't fun to play games where you expect me to be the loser every time. Let me know when you are ready to enjoy the game, win or lose, and I'll enjoy playing with you."

Planning Ahead to Prevent Future Problems

1. Discuss sportsmanship by asking questions that invite your child to find answers within himself, instead of resisting lectures from you. "What do you think it means to be a good sport? How do you feel about bad sports? What do you think is the most important thing a bad sport could do to become a good sport? What are your responsibilities when you are part of a team?"

2. Look at your own competitiveness. Are you pushing your child to win? Are you sending the message that you'll accept

BOOSTER THOUGHTS Mark is an oldest child who, by age eight, could not stand to lose at games. Dad was contributing to Mark's attitude by always letting him win at chess because he didn't like to see Mark get upset and cry.

After learning about birth order, Dad realized it was important to allow Mark some experience with losing, so he started winning at least half the games. Mark was upset at first, but Dad just let him have his feelings. Soon Mark learned that losing wasn't the end of the world, and began to win and lose with more grace. Dad felt a milestone had been reached one day when he was playing catch with Mark and threw a bad ball. Instead of getting upset about missing the ball, or blaming his dad for the bad throw, Mark used his sense of humor by commenting, "Nice throw, Dad. Lousy catch, Mark."

nothing other than being the best? Are you yelling at the coaches or coaching from the sidelines? Do you lecture your child after a game, pointing out the errors? Keep in mind who is playing the game—you or your child.

3. Show faith in your children to learn over time how to experience disappointment with grace. Share your successful handling of disappointments with your children. Tell them what you learned from the experience and how you think that has helped you in life.

4. Play cooperative games with your children that don't involve winning and losing. There are many books at your local bookstore with ideas for noncompetitive activities.

5. Invite children to think about self-improvement instead of competing with others. Find stories from Olympic winners who share their desire to keep doing their personal best—whether they win or lose.

Life Skills Children Can Learn

Children can learn that it is okay to be disappointed when they don't win, and that they can deal with it. They can be invited to think about how others feel when they lose, and how considerate it is to lose with grace. They can experience the joy of working together as part of a team.

Parenting Pointers

1. Show gratitude and joy in participating in games for the fun of it.

2. Some coaches and teams are more destructive than beneficial for your children when they overemphasize the importance of winning. Don't hesitate to remove your child from such an experience if that is what he wants.

POTTY TRAINING

"I hear so many conflicting ideas about toilet training. What is the Positive Discipline way?"

Understanding Your Child, Yourself, and the Situation

Toilet training has become an issue that is blown out of proportion in our society. It can be the origin of feelings of guilt and shame, power struggles, revenge cycles, bids for undue attention, and competition

between friends to see whose child is potty trained first. If you simply *don't worry about it,* your children will become toilet trained in due time just because they will soon want to copy what everyone else does. However if you are still having challenges with children over the age of three and it isn't a medical or sexual abuse problem (see Sexual Abuse), you may have helped create a potty power struggle.

Suggestions

1. Wait until after your child is two and a half years old before you even start toilet training—unless he begs to start sooner. If your child trains himself sooner, lucky you. Notice the words *trains himself.* When most parents say "my child is potty trained," what they really mean is "I'm potty trained. I'm trained to remind and nag and to catch him looking like he is ready. I'm trained to hand out the M&Ms and to put stars on his chart every time he pees or poops in the toilet."

2. When introducing your child to toilet training, get a small potty chair that he can manage by himself. At first let him sit on it for as long or short a period of time as he wants without having to do anything. He may enjoy having a stack of books to read by his potty.

3. During warm weather, take your child and the potty chair out in the backyard. Let him play naked while you sit and read a book or simply watch. As soon as he starts to urinate, put him on the potty chair. Say, "Way to go." You may have to do this often before your child learns the socially appropriate place to urinate and defecate. If you are okay with a little mess, you can do this indoors too.

4. Lighten up and make toilet training fun. One parent emptied the toilet bowl and painted a target in the bowl. His son could hardly wait to try to hit the bull's eye. Another made potty time a mom and son affair. Both sat on their respective pots reading a book.

5. When you introduce training pants, do not humiliate or shame your child when he has an accident. Don't put him back in diapers. Simply help him clean up. Say, "It's okay. You can keep trying. You will soon learn to use the potty chair."

6. Avoid rewards and praise like stars on a chart or candy treats. Instead use encouraging statements, such as the ones above. Rewards can become more important to your child than learning socially appropriate behavior.

7. If you are engaged in a potty power struggle with a child between age three to four, disengage. Teach your child how to take care of herself (clean up her messes and use the washing machine) and then mind your own business. That may sound harsh, but you'll be surprised how quickly the problems go away when you become unconcerned.

BOOSTER THOUGHTS The mother of a two-year-old told her daughter, "This weekend we're going to work on potty training. Whenever you feel the urge, let me know, and we'll go in the bathroom together and you can sit on the potty instead of going in your diaper." All weekend, she gave her daughter her complete and undivided attention, waiting for signs or signals from her daughter. By Sunday night, her two-year-old was completely potty trained. Though she had a few mistakes from time to time during the following year, she mostly used her potty chair willingly and on her own.

Planning Ahead to Prevent Future Problems

1. Keep using diapers (without even talking about toilet training) until your child is old enough to talk about it. (You may be surprised by how early they ask to use the toilet like Mommy and Daddy or their friends who don't wear diapers.) You can then work out a plan together that might include pull-ups as a transition stage.

2. If your child is still not toilet trained by the time she is three years old, be sure to get a doctor's evaluation to see if there is a physical problem. If there is not a physical problem, you may be involved in a power struggle. Guess who will win! Stop nagging. Allow your child to experience the consequences of his choice with dignity and respect. During a calm time, teach your child to change his own clothes. When the pants get wet or soiled, kindly and firmly take your child to his bedroom to find new clothes. Then lead your child to the bathroom and ask if she would like to change alone or with you there to keep him company. (Do not do it for him.)

3. If he refuses (which is unlikely if you have truly dropped the power struggle), ask, "How does it feel to have soiled pants? What ideas do you have to solve the problem? Where are the places you can play when you have soiled pants?" (See the next suggestion.)

4. During a calm time (when your child is dry) brainstorm with her places she can play when she's not in clean pants. Outside or in the bathroom (have some games in a drawer) or a basement might be appropriate. Be sure this is not a humiliating experience, but her choice. "You can change your soiled pants or play in one of the places we agreed on."

5. Teach your child (age four and older) how to put soap in the washing machine and push the buttons to wash his own clothes.

6. Find a preschool where the staff is willing to handle toilet training. It can happen quickly when the facility has small toilets that children can use themselves and children have many opportunities to watch each other use the toilet successfully. Many preschools also have frequent toilet routines that help children learn quickly.

Life Skills Children Can Learn

Children can discover that they can learn socially acceptable ways to handle normal life processes in due time without guilt and shame. Mistakes are nothing more than opportunities to learn.

Parenting Pointers

1. Children often feel frustrated and powerless when faced with expectations they don't feel they can live up to. This is often the reason behind their misbehavior. Children may try to prove they have power in useless ways—by refusing to do what you want.

2. It hurts when parents don't give unconditional love. Children may want to hurt back without realizing that is their hidden motivation. One way to hurt parents is to refuse to do what is important to them.

3. Take comfort in knowing that your child will probably be toilet trained by the time she goes to college—and even much sooner when power struggles are eliminated. Relax and enjoy your child.

POUTING, COMPLAINING, AND OTHER NEGATIVE BEHAVIORS

"My child pouts or complains when she doesn't get her own way. It is most annoying when I have been doing so much for her all day, and all she can do is complain and pout about how awful her life is and how she 'never gets to do what she wants.' When I get angry and remind her of all the good things she does have in her life, she gets more sullen and moody, and pouts and whines until I threaten her with taking away something she really likes if she doesn't stop immediately."

Understanding Your Child, Yourself, and the Situation

A pouting, whining, negative child usually has a controlling or easily manipulated parent. The child has learned an unhealthy way to get her needs met, or to have some power over her life. We all get frustrated when we don't get what we want. It is worse when we don't seem to have any control over the situation. However we all need to learn healthy methods for control and healthy ways to deal with our feelings when we don't get our way.

Pampered children often pout because they get their way most of the time and don't know how to handle it when they don't. Controlled children don't learn to say what they want or feel, and so they may believe the only way they can get what they want or feel powerful is to pout, whine, or complain. Scolding, threatening, shaming, or punishing a pouting child only deals with the symptom and is disrespectful. Learn to use non-punitive methods that allow children to experience their feelings and still deal with the situation without diminishing their self-esteem.

Suggestions

1. Do not scold, threaten, punish, or shame your children by calling them names or using guilt.

2. Take a look at your own behavior. If you demand compliance without giving your child a voice, learn methods to invite cooperation respectfully by trying one of the following:

   a. "Now that you have identified the problem, what ideas do you have that you can do to solve it?"
   b. "I notice you are complaining a lot. Do you just want me to listen or do you want me to help you brainstorm for solutions?"
   c. "I'm willing to listen to complaints if they are followed by ideas to solve the problem."
   d. "Would you like to put this problem on the family meeting agenda so we can all hear your feelings and then all brainstorm together for solutions?"

3. If your child pouts, maintain your routine and have faith in her to work it out. Ignore the pouting and proceed as planned. For example, go to the car, saying, "I'll be waiting in the car. I know you are disappointed, but I have faith in you to work it out." When you handle your child and the situation with dignity and respect, often it doesn't take more than a few minutes for her to realize pouting isn't effective.

4. Sometimes it helps to just listen to your child's complaint. Then verbalize the feelings, "I know you are disappointed and upset. I feel that way too when things don't work out the way I wish they would." Then use action instead of words.

5. Say, kindly and firmly, "I know you feel upset. I don't blame you, but we still need to _____." Then offer a limited choice: "Do you want to get your things, or do you want me to?" "Do you need three minutes or five minutes to adjust to the idea of leaving?"

BOOSTER THOUGHTS Mrs. Maxwell became exasperated with her seven-year-old daughter Jenny's increasing pouting. She decided to try discussing the problem at a family meeting. When Mrs. Maxwell brought up the subject of pouting, Jenny said, "Well, I don't like it when you are so bossy."

Mrs. Maxwell felt defensive for a minute, but then she thought about it and said, "I think you are right. Let's put that on our list of possible solutions—for me to stop being bossy. What other solutions can you think of?"

Since Mrs. Maxwell was willing to admit she was bossy, Jenny said, "Well, I could stop being so mad at you when you ask me to do something."

Mrs. Maxwell said, "Wow, are we ever making progress. And I can make sure I ask you respectfully. What other ideas can we think of to help me not be so bossy and you not be so mad?"

They discussed planning ahead, allowing people to feel disappointed and then have a few minutes to adjust to change, and verbalizing their feelings respectfully. They decided to try all these plans. They also decided to use nonverbal signals to let each other know when they were "misbehaving." When Jenny thought her mother was getting too bossy, she would put her hands on her hips and wink at her mom. When Mom thought Jenny was getting too mad and pouty, she would put her hands over her heart and wink at Jenny.

They had created such a sense of fun around the problem that they could hardly wait for the other to boss or pout. They would then give their signal and both start laughing. The good feelings they created made it easy to work together and solve the problem.

Planning Ahead to Prevent Future Problems

1. Practice methods that allow children to have healthy power over their lives, including choices, family meetings, joint problem solving, and planning ahead with the children's help.

2. When you are planning an outing, discuss it before you go. Talk about the time you will be leaving. Ask your child to help you come up with a plan that will make leaving easier for her.

3. During a family meeting, discuss the issue of being disappointed when things don't turn out the way we hope. Invite everyone to brainstorm on ways to deal with this and how to support each other.

4. Another subject to discuss during a family meeting is the matter of feelings (see Crying). Remind everyone that sometimes it takes time to experience feelings before deciding what action to take.

5. Do not pamper your child or be a permissive parent (see Overprotection, Spoiling, and Rescue). Children who are pampered often develop the belief that "Love means getting others to let me have my way" and will develop avoidance skills instead of cooperation skills.

6. Do not use excessive control with your children. Children who are overly controlled often become either pleasers or rebels. Pouting could be a mild rebellion on the part of your child if you are using too much control instead of advance planning and problem solving with your child.

7. Present the following motto to your family: "We are not interested in blame. We are interested in solutions." Avoid blame yourself and help your children focus on solutions.

Life Skills Children Can Learn

Children can learn that things don't always work out the way they want, but that they can handle that. They can learn that their feelings are acceptable but can't be used to manipulate others. They can learn that their parents support them in adjusting to situations with firmness and kindness.

Parenting Pointers

1. It is important to help your children develop and maintain healthy self-esteem while being firm about what needs to be done.

2. Watch your own behavior. Instead of pouting or complaining, use self-discipline when your children are out of control. Instead of reacting to provocation, act thoughtfully with long-range goals in mind. See the big picture: the important thing is to help your children develop and maintain healthy self-esteem no matter what the situation.

PRACTICING (PIANO, DANCE, SPORTS, AND OTHER ACTIVITIES)

"My child wanted to take piano lessons, but now she won't practice until I threaten to take away some privileges. I wish my mother had made me practice so I could play the piano today. I don't want my child to say that about me when she gets older. I hate the battles, but I think it is important for her to practice."

Understanding Your Child, Yourself, and the Situation

It is normal for children to think they want to do something and then change their minds—either because it is harder than they thought it would be or because they don't like it as much as they thought they would. Parents often want their children to accomplish the things they didn't accomplish. Some parents think it is a character defect to start something and not finish it; others may be upset about spending a lot of money to help a child take up an interest and see the money as being wasted if the child changes his or her mind. This is one of those areas where it is important to look at who has the issues that need to be solved.

Suggestions

1. If you have regrets from your childhood, take music lessons yourself and practice until you can play as well as you would like. Then you can stop blaming your mother.

2. Take lessons with your child and practice with her.

3. Be willing to spend the practice time sitting with and paying attention to your child, or at least in the same room.

4. Get into your child's world and explore what is really important to her. Help her explore what is important to her with curiosity questions such as "How do you feel about playing the piano? What does it take to accomplish what you want? What are some of the problems you have with practic-

ing? What ideas do you have to solve some of these problems? How long do you think it will take to get over the hard part so it becomes more enjoyable? How do you think you might feel as an adult if you don't take the time to practice now? What help do you need from me?"

5. Share your own childhood feelings about practicing. Be honest about your agenda—trying to encourage your child to avoid mistakes you think you made. Be sure this doesn't sound whiny or preachy—but is heartfelt sharing. Respect the possibility that your child may not be impressed.

6. Help your child have realistic expectations by telling stories of how it takes time to learn something new. Set up an agreement that your child can't quit an activity until he or she has tried it out for a month, four times, etc. Be supportive and unconditionally loving when your child changes her mind.

BOOSTER THOUGHTS At a parenting class, a group of parents were talking about practicing and how long to expect a child to stick with a new hobby or sport. One of the parents was in a power struggle with her child about practicing the flute. She insisted her child continue with the flute and practice daily, because she didn't think her child was old enough to know what was best. She asked the group what they thought.

One of the parents said, "There are times when, as parents, we see the value of music lessons and our kids don't. Making a deal with our kids often motivates them to get started. Since certain physical skills and eye-hand coordination are more effectively learned in childhood, we want them to take music or dance lessons. We worked out a system with our kids where they agreed to take lessons until they reached a certain level of skill (for example, being able to play a piece of music at a given level), and this seems to be satisfactory for all of us."

Another parent said, "With our children, sometimes the agreement is to try out a class or instructor for three to ten lessons. If at that time our child remains disinterested, she can drop the class. We know of children with great talent who have learned to hate music or dance through being forced to fulfill someone else's dreams, and we don't want our children to end up angry and resentful at being forced to practice or perform."

One of the fathers said, "I was delegated to take my son to swimming lessons. We really wanted him to learn because we recently purchased a fishing boat and want to feel safe with him on board. My son was very enthusiastic about learning to swim until the instructor told him he had to put his face in the water and blow bubbles. He took one look at me and started screaming and crying and said he wanted to get out of the pool. I was standing on the side watching in agony and wondering what would be best. The instructor, a high school student, looked at me and said, 'Why don't you go get yourself a snack or a coffee and come back in fifteen minutes. I know your son can work this out and he'll be fine.' I figured another fifteen minutes wouldn't kill either of us. I heard my boy screaming all the way to the snack bar, but when I came back, he was blowing bubbles with his face in the water like a regular fish. For the next few lessons, he fought me a little, but I remembered those bubbles and told him I knew he'd be fine and we'd just stick with the program till the series was over. At the end of the series, he came to me with a grin and said, 'Can we sign up for more lessons?' "

Planning Ahead to Prevent Future Problems

1. Make an appointment with a professional musician, dancer, or athlete, and let your child talk to this person about his or her experience with practicing.

2. Take your children to concerts (including rock music concerts) or other events featuring their interests and then let them follow their own inspiration about what to do.

3. Work *together* on a practice schedule. Make an agreement that feels good for both of you. Then don't get upset when your child doesn't keep her agreement, because this is normal. Simply use follow-through. (See Part 1, page 5.)

4. Get an agreement from your children that they promise not to blame you when they grow up for not making them practice.

5. Be willing to let your children try out many different activities to help them find their areas of interest.

6. Don't compare children to each other or anyone else. Allow space for them to follow their hearts.

Life Skills Children Can Learn

Children can learn that their parents care about what is important to them. Parents will help them figure out what they want and what they need to do to accomplish it.

Children can figure out ways to conquer the hard parts of what they want to do. They can change their minds and still experience unconditional love.

Parenting Pointers

1. Practice time could be an opportunity to spend special time with your children. Feeling your love and interest in taking the time with them might motivate them to look forward to this time.

2. Many children don't know how to follow their own hearts because they are so busy living up to the expectations of others—or rebelling against those expectations. Provide lots of opportunities for your children to explore what they really want and how to achieve it.

PRESCHOOL AND DAY CARE

"I have been thinking about sending my child to preschool, but I don't know if it will be good for her. How can I know if my child is ready for preschool, and how do I find a good one?"

Understanding Your Child, Yourself, and the Situation

Some parents do not have the option to stay home with their children and must find all-day child care. But even if you do stay home, preschools can be beneficial for both children and parents, depending on the age of the child and the quality of the preschool. Children as young as two can benefit from spending a few hours away from Mom and Dad. In a good day care or preschool, children spend time with other kids in a child-oriented environment and start learning self-reliance in small steps. Reputable university studies have proven[15] that children do very well at a "good" preschool. This knowledge may help you feel confident about your decision to have your child attend a "good" preschool. It can also be healthy for Mom and Dad to have a few hours away from the children to pursue interests of their own and to learn that their children can survive without them.

Suggestions

1. Once you have done your homework to find a good preschool (see Planning Ahead 1 below), have confidence in your decision. Children absorb the energy of your attitudes and react to them. If you feel fearful, so will your child. If you feel guilty, your child may sense an opportunity to use manipulation.

2. A relaxed morning routine will help so your child doesn't feel the stress of rushing. Leave early enough to allow five to ten minutes for transition when you take your child to preschool and when you pick her up.

3. When arriving in the morning, let her show you some of her favorite things and/or introduce you to her friends. At departure time, let her show you things she has done during the day.

4. If your child has a difficult time when you leave (crying or clinging), leave as quickly as possible. Children usually adjust very soon after their parents leave. It might help to give him something of yours to hold in her pocket (an earring, a handkerchief with your perfume or aftershave lotion) until you return. Remember, your confidence is key.

Planning Ahead to Prevent Future Problems

1. Find a good preschool.

   a. Check the credentials of the people supervising and working in the preschool. The minimum requirement should be a two-year degree in an early childhood education program.
   b. Interview the preschool staff members regarding their discipline policies. Make sure they do not advocate punishment or any kind of discipline that is humiliating or disrespectful to children.
   c. When you find a preschool that seems good to you, ask if you and your child can spend at least three hours at the school so you can observe the school in action and

how your child responds to it. This also gives you an opportunity to find out if what the staff members say is what they do. If this is against school policy, find another school where observation is welcome.

2. You may want to consider sending your child to a parent cooperative preschool. At a co-op you can share the school experience with your child, save money, and be involved in parent education classes. However if you have an extremely possessive child who does not want to share you with other children, a co-op could be a stressful experience.

3. For children two to three years old, two to three mornings a week is ample time for a good preschool experience. For ages three to five, most children do fine extending their preschool time to five mornings or three days a week. Use your judgment about what works for you and your child. And if you require full-time child care, know that your child will be fine if you have taken the time to find a good preschool.

4. Prepare your child for separation. Take time for training by role-playing. Pretend you are going to the door of the preschool and ask your child if she will give you a big hug before she goes to school. Then have her pretend that she is clinging to your leg and crying. Then let her know she has a choice when you go to school—to give you a hugging good-bye or a crying good-bye. When following through, your actions speak louder than words.

Life Skills Children Can Learn

Children can learn that they feel safe and loved by their parents and are capable of enjoying themselves when apart. Their parents care about them, but don't let them be manipulative. Their parents like to spend some time away from them, but that doesn't mean the parents don't love them.

Parenting Pointers

1. Many parents rob their children of the opportunity to develop courage, self-confidence, and self-reliance, all in the name of love. They overprotect their children instead of letting them experience a little discomfort and learn that they are capable of handling it.

2. Kids pick up on your faith or lack of faith in them and in yourself. If you treat them as helpless and get hooked by their crying or other kinds of manipulation, they will act helpless and manipulative. This does not mean you should not listen to their concerns during calm times. If your child cries when you start to leave, give her a hug, say, "I'll be back in three hours," and leave.

BOOSTER THOUGHTS A young mother chose two preschools that sounded perfect for her son. After observing one of the schools, she realized that the school personnel didn't practice their stated philosophy. They expected two-year-olds to sit on chairs for longer periods of time than is appropriate for that age and then treated the children as though they were misbehaving when they didn't comply.

After spending three hours at the second school with her son, she was delighted. They had many routines to help the children feel capable. After shopping for groceries, the school director backed her station wagon into the yard and let the children each carry one item at a time into the kitchen. The children took turns helping the cook prepare a hot lunch. They were allowed to dish up their own food. When they finished eating, each child scraped and washed his or her dishes. They had small toilets and her son seemed to enjoy "going" with the other children and then washing his hands at the small sinks as part of the routine. When it was time to go, her son did not want to leave. He obviously enjoyed the many opportunities to be involved and feel self-reliant.

◎

Two-year-old Mandy's child care provider called Mandy's mom, Susan, almost daily saying that Mandy was crying and wouldn't stop. She tried comforting Mandy, held her on her lap, and talked to her, but the little girl was inconsolable. Mom was a wreck because she couldn't leave work to pick up her daughter and she had researched long and hard to find this place and believed it was an excellent facility. What should she do?

Susan asked her friend Patricia for advice. Patricia asked Susan if Mandy cried when she left her there in the mornings. "Yes, she starts crying as soon as I head for the door, so I sit and wait till she stops and then I sneak out. Sometimes I wait for a half hour. I guess the minute she notices that I've left, she starts up again and won't stop for anything."

Patricia said, "I have a suggestion. Ask the teacher to meet you at the door and take Mandy inside immediately. Give her a quick kiss and walk away. I bet she'll be fine. I think you are creating this problem by hanging around so long."

Susan was desperate, so she took her friend's advice and amazingly, that very same day was the last day Mandy cried at day care.

PROCRASTINATION

"I can count on my son to say 'Later' or 'In a minute' to any request I make. I would fall over if he ever did anything immediately. His father procrastinates all the time too, and it drives me crazy. Is this genetic?"

Understanding Your Child, Yourself, and the Situation

Procrastination is not genetic, but it can drive others crazy. Even the procrastinator gets irritated by his or her own behavior. Procrastination is a socially acceptable way of saying, "I don't want to and you can't make me." This is a form of passive power. It is normal to procrastinate when we know we "should" do something we don't want to do but are supposed to do according to someone else. Subconsciously you think that if you wait long enough, maybe the hated activity will simply go away. Procrastination can also be an unconscious way of getting recognition, revenge, or avoiding tasks that seem too

hard. People who procrastinate are probably unaware of the purpose behind their behavior. If left unchecked, it can become a lifelong habit.

Suggestions

1. One of the most powerful things you can do to reduce procrastination is to get children involved in the creating of routines (bedtime, morning, homework, mealtime, etc.) and making sure each activity has a deadline. Routines become part of the normal flow of events that doesn't leave room for procrastination. (See Establish Routines in Part 1, page 17.)

2. If your children procrastinate anyway, allow them to experience the consequences of their procrastination without bailing them out or reminding them. For example, your child might have to wear a dirty shirt if she procrastinates about getting her laundry done, or your son might have to ask his friends to wait for him to go to the park until he finishes mowing the lawn. You don't want to punish your child—make sure that consequences for not meeting deadlines are logical. Remember that "allowing" consequences is very different from "imposing" consequences.

3. If your child forgets to do something on time or procrastinates and then is upset at the deadline or with the consequence,

listen with empathy but don't fix the situation. Many children only learn when they experience the consequences themselves instead of being told what might happen.

4. Don't ask questions that can be answered with yes or no unless you are willing to take no for an answer. For example: "Do you want to do your homework now?" "No." Instead try offering a choice as one way of sharing power: "Do you want to do this in five minutes or in ten minutes?"

5. If you say something, mean it—if you mean it, follow through. If you make a request and your child says, "Later," say, "That isn't one of the choices. Do it now. Call me when you're done, so I can check your work." Then physically stand and wait until she starts moving.

Planning Ahead to Prevent Future Problems

1. Look for areas where you are bossing your children and expecting them to do as you say instead of setting up opportunities for their input or for them to have a choice. Children are more willing to do things when they have advance warning—and especially when they have been respectfully included in the creation of the plan.

2. Get agreements ahead of time from your children and let them be part of the planning process (see Establish Routines in Part 1, page 17, and Chores).

3. Don't leave lists of jobs for children to do while you are at work and expect them to be done before you get home. It is better to create deadlines that you are around to enforce (see Use Follow-Through in Part 1, page 5).

4. Ask your children if procrastination is a problem for them and if they would like help with it. If they do, help them think through a project, starting backward from the deadline and planning a timeline for all the steps that need to be done.

5. Create situations where your children can make mistakes and you help them learn from the consequences. For instance, if your child said she would complete a project before leaving to play with her friend and the project isn't done, don't remind her. When it is time to go, tell her she needs to call her friend and let her know she will be late, because she has a project to finish first.

Life Skills Children Can Learn

Children can learn what will happen if they put things off. They can develop skills in planning and organizing so they get things done. They can learn to set

BOOSTER THOUGHTS Marcie's son, Josh, had great computer skills. Marcie asked him if he would help her install a computer program. He said, "Sure, as soon as I have time." Marcie knew Josh was busy with projects of his own, but every time she asked for his help Josh seemed to have an excuse. Finally she asked, "Josh, I'm happy to wait until you have time to help me install this program, but it would help me a lot if you would help me set my wait-o-meter by letting me know a time that works for you. Then my wait-o-meter starts clicking and I won't bug you because I know you'll do it when you say you will." Josh grinned and said, "Okay, Mom. I'll do it in twenty minutes." And he did.

deadlines for themselves. They can also accept that it is okay to say no to something that is of interest to a parent but not to them. In this way they don't have to procrastinate as a way of avoiding doing something they hate.

Parenting Pointers

1. If you think your child is putting something off because the project seems too overwhelming, help her find small steps to get started. Let her know that mistakes are wonderful opportunities to learn and grow and that she doesn't have to be perfect.

2. Respect your child's style. Some people work better under pressure. What seems like procrastination to you may just be a child waiting for the edge of anxiety to help her finish a project.

PROPERTY DESTRUCTION

"My daughter threw a ball through her window in a fit of rage. What should I do?"

Understanding Your Child, Yourself, and the Situation

Children are going to break things and damage property in the course of their growing up. Most times this will happen by accident. Sometimes children damage property (such as drawing on a wall) just because it seems like a lot of fun at the time. Occasionally children may seek revenge or express their anger by damaging property. In either case it is up to parents to help their children repair or replace the damaged property without punishing children or protecting them from the consequences of their acts.

Suggestions

1. Avoid overreacting and yelling at your children, calling them names like clumsy or stupid.

2. Involve your children in the cleanup. Work with them to repaint a wall, use soap and water to take off pencil marks, or scrub a floor. Children don't have to suffer to learn. Don't punish them for making a mistake, but show them how to rectify it.

3. If it costs money to repair damaged property, you could advance the money and collect payments on a weekly basis from their allowance in amounts your children can afford. You may wish to

cover part of the cost and let them cover the rest. Keep track with them in a payment book. Perhaps they can do extra chores or work for you to help pay off the debt. They can choose how to pay, but not whether to pay.

Planning Ahead to Prevent Future Problems

1. Are you too fussy about your home and forget that children are children? Do you have a special place where the kids can play and where, if they spill or drop things, it won't destroy valuable property? If not, create one.

2. Reach agreements with the kids about where they can ride bikes, play ball, roughhouse, paint, or do other activities that have the potential to cause damage.

3. Put up large sheets of paper that children can draw on, so they don't need to draw on walls. Have young children paint or color at the kitchen table with newspapers underneath to avoid dirtying the floor or carpet. As soon as they are old enough, include them in the preparation so they learn about protecting property.

4. Let your children help decorate their rooms, picking colors, themes, bedspreads, pictures, and room arrangements. Use materials that are age appropriate so you don't have to worry about spills and marks from toys and shoes.

Life Skills Children Can Learn

Children can learn that it is okay to make mistakes and that they can fix their

BOOSTER THOUGHTS Eight-year-old Mary was with some friends who decided it would be fun to throw ripe oranges at a neighbor's car. The neighbor caught them and called Mary's mother. She promised to get back to him.

Mom sat down with Mary and asked in a curious tone of voice, "What were you thinking when you threw the oranges at the car?"

Mary said, "We just thought it would be fun. I'm really sorry."

"Imagine you are sixteen and used all the money you have saved to get a car," Mom said. "If someone threw oranges at your car, what would you want them to do about it?"

"I would be so mad. I would want them to go to jail."

"I don't think our neighbor wants you to go to jail. Can you think of anything else you could do to correct your mistake?"

"Well, I could offer to wash his car," Mary said.

Mom said, "I'll bet that would work, and it would take a lot of courage to admit your mistake and to correct it. Do you want to call him and ask, or do you want me to go with you in person?"

"I'm going to see if my friends will go with me," Mary said. "They threw the oranges too, so they should help."

"Good idea. Let me know how it goes."

Mary's friends were not excited about the idea until Mary asked them how they would feel if someone threw oranges at their car. "I think we should have the courage to correct our mistake," she said.

And they did.

mistakes without suffering pain or humiliation. Children can also learn that they are responsible for their actions and that others will not experience the consequences instead of them. They can learn social skills and manners about where it is appropriate to participate in different activities.

Parenting Pointers

1. If you suspect the property destruction is not an innocent mistake, be aware of the goals of your children's behavior and look for the beliefs behind the behavior (see Part 1, page 25, Help Children Feel Belonging and Significance).

2. Don't let your children find they can push your buttons or draw undue attention by drawing on the wall or other destructive acts. Children love watching their parents fly out of control and may find it worth destroying property to get a rise.

3. If your children are feeling hurt and destroying property to hurt you back, give them lots of hugs along with the cleanup time. Do not perpetuate a revenge cycle. Let them talk about their feelings and what might be hurting them.

ROOMS (MESSY)

"My children refuse to clean their rooms. They have dirty clothes under the bed, dirty dishes and spoiled food on their dressers, and toys strewn everywhere. No matter how much I nag and complain, we don't seem to make any progress on their rooms."

Understanding Your Child, Yourself, and the Situation

Messy rooms and unfinished homework are two of the biggest complaints we hear from parents of children of all ages. These issues become a real battleground in many families. Often children share rooms, and this becomes another whole reason for fighting. Some families are comfortable letting the children keep their rooms the way they like them, but it is possible to have a semblance of order in your children's rooms if that is important to you. Helping your children organize and clean their rooms can be worth the effort, as children learn many valuable life skills through this process. To succeed, however, requires commitment to time for training and ongoing supervision on your part.

Suggestions

1. With young children, it is important to clean with them so they don't become overwhelmed. Sit in the middle of the room and pick up a toy, saying, "I wonder where this goes? Can you show me?" Wait until the child puts the toy away and then start over. Do this at least once a week.

2. Many preschool children collect scraps of paper, rocks, string, and other treasures. It is okay to remove these objects when your child is out. If she objects, let her help sort the items, but usually young children don't miss the clutter and just start collecting again. When children get old enough to notice and care, be respectful of their treasures and leave them alone.

3. You may be part of the problem if you buy your child too many toys. That is easily corrected. Suggest that she choose some to put on a shelf and take down

later. You might also suggest that your children clear out toys they no longer play with and give them to a charitable organization, for other kids to enjoy.

4. Do not bribe or reward children for doing what needs to be done. Caring for their rooms is their job to help the family, and they don't need a prize to do it. Do not connect allowances to cleaning rooms (see Chores). By the same token, do not threaten to take away your children's possessions if they don't take care of them.

5. Some parents choose to ignore messy rooms. They allow children to keep their rooms any way they want, but get them involved in solutions to keep common rooms clean.

6. Another possibility is to give your child a choice, "Do you want to clean your room or do you want me to? If I clean, I get to throw away anything that seems worthless." Another choice could be, "Do you want to clean your room, or pay a housekeeper out of your allow-

ance?" Your tone of voice will determine whether or not the choice is received respectfully or as an invitation for a power struggle.

7. For children who argue over sharing a room, suggest they work it out together or at a family meeting.

Planning Ahead to Prevent Future Problems

1. Let your children have a say in how their rooms are decorated. Children have distinct taste in colors and decor, and it is important that their rooms be theirs and not yours. Make sure they have plenty of containers and shelf space for their toys and possessions.

2. With children ages two to ten, it often works to say, "Here is how your room needs to be kept. You may play with your toys or move things around, but put them back the way the room is set up when you are done." Some children are perfectly happy to comply with your wishes when stated unemotionally. If your children want more say, use the other suggestions.

3. During a family meeting set up a routine with your children for cleaning rooms. With school-age children, one that works well is to have the room cleaned before breakfast. If the child forgets, simply turn her plate upside down as a nonverbal reminder to go clean her room

before joining the family for breakfast. When children take part in making the plan, they will cooperate in following through with it. Be realistic about what you consider clean. If children push things under the bed or pull the covers up over wrinkled sheets, let it go.

4. As children get older, it works better to have one day a week when they clean their rooms. They need to return dirty dishes to the kitchen, put their laundry in the laundry basket, vacuum, dust, and change their sheets. Having a deadline that you enforce works best. For instance, the room must be cleaned before dinner on Saturday. If you aren't around to enforce the deadline, don't expect your children to clean their rooms.

5. Twice a year go through your child's clothing with her to remove clothing that no longer fits and donate it to a charity like Goodwill or the Salvation Army. You can also put away clothing that is out of season.

BOOSTER THOUGHTS Krista and her brother, Tom, loved to decorate their rooms. Every two or three years, their tastes would change completely—from circus themes and kittens to baseball players and ballerinas to rock stars and movie heartthrobs. There were times when posters covered every square inch of wall and ceiling space and times when the walls were painted hot pink or black. The rooms reflected their unique personalities, interests, and tastes.

Tom and Krista helped paint their rooms and pick out fabrics for drapes and bedspreads. The posters they wanted would be at the top of their birthday or Christmas wish lists. On occasion they could be found moving their furniture around into some new arrangement. Some years the rooms were orderly and clean; other years they collected chaos and confusion. Each room usually boasted at least one sign on the door announcing "Come In," "Keep Out," or "Beware."

These two children were encouraged to be themselves and express the ways in which they are unique. They loved the opportunity to express their individuality, and their parents enjoyed watching each new aspect of their personalities develop. We wish this for you and your children.

6. You may wish to have a discussion about your minimum standards for a room, especially as your children get older. You might say, for instance, "I'm not happy with the situation, but I'm willing to live with your room the way you like it as long as my minimum standards are met. They are that the dirty dishes be returned to the kitchen once a day, that the floors get vacuumed once a week, and that the sheets are changed on weekends."

Life Skills Children Can Learn

Children can learn how to maintain a routine, contribute to the family, organize and care for their possessions, and cooperate. They can also explore their own taste and express their uniqueness in the decoration and organization of their rooms.

Parenting Pointers

1. A clean room may be high on your priority list, but very low on your child's. If you choose to make this a battleground, your child may keep a messy room just to win the battle. Keep perspective— remember that many neat adults were once messy children.

2. Don't worry that your friends will look at your children's rooms and wonder about your housekeeping. Your friends can tell the difference between your standards and your children's.

SCHOOL PROBLEMS (*SEE ALSO* HOMEWORK)

"*My child was caught cheating at school. Now I have to go to a parent-teacher conference. I feel intimidated and embarrassed that I am failing as a mother. How can I make my child behave at school? He is fine at home.*"

Understanding Your Child, Yourself, and the Situation

School problems indicate another area where you may need to deal with the belief behind the behavior as well as the behavior. There are so many different reasons for misbehaving at school. Usually they are related to wanting power or revenge, although some kids who are failing in school decide they can get recognition as troublemakers or decide not to try at all instead of trying and failing.

Too often we assume children are at fault when it could be that the school environment encourages competition, does not provide opportunities for children to be involved in learning respect and problem-solving skills, or does not honor different learning styles. Your child may be treated disrespectfully by a teacher who is punitive and shaming. Some children are unable to function in an environment of disrespect and need a parent who is an advocate to help them find a safe place to learn. Perhaps your child is afraid to go to school because of a bully or gang situation.

Suggestions

1. Spend some time getting into your child's world to discover the belief behind the behavior. Sometimes this just takes hanging out and asking questions, and listening to your child's side of the story.

2. Approach the situation in a positive way. "It must be very important to you to do well in school if you are willing to cheat to achieve that goal. How does that help you or hurt you in the long run? What else could you do to achieve your goal?"

3. Engage in joint problem solving. Together decide what the problem is and what some possible solutions are.

4. Tell the teacher that you prefer a parent-teacher-child conference. Since the conference concerns your child, it will be more effective if she is present to help with understanding the problem and working with you on solutions. Suggest that the tone of the conference be "We are not looking for blame. We are looking for solutions." Let your child give her perceptions of the problem and possible solutions before the teacher and you do. Children usually know what is going on, and they feel more accountable when they tell instead of being told. Be sure to also discuss all the things that are going well, again starting with the child.

5. Discussion may be enough. Too often we focus on consequences or solutions and undervalue the power of understanding that may be gained by a friendly discussion. When children feel listened to, taken seriously, and loved, they may change the belief that motivated the misbehavior.

6. With some children, switching teachers or finding a new school may be the road to school improvement. Don't hesitate to help your child make those changes if you and your child feel they will help.

Planning Ahead to Prevent Future Problems

1. Take the time to visit the school. Sit in classrooms and see what it feels like. Are the teachers encouraging or discouraging? Do they use a system of punishments and rewards that is humiliating to some children and invites rebellion in others? Do teachers use class meetings to get children involved in finding solutions to problems? If not, are they open to this possibility?

2. Give your child information, not lectures, about why you think a good education is important. Use emotional honesty to share your values. "I feel _____ because _____ and I wish _____."

3. Create closeness and trust. Lectures and punishment create distance and hostility. Getting into the child's world and actually listening create closeness and

trust. A foundation of closeness and trust is vital for positive parenting tools to be effective.

4. Take responsibility for your part in creating the problem. Taking responsibility does not mean that you should feel guilty, but you should try to gain insight and awareness of what you create. Is your child feeling conditional love: "I'm loved only if I do well in school"? Is she feeling too much pressure to perform up to your expectations? If children see us taking responsibility for anything we've done to help create the problem, they may be willing to take responsibility for their part.

5. Decide what you will do and let your child know in advance. "I have faith in you to work out your problems at school. When the teacher calls, I will hand the phone to you. I will not lie for you when you skip school. I will listen, and I will offer suggestions only when you ask me to."

BOOSTER THOUGHTS Sixteen-year-old Diane started sleeping in every morning. Her mother became involved in a battle to get Diane out of bed and off to school on time. A full-fledged power struggle evolved with Mom yelling, lecturing, and even trying to pull Diane out of bed. Diane would yell just as loud. Finally one morning Diane shouted, "Leave me alone! I hate you!"

Mom was stunned, but fortunately that comment reminded her of some concepts she had learned in a parenting class the previous year. She remembered that sometimes the most important thing is to create a relationship of closeness and trust instead of distance and hostility. She decided to stop trying to control Diane and to support her daughter in her decisions with unconditional love.

The next morning Mom did not try to wake Diane up, but allowed her to sleep in. When she finally woke up, Mom sat on the side of her bed and said seriously, "Honey, since you don't want to go to school, why don't you just drop out and get a job?"

Diane was surprised by this change of attitude and support from her mother. The power struggle dissipated and Diane started sharing with her mom. She said, "I don't want to drop out. It's just that I've gotten so far behind that I can never catch up, so why bother? It doesn't seem to matter what I do; my teachers just keep penalizing me. It's hopeless. I wish I could go into continuation school where they let you work at your own pace."

6. Some children do poorly in school because their parents are too controlling and try to manage their schoolwork and school experience. Try backing off and watching to see what your child will do without your constant nagging. Wait a week, observe and then discuss what you have noticed with your child.

Life Skills Children Can Learn

Children can learn that they are accountable for their choices. Their parents help them think through what happened, why it happened, and what they can do if they want different results. Most important they can realize that they are loved unconditionally and can learn from their mistakes without guilt and shame. Children also learn that their parents care enough to look at both sides of the story.

Parenting Pointers

1. It can be difficult for parents to face teachers who seem to be blaming them

"Well, why don't you do that?" her mom asked.

Diane said, "Everyone thinks you're a loser if you go to continuation school."

"What do you think?"

"Well, I am losing now," said Diane. "If I went to continuation school, I know I could catch up. The problem is you have to get kicked out of regular school before you can go to continuation school."

Mom said, "Why don't you go see your counselor and see what you can work out? I'll be happy to go with you if you need my support."

They went to see the counselor and he suggested that instead of continuation school, Diane try individual study for a semester. Diane was excited about this plan and worked very hard to catch up so she could go back to her regular school for her junior year. Her counselor told her he had never seen a student do so well in individual study and commended her self-discipline.

Diane appreciated the unconditional love and respect she received from her mother and the encouragement from her counselor. When they worked with her instead of against her, Diane was motivated to end her downward spiral and pursue a productive plan.

for their children's behavior. It helps to make a conscious decision to be more interested in your child than in your ego.

2. Teachers often feel defensive and intimidated too. When you set up a positive parent-teacher-child conference, show compassion for the teacher instead of defensiveness. Someone needs to break the chain of defensiveness and create a chain of mutual concern for everyone involved.

SELF-ESTEEM

"My child is convinced she is ugly. She has such a poor opinion of herself. How can I help raise her self-esteem?"

Understanding Your Child, Yourself, and the Situation

Self-esteem—the collection of pictures children carry around of who they are and how they fit in—is formed early in life. Even though children make these decisions internally, parents have a tremendous influence on the unconscious decisions children form. The ways parents communicate, both with words and actions, helps children form healthy or unhealthy decisions about themselves. Children usually form healthy self-esteem decisions when parents demonstrate that they believe their children are capable by giving them opportunities to experience their capability. They thrive when parents create an environment where children are allowed to contribute, and when they let children influence what happens to them by participating in decision making. Children usually make unhealthy self-esteem decisions when they think they are loved conditionally, or when parents do too much for them so they don't experience their capability. As a parent you may think your children are great just the way they are, but what is more critical is what your children decide.

Suggestions

1. When your child expresses feelings of low self-esteem such as "I'm stupid," just listen and validate her feelings. Have faith in her to get through this period without being rescued—which will ultimately increase her sense of self-esteem.

2. Don't try to convince your child that she should feel differently. A comforting hug is enough.

Planning Ahead to Prevent Future Problems

1. Never, ever call your children names. Do not call them stupid, lazy, irresponsible, or any disrespectful put-down. When there is a problem, focus on finding solutions instead of placing

blame. Separate the deed from the doer and deal with the behavior, making it clear that you love the child, but you don't like crayon drawings on the wall. Remember that mistakes are opportunities to learn and grow and not character defects in your children.

2. Also avoid the use of praise. Praise may seem to work when things are going well and the child is succeeding. However your children may be learning to be "approval junkies." This means they believe they are okay only if someone else tells them they are. If you overuse praise, what do you do when your child is failing? That's when she needs encouragement the most— some word or gesture that lets her know "You're okay!"

3. Children are forming their ideas and opinions every day. How they think today may be different from how they think tomorrow, but they still need their parent's ear and support. They need validation that their opinions are listened to and taken seriously.

4. Do not compare children to each other. Each child is a different, unique person and is valued and belongs just the way he or she is.

5. Watch out for having overly high expectations for your children or making your love conditional on their behavior.

6. Hold regular family meetings so children have a place to air their opinions and to be reassured that they belong and are significant. Brainstorm for solutions to problems so they learn that mistakes are opportunities to learn. Plan opportunities for them to contribute and experience their capabilities.

7. Spend special time with each of your children alone, reminding them of their uniqueness and how much you appreciate their special qualities.

8. Don't play favorites.

9. Be sensitive to situations where your children are being put down by siblings, teachers, classmates, friends, and other family members. Talk to your children about their feelings and share yours. Let them know that some of the mean things people say and do are about their own insecurities and have nothing to do with them.

10. You may choose to remove your child from a classroom if a teacher uses methods that are detrimental to the

BOOSTER THOUGHTS There are times when staying positive about teenagers can be a real challenge. In the case of sixteen-year-old Jesse, his family members were all having a hard time for various reasons. His mom was angry because his grades were declining. His grandmother was worried about him because he had pierced his ear. His father was upset that he didn't follow through on his commitments, and his stepmother was ready to choke him for leaving his laundry in the washer, dryer, hallway, and car.

Thank goodness for Grandpa! Just when he was needed the most, he came to visit. He watched everyone nag, lecture, and avoid Jesse, and in his grandpa way he didn't say a word. But out of nowhere, Jesse started finding notes in the strangest places, and they all said the same thing: "Jesse, you're all right!"

There were times when the family would be sitting around the table and Grandpa would look at Jesse and say, "Jesse, guess what?"

Jesse would grin from ear to ear and say, "I'm all right?"

"Right, and don't forget it."

development of healthy self-esteem. However there is a fine line between overprotectiveness and alertness to a negative environment.

11. Don't forget to have fun with your children.

Life Skills Children Can Learn

Children can learn that they don't have to prove themselves to be loved, and that they are good enough the way they are. Also they can learn that they are capable of solving problems, handling the ups and downs of life, and making a contribution.

Parenting Pointers

1. Value the uniqueness of each child. Avoid comparisons and work at finding out who your children are instead of trying to get them to live up to a picture of who you think they should be.

2. Work on your self-esteem. The better you like and accept yourself with all your mistakes and shortcomings, the better model you give your children about self-acceptance.

SEPARATION ANXIETY

"My son clings to me whenever a stranger is nearby. He won't leave my side when I drop him off at day care. He even cries when my husband tries to comfort him. He wants me to hold him all the time. Is this normal behavior? I'm planning to go back to work full-time and I have no idea how I can if it's going to be too hard on my son."

Understanding Your Child, Yourself, and the Situation

If you have created a world in which your child is used to other people right from the beginning (such as extended family), your child might never have this problem, or you might experience it in extremely small doses. However if you have been the center of your child's world and she has had minimal contact with others, she will be reluctant to leave your side. When your child clings to you, you may experience guilt, thinking you should be with her all the time. She will sense your lack of confidence and will absorb this energy and act accordingly. On the other hand, if you feel confident of your child's ability to adjust to others, she will sense this and adjust more quickly. If you or your child has been sick or if there has been a transition in the family, clinging may be your child's way of trying to feel safe. If you aren't used to introducing your child to new activities

and people, it will take time and patience and small steps to make the transition. Follow the suggestions below both for your sake and for your child's.

Suggestions

1. If your child clings to you, set up situations where your child can get used to new people and situations while you are present, but in the background. (For example, visiting with a friend while your child plays with or near others.) Then leave your child with others for short periods of time until she gets used to you being gone.

2. Explain to your child what or where you'll be going, who will be there, how long you'll stay, and any other details that can help him know what to expect. (If your child is preverbal, he will still "sense" that you are prepping him.)

3. Tell your child that you understand he's afraid and that it is okay, but it's not okay to miss out on new people and places. That isn't one of the choices.

4. Walk away quickly and trust that your child will stop crying once you have left the scene and the child care person redirects her to other activities.

5. Don't shame or humiliate your child. Don't let your child avoid new people or situations either.

Planning Ahead to Prevent Future Problems

1. When you spend plenty of quality time with your child, she will not suffer traumatic effects by spending time with others (even though she may need to experience tears before she learns she can handle it). On the other hand, if you are so busy with your life and job that you don't have time to spend with your child, she may have good reason to experience separation anxiety.

2. Create situations from birth on where others care for your child and spend time with her when you aren't around, or when you are there but involved in some other activity. Make sure you share the parenting with your partner.

3. Let your child know that you'll be going somewhere and that if she is uncomfortable, that's okay, but you'll still do the activity. Repeat it often until it feels more comfortable.

4. Let your child sit on the sidelines and watch until she gets a picture of the new situation.

5. Allow for differences with your children and don't expect all of them to adjust to new people and situations at the same pace.

6. When you go on an outing such as shopping, bring a friend along to interact with your child so she gets used to others.

7. If your child has given a situation or person a fair try and still hates it, you might need to look for a different activity or caregiver.

BOOSTER THOUGHTS Maria is a single working parent who feels bad about having to work, having to put her three-year-old daughter in day care, and missing out on so much with her child. When Audrey started preschool and cried when she left, Maria decided that her daughter was suffering from separation anxiety and that it was her fault for being gone so much.

Fortunately for Maria, her boyfriend, Tom, talked her out of doing anything extreme and offered to take Audrey to school each morning. When he dropped Audrey off, she didn't shed a tear. He also encouraged Maria to take two evenings a week for herself to work out at the gym and he promised to make the evenings a lot of fun for Audrey. He and Audrey cooked mac and cheese together, gave the dog a bath, and read her favorite books. By the time Mom got home, Audrey hardly looked up from the stories until her mom came over and gave her a big hug.

Life Skills Children Can Learn

Children can learn that it's a big world filled with interesting people and places and activities that will enrich her life. She can learn that it is natural to feel nervous at first and be reserved, but that with practice and time, she can be more comfortable and at ease. She learns not to give up on herself.

Parenting Pointers

1. If you want your child to feel comfortable in the world, you need to help it happen by introducing your child to new people and places and activities. If you feel nervous about being out and about, perhaps you and your child can learn together.

2. Beware of thinking you are the only person in the world your child can relate to. You'd be depriving your child of a lifetime of wonderful experiences.

SEX EXPLORATION AND SEX EDUCATION

"I caught the neighbor boy and my five-year-old daughter with their pants down. I don't want to punish her, but I don't want her playing around sexually. I don't know how to teach her propriety regarding sex."

Understanding Your Child, Yourself, and the Situation

Today is a very different world from the one in which we grew up. Now there are extremes—kids who are vowing to stay celibate until they get married, and kids who think of "hooking up" with someone at a party is an activity as common as going to a movie. The media glorifies and glamorizes sex, so culturally, kids are bombarded with "be sexy" and "have sex" messages on a regular basis. You may have very different values from your children, and you might even think that your children will follow your values because you are the parent. If that is your thinking, you may be cutting yourself off from being the kind of consultant your children desperately need as they struggle with their own views about right and wrong.

With younger children, good sex education can help a child have information about how the body parts work, what is normal and what is not, how babies are made, what it means to be a sexual being, and the confidence to say no to an older child or adult who wants to take advantage of him or her. As children get older, good sex education is having the ability to open a nonjudgmental dialogue with your kids and keep the conversation going.

Suggestions

1. When you catch your child exploring sex or sex organs with another child of a

similar age, this is a clue that he or she is ready for sex education. Do not scold, embarrass, humiliate, or shame your child. Let him know it is okay to be curious about sex and all the body parts. Tell him that you will answer questions and explain how things work, but you do not want him playing "doctor" or "show-and-tell" with other children because the sex organs are a private part of the body.

2. Talk about respect for self and others. It is not respectful to involve other children in sexual displays or exploration.

3. Avoid punishment, as this is likely to provoke kids to take their sexual explorations "underground." With teens this is especially crucial. Once you start grounding and taking away privileges, your kids will find ways to work around you and defy your rules, thus losing any chance you might have of being a consultant to them and doing harm instead of good.

4. Ask your child what questions she has about sex or the penis or vagina or breasts (use the correct words). Answer the questions honestly and without embarrassment if you can. Do not give more information than she has asked for, unless you feel it is needed. Use your common sense to help you know how much your child can understand.

5. Go to the library together and check out some good books on sex education, suitable for your child's age level.

Planning Ahead to Prevent Future Problems

1. Find some good sex education books designed for small children and start reading them to your children when they are two or three years old. At this age they won't understand much of what you are reading, but will still enjoy the book. When they are older and the neighborhood kids try to give them information, they will be able to say, "Oh, I already know all about that."

2. For ages three to ten, while you are tucking your child into bed at night, occasionally ask, "Do you have any questions about how your body works?" The answer will usually be no, but you are establishing that sex and conversations about how the sex organs work are valid topics of conversation, just like school or toys.

3. For ages six to eighteen, children today see more explicit sexual interaction on television and movies in one weekend than their grandparents could have imagined in an entire lifetime. They need to have open conversations with adults about what they are seeing. Communication needs to go both ways. Ask your kids what they think and feel without lecturing or judging. Then tell your kids what your thoughts and feelings are. You can draw them out by asking curiosity questions: "What do you think about what you are seeing on television? How do you feel about it? What conclu-

sions are you making?" Share your own thoughts and feelings too.

4. As your children grow older, give them information about why they will benefit from postponing sexual activity—as they grow up they will have greater emotional maturity and wisdom so that they don't end up being disrespectful to themselves and/or others. Hopefully they will have the self-confidence and self-love to do what feels right for them, instead of feeling that they have to please others at their own expense. Kids need to know that if someone says, "If you love me, you will have sex with me," or "If you don't have sex with me, I'll find someone else who will," they should run in the other direction as fast as they can.

5. If your children have decided to be sexually active in spite of your feelings, make sure they are protected against unwanted pregnancies and sexually transmitted diseases.

BOOSTER THOUGHTS A little girl suffered as a child because she could not discuss sex with her parents—they were too embarrassed. When she was six years old, a neighbor boy wanted to show her how to "fuck," a word she didn't understand. He took her to a barn and told her to pull her pants down and squat. He then proceeded to urinate on her bottom. Later the little boy told all the other kids that he had "fucked" the little girl. This information followed her all through elementary and high school. About once a year she became the topic of ridicule. The kids would chase her around the yard and tease her about having babies in her belly. In junior high the kids would pass notes about her and giggle. As she matured she started getting propositions from other boys, who believed in her bad reputation.

Her sex education was so lacking that this little girl did not know she had not had sexual intercourse or that, even if the little boy had known how, it would not have been her fault and she was not bad. The little girl is now a woman and can laugh about it, but sex education or honest communication with her parents could have saved her a great deal of pain.

As parents you may ask yourself what your ultimate goal in giving sex information is. Is it just to inform? Probably not. Is it merely to help your child keep out of sex difficulties as she matures? No, it is more than that. Shouldn't the goal be to help your child to look at sex in such a way that she can one day grow up to have a happy, successful, and responsible sex life? If you keep this goal in mind, it will help you to know what to say to your child and how to say it.[16]

6. You should not use the threat of AIDS or other sexually transmitted diseases to instill fear and guilt that often invites kids to rebel. Information about these diseases should be given in a matter-of-fact way that encourages kids to listen and make intelligent decisions.

7. Tell your children you will explain any word they hear that they do not understand, and that you want them to ask you questions if their body does things they don't understand, like discharges or emissions or menstruation. It is best to let your children know ahead of time about these things and that they are normal, so they don't have to live in fear of being weird or having some life-threatening disease. Be calm no matter what they ask, and don't pass judgment on the friend who said the word. If you need help answering questions, ask the physician to answer what you don't know or find books and other resources to put your child's mind at ease.

Life Skills Children Can Learn

Children can learn that sex is a wonderful part of them and of life and that their sex organs and their functions are normal and not to be feared or be ashamed of. They can learn it is okay to discuss anything with their parents, who will give them honest and helpful information. With the right kind of information, they can make the right decisions for themselves, no matter what anyone else thinks.

Parenting Pointers

1. If you are embarrassed about sex or think it is bad, this is the message your children will receive. They may adopt your attitude or simply decide to hide their feelings, questions, and actions from you. It is not what you say, but how you say it, that has the greatest influence on your children.

2. A study of 1,400 parents of teenage girls in Cleveland found that 92 percent of the mothers had never discussed sex with their daughters. If you are uncomfortable talking about sex, share that with your child and why. Then talk about it anyway, or offer the services of a responsible adult to whom your child can talk to get another perspective. This might be a counselor or family member or friend.

SEXUAL ABUSE

"I can't pick up a newspaper or magazine without seeing a story about a child being sexually abused. How do I protect my children from having something like that happen to them?"

Understanding Your Child, Yourself, and the Situation

We wish the world was such that we didn't have to include a chapter on sexual abuse.

Reading this section may seem frightening or exaggerated. Unfortunately the statistics are overwhelming—one in four people have experienced some kind of sexual molestation or violence. It may be that the incidents of child sexual assault are growing, or perhaps the number being reported is growing. When children are sexually abused, the effects on their personality can be lifelong, and most of the time the effects are devastating. Most children who have suffered abuse have decided it was their fault and that they are bad. They spend a lot of time hiding because they think they are different and live in fear of others finding that out. In some cases, the memories they have of being abused fade, but the feelings and decisions stay. Later in life they may start having flashbacks of abuse and think they are going crazy. There are many things we can do as parents to both protect our children and to help them if they are abused. Please take this information very seriously if it affects you or your loved ones.

Suggestions

1. Children are people and not sex objects. It is incredibly damaging to use a child as a sex partner. If you are doing this, stop and call for help. You are not a bad person, but your behavior is wrong and you need to find out how you can get better. There are agencies and people who are trained to help both you and your child.

2. If you suspect that your child is being abused sexually, get help, even if you suspect it is your own spouse. Resist the desire to keep your fears a secret and try to handle this alone or hope it will pass. This is called "silence and denial" and only makes things worse over time. If you feel threatened that the abuser will hurt you if you tell, get professional help. They deal with these issues daily and are there to stop the abuse and protect you and your children and help the perpetrator.

3. If your children are hinting about being abused or complaining of physical problems in their genital area, take their complaints seriously and get help. If you notice bruises, cuts, or infections, your child may be the object of sexual abuse. Reassure your children that they won't get in trouble if they talk to you, that you are there to help, and that you believe them if they say someone is abusing them, and that you don't think they are bad.

4. Minimizing or ignoring children's cries for help is a serious mistake. Most

children who are being abused have been told that if they say anything, they'll break up the family or everyone will think they are bad, or someone will get hurt. It takes a tremendous amount of courage for children to break their silence and share the secret, so take them seriously.

Planning Ahead to Prevent Future Problems

1. Talk to your children openly about the possibility of sexual abuse. Tell them there is a difference between the touch that gives and the touch that takes away, and that no one should be touching their private areas. If they are uncomfortable with the way anyone touches them, make sure they know it's okay to say no, even if that person is a grown-up. Show your child how to firmly and loudly say, "STOP!" Keep communication open so they feel free to tell you if something is wrong.

2. Tell your children that they are people and their bodies are precious and belong to them and that no one has the right to hurt them, put things into their bodies, or make them perform sexual acts.

BOOSTER THOUGHTS A young child was molested by a grown-up in her neighborhood when she was about five years old. The molester told her that if she ever told anyone, they would die and it would be her fault. He also told her that if he found out she told, he would chop her in pieces and put her in the bean pot and cook her parts for dinner. He told her she could never tell a soul till she was fifty years old.

When she was forty-eight, she started having flashbacks and anxiety attacks, but she didn't know why. Her memories of the incident were forgotten and blocked, and now she was terrified as she remembered the incident. After a year of therapy, she was able to get in touch with the incident and with great fear, talked about it with her therapist. She called her therapist daily for several weeks to make sure he was still alive, because she had told before her fiftieth birthday.

This is one small case study of some of the pain and agony a person goes through after being molested. Much of this could be prevented with open communication, information, and an environment where children know they won't get in trouble when they talk to their parents and that their parents are there to help, not hurt them.

3. If your children are acting strangely, talk to them about secrets and let them know they can trust you and can tell you if someone has been telling them to keep a secret. Get secrets out in the open. If you suspect something happening, use the words openly with your child, for instance, "I'm wondering if when your uncle kisses you he is putting his tongue in your mouth," or "Has Daddy ever asked you to kiss or suck on his penis?" or "Did the babysitter put something inside your vagina? It looks red and sore."

4. Watch for revenge cycles between siblings. Sometimes an older sibling will sexually abuse a younger sibling as a way of hurting back if they think the younger child is more loved, spoiled, or special. Teenage siblings may think their younger siblings are a safe place to practice sex. Let them know this is not acceptable behavior. Talk about this in front of all the children at the same time. Get professional help immediately if one of your children tells you that a sibling is molesting her.

Life Skills Children Can Learn

Children learn they are people and have the right to decide what happens to their body and that there are people who will take them seriously, love them, and help them if someone is sexually abusing them.

Parenting Pointers

1. If you were molested as a child or molested someone, you need to get help with your issues, as it is very difficult to be there for your children when you have unfinished issues about your own sexual abuse.

2. When you raise children to be assertive, taken seriously, and given opportunities to contribute to the family and discuss their ideas, you are indirectly preventing sexual abuse. Children who know they are worthwhile people, who believe that they have rights and that their feelings are legitimate, and who are given information about the possible dangers are not good candidates to be molested.

3. Do *not* underestimate the manipulative nature and sneakiness of a perpetrator (the molester). This person thrives on getting you to believe he is innocent and that your child is making things up.

SHARING/SELFISHNESS

"My child refuses to share his toys with anyone. When his friends come to play, he grabs toys out of their hands and yells, 'Put that down, don't touch it, it's mine!' The other day he hit his sister when she picked up one of his books. She ran screaming to her room while he yelled at her, 'Leave my things alone!' "

Understanding Your Child, Yourself, and the Situation

Sharing is not an inborn trait; it is learned. Sometimes parents expect sharing before it is developmentally appropriate. (Many adults still don't like to share.) If there's more than one child in a house, there will probably be fights about sharing. This is natural, but that doesn't mean parents should ignore it. Too often the parents' solution to this problem is to tell the child, "You should share your toys or no one will like you," or "How can you be so selfish?" It is important to separate the child from the behavior and make sure the message of love gets through. You must also teach children when it is appropriate to share and when it is okay not to share—and how to find win/win solutions.

Suggestions

1. Don't expect children to share before the age of three without lots of help. Sometimes they seem very generous, and other times they don't want to share anything. You may need to have more than one desirable toy around in case of conflicts, or use distraction to get small children interested in something else. Even after three, sharing is not always easy. (Don't you have some things you don't want to share?)

2. When children are under three, it often works to distract them either by offering something else for them to play with or to do. With older children, it is okay to ask them to put a toy they are fighting over on a shelf until they can work out a plan that works for both of them and can share it without fighting.

3. If your children are being bothered by infants or toddlers who get into their toys, help them find a place to play that is out of reach of little fingers.

Planning Ahead to Prevent Future Problems

1. Have toys that are for sharing, like table games, croquet sets, art materials, etc.

2. Share something of yours with a child saying, "I'd like to share this with you." Also make your expectations clear about how you want the item used and returned. You may be pleasantly surprised to notice that from time to time, your child might share something with you without being asked. When that happens, make sure you say, "Thank you so much for sharing. You're really getting good at that."

3. It is easier for children to share some things if they don't have to share everything. Help your child find a special shelf or box for those things she doesn't wish to share. Make sure that the family guideline is that "We don't go in someone's room or use their things without their permission."

4. A child should not be required to share a toy that belongs just to her if she doesn't want to. If your children are having friends over, discuss ahead of time which toys they are willing to share. Suggest that they put away the things they don't want to share. Discuss with your child the difference between sharing their own toys and the toys they find at other people's houses or at pre-school or day care. Sharing in those situations can make or break a friendship.

5. Set an example of respect for private property and that people don't always have to share everything by saying to kids who want to use something you own, "This is mine and I'm not ready to share it right now. I have other things I'm willing to share, but not this." If you do decide to share something very special to you, make your expectations clear about how you want it used and returned. If objects haven't been returned to you in the past, ask for collateral, like a favorite toy or video game. Return the collateral when you get your item back.

6. Use the family meeting for kids to discuss their feelings about sharing. Once a month include a sharing segment in your family meeting, and have everyone talk about when they've shared something and how it made them feel.

BOOSTER THOUGHTS When June was a kid, her mother told her she was selfish because she didn't want to share her toys with her younger siblings. That was Mom's anger talking, and it worked to get June to do what her mom wanted. Being a textbook firstborn child, June decided that what Mom said was true and that she was selfish. June also decided that it wasn't okay to have anything that was solely hers or do anything that was just for her.

When June got married, she deferred to her husband whenever he implied she was selfish. Because of this June carried a lot of resentment that she never dealt with, and her resentments created many problems in her relationship with her husband. When children came along, June sacrificed for the kids and put her needs aside, not wanting to be selfish. In addition to building resentments about being a parent, June inadvertently trained her children to be spoiled, demanding brats by pampering them and never saying no.

June's story is not uncommon. Many adults are still living with the labels they were given as children. Always remember to respond to the *behavior* and never call a child names or label them, or you can do more damage than you know.

Often the family can work out a schedule to rotate popular family toys such as video games. If the kids still can't share them without fighting, it is okay to put the toys off limits until they or the family come up with a win/win solution.

7. Teach that sharing includes more than material possessions. It could include sharing time, sharing feelings, or sharing ideas. While tucking your children in bed at night, invite them to share their saddest time of the day and their happiest time. Also share your saddest and happiest moments of the day.

Life Skills Children Can Learn

Children can learn that there are times for sharing and times to respect not sharing. They can learn that sharing includes much more than sharing things.

Parenting Pointers

1. Children need to have privacy and boundaries that others respect. They should not have to share everything with everybody.

2. Do not tell children they are selfish or label them with any other disrespectful term. Make sure you say instead, "I'm unhappy with the way you fought with your sister over the game."

3. When someone calls another person selfish, could it be that the name caller is not getting her own way?

SHOPPING WITH CHILDREN

"I can't afford a babysitter when I go to the store, so I have to take my children with me. They run around, hide, and throw tantrums until I buy them a toy or a treat. I see other children with their parents and they seem so well-behaved. Is there something wrong with my kids?"

Understanding Your Child, Yourself, and the Situation

We see as many misbehaving parents at grocery stores and shopping malls as we see misbehaving children. We see parents yelling, spanking, making demands that are inappropriate for the age of the children, giving in to demanding children, and using bribery. Some children don't look forward to going to the store any more than their parents look forward to taking them. But there are some ways to make shopping more enjoyable when your kids have to go with you.

Suggestions

1. Discuss the behavior you expect from your children before leaving home. Many children do not know what their parents expect. Let your children know in advance what you will do, and then if they misbehave quietly take them to the car and let them know they can try again when they are ready. Then keep

your mouth shut, read a novel, and give them time to calm down. If they don't calm down, you may need to leave and try again another day. This works very well if you let them know in advance what will happen if they misbehave, are kind and firm, and don't add lectures or shame.

2. If there are carts with children's seats or strollers, put your children in them. If they climb out, tell them it is not okay and return them to their seat. Follow through with action and as few words as possible. Children know when you mean what you say.

3. Do not leave children unattended in the car or a store to wait for you, even for a few minutes. It is unsafe and very frightening to the child.

4. If you can, give the kids a job to do, such as helping push the cart, finding the can or box you are looking for at the grocery store, or help carrying packages. Hand toddlers your purchase and let them drop it into the cart.

5. If your children run away, go after them and then have them hold your hand, or the cart if at the grocery store. The quicker you follow through by acting (instead of yelling orders at the kids from another aisle or ignoring them), the more they know you mean what you say.

6. Be flexible and willing to cut the trip short if the kids are too unruly. There are times when you may have to leave your purchases and try again another time. If your child chooses a store to have a temper tantrum, you can wait quietly until they are done, hold them firmly while you finish paying or hug them until they calm down. Do not let water power influence you.

7. If your kids want to buy anything for themselves, it's time to start them on an allowance (see Allowance).

Planning Ahead to Prevent Future Problems

1. When children help plan menus, they are more interested in finding ingredients at the grocery store.

2. If the kids have a clothing allowance, make a date to spend special time shopping with them one on one, instead of trying to combine their trip with shopping of your own. Don't rush them.

3. Suggest the kids pick a toy or a book they can take along in case they get bored.

4. Do not promise treats or toys as a bribe if the kids will behave. If you want to create a routine of doing something fun after shopping, make sure it's not dependent on your children's behavior. Shopping can be a lot more fun if the kids know that first you shop and then you stop for hot chocolate or some other kind of treat.

5. Give children an allowance. If they want special treats, tell them they have an allowance. If they can't afford an item, help them figure out how to save for it instead of advancing them money.

6. If you aren't shopping for your children and it is at all possible, you might want to ask a friend to watch them, have your mate handle child care, or put the kids in day care.

7. Explain to your kids that there are times you have to take them shopping, and that you understand it may not be a lot of fun for them and you appreciate their help. Ask if there is anything you could do to make the trip more enjoyable.

Life Skills Children Can Learn

Children learn about give and take and how to entertain themselves. They also learn how to find their way around a store, help the family shop, and cooperate.

Parenting Pointers

1. It is humiliating and disrespectful to yell at your child, spank, or threaten them in public. (It's humiliating to do the same

BOOSTER THOUGHTS Some children love browsing through bookstores and shops and others hate it. Kids who have had exposure to shopping in short bursts and who have control over their money and get an allowance tend to enjoy shopping more than those who get dragged along without any consideration for their needs.

One family decided to help their teenaged sons, who hated shopping, learn that a shopping trip can be fun. They planned a day in San Francisco with no other agenda than to have a fun activity shopping. They took the kids out to lunch, let them ride up and down the escalators at a large department store, stopped in pet stores, comic book stores, and dime stores. They did everything they thought the kids would like—even riding the cable cars.

The boys were crabby, complaining, and sullen the whole day. Why? No one had thought to ask the boys if they would like to participate in this activity. It was assumed they would love the experience, but because they weren't part of the planning, they felt forced and controlled and reacted accordingly. If the parents had asked them in advance and gotten their help in planning out the day, they might have felt more involved and the day might have had a very different outcome.

thing at home, but worse when there is an audience.) You can let them know you are angry and will talk about what is bothering you in the car, at home, or at a family meeting.

2. If you keep shopping trips with children short, they are more likely to look forward to going with you. Be sure you plan times when your children are not tired or hungry.

SHYNESS

"My child is so shy. Whenever people talk to her, she hides her head behind me and won't answer them. Everyone acknowledges how shy she is. Does this mean she has low self-esteem? What can I do to help her with this?"

Understanding Your Child, Yourself, and the Situation

There are some who think that children are born shy. Children may be labeled shy when they act in an introverted way. Children often accept a label that is given to them and then may use it to get undue attention, for passive power, to get revenge when they feel hurt, or as a way to give up when they feel discouraged. Also shyness may be a behavior that has an unconscious purpose. In some cases the child may have an outgoing, sociable sibling and the shy child may have unconsciously decided that she had to find another way to belong in the family. Being an introvert has nothing to do with self-esteem. Low self-esteem comes from not being accepted for who you are.

Be careful what you create—if you label a child as "shy" you might be condemning them to go through life as a shy person, which can have devastating effects, including loneliness, alienation, and a fear of trying new situations. Try the suggestions below instead of labeling your child.

Suggestions

1. There are times when it makes perfect sense for children to hold back, especially if they are checking out a new situation, if they don't feel like interacting, or if they are being pushed to act according to someone else's standards. They should be allowed to approach those situations with caution without being labeled shy.

2. If your children do hold back, don't speak for them or try to coax them to talk. Simply go on with the conversation and trust that they will enter in if and when they are ready.

3. Don't introduce your child as shy or tell others she is shy when she refuses to talk.

4. Look for ways you may be trying to force your child to act a certain way.

You may be in a power struggle, and she is using the passive power of silence to show you that you can't make her do what you want. Back off. She may be using "shyness" as a way to feel special because it creates so much attention. Let your child be who she is and have her own relationship with others without you getting in the middle.

5. Don't let your child's shyness be an excuse to stop her from doing things she needs to do. Tell your child "It's okay to feel uncomfortable, but you still need to

BOOSTER THOUGHTS Norma and Doreen enjoyed getting together once a week for coffee. Doreen's four-year-old daughter Vicki usually accompanied her mother to Norma's house. When Norma said, "Hi, Vicki," Vicki hid behind her mother's leg and Doreen explained, "She's shy."

When Norma asked Vicki, "Would you like some nice juice and a cracker?" Doreen answered for her daughter. "She's too shy to talk, but I'm sure she would love some. Why don't you set it out for her and she'll help herself, won't you, honey?"

When Norma asked Vicki if she would like to play with the other children, Vicki said, "I can't. I'm shy."

Norma invited Doreen to a parenting class where she was introduced to the Four Mistaken Goals of Behavior. When discussing the four mistaken goals, the instructor explained that if you feel annoyed by a behavior it is a sign that the child thinks she belongs only if you are noticing her and that behavior is an attempt to get you to notice her. Doreen realized she did feel annoyed by Vicki's shyness, but kept feeding it by giving her so much undue attention.

Doreen stopped telling other people Vicki was shy and stopped talking for her. She told Vicki, "I notice that there are times when you choose not to answer when people ask you a question. That's okay with me, but it would help if you would tell people you don't want to talk. When you are quiet, I'm going to guess that you don't feel like talking unless you tell me otherwise, and I'll go about my business. I love you whether you talk or not. You let me know if you want something."

Within a short time, Vicki stopped acting shy. Doreen later told Norma, "I don't know for sure when she stopped acting shy. I became so unconcerned about her choice to act that way that I hardly noticed when she did it or when she stopped. I started focusing on her strengths and the fun times we had together. I wonder if that had anything to do with it."

go to school. Are there some ways I could help you feel more comfortable?"

Planning Ahead to Prevent Future Problems

1. Teach your child that introverts have just as many strengths as extroverts. They are just different strengths.

2. Don't overprotect your child. Everyone experiences some pain in life. (Just be sure you don't add to her pain by not accepting her as she is or by overprotecting her.) The important thing is for her to learn that if she doesn't like the consequences of her lifestyle choices, it is up to her to change what she wants to change. She will feel freer to change what she wants to change when she feels that an introvert style is a valid choice.

3. Talk with your children and try to get into their worlds to find out if their behavior is a problem for them. Ask if there are ways you can help them feel more comfortable around others.

4. Talk about your child's behavior instead of labeling her shy. For instance, you might say to your child, "I notice that when people say 'hello,' you hide your head behind your hands. Do you do that because you think it's a game, or do you do that because you want them to leave you alone? If you would like them to leave you alone, perhaps you could tell them, 'I don't feel like answering any questions right now.' "

5. Don't try to force your children into situations that they aren't ready for. Help them find small steps they can take to feel more comfortable. Don't try to make them perform (sing songs, play musical instruments, etc.) in front of your friends or relatives.

6. Create a safe environment where she can learn to speak up at home and then allow her to make the choice about whether or not she wants to speak up away from home. One way to do this is through regular family meetings where she can learn to express her feelings in front of others, to give and receive compliments, and to brainstorm for solutions to problems.

Life Skills Children Can Learn

Children can learn that they can behave in ways that feel comfortable without being labeled or pushed to do something they don't want to do. They can also learn to say what they want instead of expecting people to read their minds.

Parenting Pointers

1. Some people choose a quiet, introverted lifestyle. We need to accept and respect different lifestyles.

2. Familiarize yourself with the Four Mistaken Goals of Behavior and decide if your child is discouraged and wanting attention, power, revenge, or to be left

alone. How you encourage a child should be related to her form of discouragement. (See Part 1, page 25.)

SIBLING RIVALRY (*SEE ALSO* FIGHTING, SIBLINGS)

"We recently took our two boys on a trip with their cousin, who is an only child. The three boys spent the entire trip vying for position and trying to find their special place in the group. Is this normal?"

Understanding Your Child, Yourself, and the Situation

Everyone needs to feel that he or she belongs and is significant. The first place children make decisions about how they belong is in their family. Children are good observers, but poor interpreters. When a new baby arrives, the older child often believes "Mommy doesn't love me as much as the baby." As children get older, they

often mistakenly believe that only one person in a family can have a certain claim to fame. If a child thinks his sibling already has the place of being athletic, she may decide to be studious, musical, or a social butterfly. Children often develop typical characteristics based on their birth order. The oldest child usually tries to be first and the boss; the second looks for the injustices and often becomes a rebel, or may try hard to catch up with the first; the youngest thinks he is entitled to extra attention; and the only child wants to be special. If adults are trying to control a situation where kids are trying to find ways in which they are unique, it is wasted effort. The kids will find their own ways to belong and feel significant.

Suggestions

1. Get into your children's world. The oldest usually feels "dethroned" when a new baby arrives just as you would if your spouse brought home a new lover. The youngest often feels inadequate when comparing herself to the capabilities of the oldest. Understanding how they might feel helps you interact with them with compassion. Never say, "You shouldn't feel that way." Allow children to feel what they feel.

2. Compassion does not mean sympathy. It is not helpful to overprotect your children and try to save them from the many feelings and emotions they will experience in life. Compassion helps you maintain kindness with firmness

while applying any of the following suggestions.

3. Avoid victim and bully training. This happens when you assume the oldest is always at fault (the bully) and rescue the youngest (the victim). Often the youngest starts a conflict that you don't see, just to get you to rescue her (developing a victim mentality). Treat them the same and add the word *kids* to your vocabulary. "Kids, I have faith in you to work things out," or "Kids, you'll need to go outside [or to separate rooms, or to the same room] until you find a solution."

4. Make sure that you have one-on-one special time with each child sometime during each day. If a child is jealous of another, let him know that it is okay to feel jealous, and that you want to be with each child and his time will come.

5. If the situation between the kids gets out of hand, see if you can redirect them into activities, such as contests or relays, where cooperation is more important than competition.

Planning Ahead to Prevent Future Problems

1. Give positive messages to every child so they know how they are special. For instance, with the three boys mentioned above, one was told, "You're really good at organizing activities." Another was told, "You're really good at ignoring group pressure and doing what you like." The youngest was told, "You sure have figured out how to let these big guys think they're the boss, while you get exactly what you want."

2. Find activities that stress group cooperation and teamwork. Help the kids discover that things are more fun when they include people who have different strengths. Have regular family meetings (or group meetings) where children learn to verbalize compliments for the strengths of others, and to brainstorm for solutions to problems.

3. Make it a point to let the kids know how much you appreciate the special qualities that set them apart from the other kids.

4. Don't compare the kids in a misguided attempt to motivate them to be like another child. This is very discouraging.

5. Problems result when children decide that being loved is conditional. If parents stress competition, which emphasizes comparing and judging, instead of cooperation, which stresses uniqueness and differences, sibling rivalry can get out of hand. Make sure the message of love gets through and that each child is loved for being the unique human he or she is.

6. Don't gush and make a fuss over the new baby in front of an older sibling. This enhances the belief of the older child that she has been "replaced."

7. Get rid of your "fair" button. Kids will push it and use it to manipulate you.

8. Competition among children may be increased when parents disagree on parenting styles, which feels to the children like competition among the adults.

Life Skills Children Can Learn

Children can learn how to be together, but realize that each one is unique and special. They can learn how to be resourceful and solve their own problems. Most important, they can learn that they are all loved and

---

BOOSTER THOUGHTS Pam's two children tussled on the floor, punching, threatening, teasing, and wrestling with each other. Every time she tried to get them to stop, their behavior got more intense. She was upset about the sibling rivalry and was worried that her children would never be able to get along with each other.

Her friend Rita had been attending a parenting class. She suggested that Pam accompany her to the class and bring up this problem for discussion. Pam did so and was amazed to find that the other parents all had similar situations. Knowing that brought a certain amount of relief, but Pam still wanted guidance on what to do about her fighting children.

The group brainstormed a list of suggestions. The one that Pam decided to try for a week was to think of her children as bear cubs, scuffling together. It was amazing how much less the children's behavior concerned her when she simply changed her attitude. Instead of trying to make the kids stop, she sat back and enjoyed the show. She realized that her kids were really playing with each other and having fun together. She was the only one who had been upset. As she hassled them less about it, they seemed to have less need to wrestle, although they didn't give up their fun "game" completely.

◎

Wayne Frieden and Marie Hartwell Walker capture the feelings of the dethroned child in their song, "Number One,"[17] which begins with the following lines:

Oh it's hard to be number one. And lately it's just no fun at all.
Life was so nice when we were three, Mommy and Daddy and me.

that love is not conditional on being one certain way.

Parenting Pointers

1. Sibling rivalry is normal and happens in just about every family that has two or more children. It is more intense for children who are born less than three years apart. Rivalry increases when parents are competitive, and decreases when parents cooperate respectfully.

2. If there is a change in how one child finds belonging and significance in a family, all the other children have to reevaluate their unique places as well. Often when families get into therapy, the "good" child gets worse while the "problem" child begins to behave better. This is normal until each child sorts out his or her special place in the family.

SICKNESS

"Sometimes my children get so sick it scares me, and other times I think they're just saying they are sick to get my attention or to get out of going to school. How can I tell the difference?"

Understanding Your Child, Yourself, and the Situation

It can be frightening to have a sick child, and devastating when a child faces a life-threatening illness. However most times, children recover. In some families children have learned that being sick is a way to escape from something unpleasant or a chance to get some special treatment. Claiming false sickness may be a cry for help—or a bid for undue attention. In either case it is important to deal with the belief behind the behavior as well as the behavior.

Suggestions

1. If you suspect your child is using illness as an excuse to miss school, explore this possibility in a nonthreatening way. "I don't know for sure, but I wonder if you are having some problems at school and you want to be sick so you don't have to go. If that is true, I would like to hear about it and help you work on the problems when you are ready."

2. If your child says she doesn't feel well, take her seriously. Listen to her and validate her feelings. If you have encouraged your children to say how they feel—to say "I feel scared" (or worried or uncomfortable) when that is what they mean, instead of having to say "I am sick" to get help—then you shouldn't assume your child is trying to trick you.

3. Keep a thermometer handy so you can take your child's temperature to help you decide whether or not she is sick. Underarm thermometers are now available for young children. Consider other

symptoms, too—a child can be sick without a raised temperature.

4. Many parents are so in tune with their kids that they can almost tell the minute their child gets sick. Trust your feelings and get outside help to ease your fears. Also trust your feelings when you suspect your child needs help dealing with an overwhelming situation, or when you suspect your child is simply avoiding responsibility for a situation she is afraid of. Act accordingly with confidence.

5. When your children are sick, make sure they know what is going on and how to take their medicine. Do not force the medicine, but explain why it is needed and ask your children for their help and cooperation.

6. If someone is sick, don't ignore the rest of the family or yourself. Take a break to be with the others and get some rest. Be honest with all family members about what is happening and how you are feeling.

7. Allow your children to have mental health days every now and then so they can take a day off from school without having to get "sick."

Planning Ahead to Prevent Future Problems

1. Teach your children to listen to their bodies and how to care for themselves with rest and a good diet.

2. Pay attention to your own baggage about illness. Do you think it is best to fuss over sick people or to leave them alone? Do you see illness as a hassle, or are you prepared to take it as it comes? Do you think people should "carry on" even if they are sick? Your beliefs about illness could be coloring how you treat your children and how they feel about being sick.

3. Use nonmedicine treatments as much as possible so your children don't get the idea there is a pill for everything. TLC goes a long way to help children through illness.

4. Don't suggest that your children will get sick if they don't wear a jacket when it's cold, don't sleep enough, etc., as you may be programming them to get sick instead of preventing illness.

5. Keep emergency information handy so anyone can get help quickly.

Life Skills Children Can Learn

Children can learn to listen to their bodies, care for themselves, and ask for what they need without having to use "I'm sick" as an excuse.

Parenting Pointers

1. If you get sick, make sure you have family and friends you can call to help supervise the kids and care for you.

BOOSTER THOUGHTS Several children ages eight through twelve were left alone in a new house and city while the parents went out for the evening. No one asked them if they were ready to handle this—it was just assumed that they were.

Within minutes the eight-year-old got a stomachache. The oldest called a neighbor for help and said, "I don't think she's really sick. I think she's just scared and so am I."

The parents had not told the neighbors that they were leaving their number with the children in case of an emergency. Still the neighbors took over soup, soft drinks, and Popsicles, and tried to offer some comfort.

About an hour after the neighbors left, the twelve-year-old called again. This time one of the children had a headache, and they couldn't find any children's aspirin in the house. The neighbor ran to the store for some aspirin and decided to stay with the children until the parents came home. The neighbor realized these children had been left with a bigger responsibility than they were ready for.

Children are inventive. If they are treated disrespectfully, they may figure out that being "sick" is a sure way to get a grown-up to take them seriously.

2. No matter how many preventive measures you take, children will still get sick, so accept this instead of blaming yourself or overprotecting them.

SINGLE PARENTING

"I feel guilty about being a single parent. I'm afraid my child will be deprived by not having two parents—I just don't have time to be both mother and father. I feel selfish when I take time for myself. How much will my child suffer because of my inability to do it all?"

Understanding Your Child, Yourself, and the Situation

It is a myth that children are more deprived because they live with a single parent. They could be much worse off with two unhappy parents who stay

together "for the sake of the children" and set an example of an unhealthy relationship. It is common to hear single parents being blamed when children get into trouble, yet many successful people were raised by a single parent. It is not your marital status that has the biggest effect on your children, but your attitude and your parenting methods.

Suggestions

1. You do not have to make it up to your child for being a single parent—or try to be both mother and father. One effective parent is enough. Develop a good attitude about being single. "This is how it is, and we can make the best of it and even benefit." Children will pick up the powerful energy of your attitude.

2. Don't fall for your kids' attempts to manipulate you through comparisons with the other parent. Use emotional honesty to share your feelings and state your position confidently. "People do things differently. Together we can respectfully decide how things will be done in our house."

3. Help your kids deal with their disappointment about having only one parent or their anger if there has been a divorce. Help them express their feelings and then make plans for what they want to do. (All feelings are acceptable and valuable. What they do is a different matter. Children benefit when they understand the difference between what they feel and what they do.) Help them learn emotional honesty to stick up for themselves and share their needs and wants, understanding that others may not give them what they want.

4. If your child threatens to go live with the other parent, ask yourself: Is my child just angry and trying to hurt me? Is my child trying to get out of doing a chore? Does she really think it would be better at the other parent's house? Does my child need time to build a closer relationship with her other parent?" Remember that many children from two-parent homes threaten to run away, and that this could be a normal reaction to anger. After a cooling-off period, check out the possibilities with your child. "I wonder if you were angry about _____?" Follow up by working on solutions to the problem. (See Booster Thoughts for another example of how to handle this situation.)

Planning Ahead to Prevent Future Problems

1. See the benefits of single parenting. You don't have to fight about which way to parent. It is a myth that it is always easier for two parents. They often fight about how lenient or how strict they should be, or criticize each other for not spending enough time with the children. Don't idealize other circumstances. The grass usually is not greener on the other side.

BOOSTER THOUGHTS When her children would threaten to go live with the other parent, one mother would say, "Okay, but you can leave once and you can come back once. If you want to leave a second time, that will be a permanent decision." None of her children took her up on this because they knew their mother said what she meant and meant what she said. They realized that she took them seriously and respected their right to live with the other parent, but would not be manipulated. This made them think about whether that was really what they wanted to do. After giving it some thought, they decided to stay where they were and to use their problem-solving skills at their regular family meetings.

2. Another benefit of single parenting is that children have the opportunity to feel needed. It is very important that you do not pamper your children in an attempt to make it up to them. Have family meetings (even with just one parent and one child) and get the children involved in chore plans, problem solving, and planning fun events. In single-parent families, kids definitely have an opportunity to make meaningful contributions and feel needed, listened to, and taken seriously.

3. Schedule special time with each child (ten minutes a day or thirty minutes a week) at a specific time they can count on. When you are too busy to meet all their demands, calmly say, "I don't have time now, but I sure am looking forward to our special time."

4. Create a support network of extended family and friends to help with child care, to provide male or female role models, and to have fun with.

5. Join or start a single parenting class. There are hundreds of other single parents who need support—just as you do.

6. If you are divorced and your ex-spouse is irresponsible, decide what you will do instead of wasting time with anger, frustration, and disappointment on their behavior. Accept that your ex probably won't change. If you can't rely on your ex, make a backup plan.

7. Find ways to fill your own cup and take care of your needs so you have energy and enthusiasm to enjoy your kids. Don't feel guilty about taking time for yourself. See it as a gift to you and your children.

Life Skills Children Can Learn

Children can learn that life presents all kinds of circumstances, some of which they may not like. They can learn, grow, and benefit from life's challenges. They can't control everything that happens, but they can control how they deal with what happens.

Parenting Pointers

1. Emphasizing the benefits of single parenting does not mean that problems don't exist. It does mean that idealizing a different situation and having a negative attitude do not help.

2. Your children will be influenced by your attitude. If you act like a victim, chances are that your children will feel like victims. If you have an optimistic, courageous attitude, chances are that your children will adopt this attitude also.

SLEEPING THROUGH THE NIGHT

"Our one-year-old won't stay in his own bed—he cries until we put him in bed with us. I have heard about letting him cry it out, but that seems so cruel. But now my husband and I aren't getting enough sleep—to say nothing of our alone time to talk and cuddle . . . et cetera. How can we get him to sleep through the night in his own bed?"

Understanding Your Child, Yourself, and the Situation

Many parents are advocates of the "family bed," and allow their children to sleep in bed with them regularly. If your children are in your bed by choice, that is one thing. Respect your personal choice and read no further. However too many parents allow their children to sleep with them not by choice but because they feel like they have to, and they are not happy about it. When this is the case, it is disrespectful to let your children sleep in your bed with you just because it seems more convenient than going through a training process or because you think your children can't sleep alone. It may rob them of developing the sense that they are capable and self-reliant, and you might be forming habits that will be very hard to break. It is possible to teach children to sleep in their own beds without serious trauma to their self-esteem.

If you aren't sure whether to support the notion of the family bed or not, the research by Richard Ferber, M.D.,[18] may help you decide. He proposes that children need a place of their own to sleep, whether it is their own bed in their parents' room, or their own room. In this way the child learns some valuable lessons: I can handle being in my own space. I am not the center of the universe. I am an important member of my family, but my parents are also important and need time for rest and rejuvenation.

If you have a newborn, start with the Planning Ahead suggestions to save yourself a lot of heartache. If you have already helped your child develop the habit of sleeping with you it may be time to start the weaning process through the following suggestions (see Weaning).

Suggestions

1. Countless parents have found it helpful to allow their children to cry it out, which usually takes no more than three to five days if you are consistent. This suggestion is usually the most successful in the least amount of time. However we will offer other suggestions in case you just can't stand it. Many of these suggestions are meant to help you have the courage to do what is ultimately best for your child. Remember that the mother bird kicks her baby bird out of the nest in spite of his reluctance to fly. You know why. We know that nothing is more heartbreaking for a mother than to hear her child cry. But when you remember that crying is a form of communication, you know that the crying can mean many things. Your child could be telling you, "I don't like this even if it is for my own well-being." Over and over in this book we suggest that you allow children to have their feelings without rescuing them—it's important to let them experience situations that aren't perfect so they can learn to strengthen their disappointment skills and learn that they can not only survive, but feel better about themselves than they would if they were pampered and rescued. Children have needs and they have wants. It is important to take care of all their needs, but not all of their wants. They need to sleep. They may want to sleep with you, but that may not be what is best for them or for you. Have the courage to do what is best for both of you in the long term. Your child will not feel unloved and traumatized by crying herself to sleep so long as you have spent plenty of quality time with her during the day, holding her, playing with her, etc.

2. Some people hire professionals to come into their homes and help children learn to sleep through the night. Most of these professionals follow the suggestions similar to the ones we are making. The only difference is that the parents don't have to listen to the crying. We hope you will have the courage to go through the weaning process with your child instead of leaving it to a stranger.

3. One mother had to go sleep at her sister's house while her husband took the "crying it out" duty. It was hard for him, but not as hard as it was for Mom. Another mom put a pillow over her head, turned on the radio, and cried herself for the three nights it took for her child to learn to fall asleep by himself. Another mother pitched a tent in the backyard and slept in the tent for the five days it took her child. They all reported that once their children learned to fall asleep by themselves they were happier and easier to take care of during the day.

4. Some have suggested going into your infant's or toddler's bedroom while they

are crying and patting them on the back for a while and then leaving. This has worked for some. Others have said it seems as though they are teasing their child. If you feel comfortable with this suggestion, try it. (The Booster Thoughts suggestion is different because it is done with a verbal child.)

Planning Ahead to Prevent Future Problems

1. Many people think that their baby should be asleep before they put her in her bed. They rock her, nurse her, and when she is sleeping, put her into bed. To their surprise, she usually wakes up immediately and begins to cry. We recommend instead that when it is bedtime, feed her, change her, burp her, and then lay her down while she is still awake so she learns to fall asleep by herself. You may even need to wake her if she has fallen asleep while nursing or taking her bottle. Remember that a little fussing isn't a tragedy. It could be her way of self-soothing.

2. Children are capable of sleeping through the night by the time they are three months old. (Some children achieve this milestone much earlier.) If you are nursing, by three months old your child has regulated the amount of milk she needs during the day and doesn't really need more during the night. When babies wake in the middle of the night after they are three months old, it is okay to let them self-soothe themselves back to sleep—which may mean crying.

3. Babies in neonatal nurseries, where a tight schedule is kept, sleep swaddled tightly on their backs until it is feeding time. If they cry, they are allowed to self-soothe, which they do. How many of these babies go home and *develop* a sleep problem because their parents can't stand the crying or because they believe the baby has to sleep with them? You could be creating a problem you don't need to have with your attitude.

4. There is a growing movement that suggests that babies are more comfortable and sleep better on their tummies. Others believe that babies must sleep on their backs to prevent sudden infant death syndrome. Still others suggest putting the baby on her side to sleep. We are not making a recommendation of which is best, but we do suggest you consult your physician and the parenting bulletin boards on the Web to help you sort this one out for yourself.

Life Skills Children Can Learn

Your children can learn that they are capable of handling the natural bodily function of sleeping without depending on anyone else. They can learn confidence and self-reliance. They can learn that all of their needs will be met, but not all of their wants.

BOOSTER THOUGHTS Melanie Miller, a certified Positive Discipline associate in Kirkland, Washington, shares this: The following solution was respectful to my needs—wanting that priceless half hour, before I go to bed, to be by myself. Maybe I'd read a book, the newspaper, or just sit in a quiet room. It was also respectful to my son who seemed to need a kind and loving mom to ease him into sleep.

So here's how it goes. Do your usual bedtime routine. Hopefully the routine ends with holding your son and reading a book. Then tuck him into bed and tell him that you would like to rub his back. Ask him if he would like you to rub his back for four or five minutes. Giving him a choice gives him some control in the situation. After rubbing his back, tell him that you have to brush your teeth or put on your pajamas or make coffee for the morning, read the mail . . . some boring, mundane thing that he won't want to be a part of. Then tell him that you will be back in one minute. I show my kids what one minute looks like by putting my thumb and index finger very close together. Thirty minutes would be with my thumb and finger very far apart. Sometimes they need that visual. Then be sure to be back within one minute . . . you might even want to return within thirty seconds on the first night, so that he doesn't have a chance to get out of bed and come looking for you. When you return to the room, rub his back briefly and tell him "I need to go put on my pajamas, I'll be back in two minutes." Keep repeating this process and lengthening the time until you go into his room and he is asleep. It may take a while the first few nights . . . and he may have a hard time lying in bed for one minute but don't give up. Just stay calm, adjust the time as needed, and keep repeating the process.

This worked very well with my son. He now goes to bed with just a brief back rub. I have shared it with parents in my parenting classes and they have found it effective also. Baby 1 slept in a crib covered with netting so the cats couldn't get in, with a baby monitor on day and night, and parents who hardly slept a wink as they listened for every breath. Baby 2 slept in the same crib without any netting or baby monitor, but in a room near his parents so they could hear him if he cried. The third baby slept on a different floor of the house, without a baby monitor or netting . . . and turned out to be the best sleeper of all the children.

Parenting Pointers

1. Have confidence in yourself and your decision. Confidence creates an energy that children can feel and respond to. If you have confidence and faith in yourself and your child, you will act accordingly, and so will your child.

2. Millions of babies survived before there were baby monitors that allow parents to micromanage every breath they take.

3. Remember that you need your sleep so you have the energy to give your best to your children during the day.

STEALING

"Money has been disappearing from my purse and from some of my kids' piggy banks. My twelve-year-old daughter insists she hasn't been taking it, but I notice she is buying lipstick, nail polish, and treats for her friends that she couldn't possibly afford from her allowance."

Understanding Your Child, Yourself, and the Situation

Most children will steal something at least once (most adults did too when they were children). When they do, most parents overreact. In their panic parents may accuse a child of being a thief or a liar. Parents often make the mistakes of spanking, grounding, or shaming, thinking this will prevent their children from growing up to be thieves. But judging and punishing kids only makes the situation worse. Dealing with theft can provide you with an opportunity to help your child practice thinking skills, social responsibility, and focusing on respectful solutions.

Suggestions

1. When you know your child has stolen something, don't try to trap her by asking, "Did you steal this?" Tell her, "Honey, I know you stole this item. I did that once when I was little. I felt scared and guilty. How did you feel when you did this?" Continue with more what and how questions in a nonthreatening tone: "Have you ever thought about how the store owner might feel when things are stolen? How many items do you think store owners have to sell before they make enough money to pay their employees and their rent, and still have enough left over for their needs? What could you do to help?" Many children have not thought about these questions, and you can help them become concerned for other people.

2. If something has been stolen, focus on a plan for replacing the item or money rather than on pointing fingers or calling names. Tell your child that the stolen article must be replaced, and you need her help in figuring out a plan for replacing it. If necessary advance her the

money to replace it. Work out a payment plan she can handle and deduct it from her allowance each week. Keep a payment record, so she can see how she is doing.

3. Support your child in returning stolen goods to the store. Instead of being punitive, show compassion. Tell your child, "I know this can be scary and embarrassing, but that is what we have to experience sometimes to correct a mistake." Store owners usually appreciate it very much when children are willing to admit they made a mistake and try to make it right.

4. If toys appear that you know belong to a friend of your child's, simply say, "I'm sure Billy must be missing this. Let's call him so he knows it's safe and take it back as soon as we have time."

5. Give children a chance to replace a stolen item and save face by saying, "I'm not concerned with who took the item,

just that it be returned. I trust that sometime during the next hour the item will be put back where it belongs with no questions asked."

6. If a visiting child is stealing from you, let the child know that he is welcome to play in your house as long as he doesn't take your possessions with him. If he continues to steal from you or your children, let him know that he is welcome to play outside, but not in your home, until the missing items are replaced.

7. If you suspect your child is stealing to support a drug habit, get professional help. This is too hard to deal with alone.

Planning Ahead to Prevent Future Problems

1. Many children steal because they believe they are unloved and don't belong. They think they have the right to hurt others since no one cares about them, and this hurts. It is called a "revenge cycle." Therefore it is important to find ways to let children know they are loved. Separate the deed from the doer and show love while working out a plan to fix the problem.

2. Often children steal because it is the only way they have to get what they want. Make sure your children have allowances that are realistic to cover their expenses while still fitting into the family budget (see Allowances).

BOOSTER THOUGHTS Rebecca came to a counseling session extremely distraught. She suspected her daughter Julie was stealing makeup from her and money from her brother. When the school called and said that food items were missing from a fund-raiser, that was the final straw. Rebecca was ready to send her daughter to jail.

In the past Rebecca had handled incidents of stealing by confronting her daughter. Julie had responded by insisting she was innocent, even when the money or items were in her room. Then Rebecca would get angry and call her a liar and ground her for a week.

Rebecca decided to handle things differently this time. She told Julie the school called to say she was short on her food deliveries for the fund-raiser. Rebecca said she would be happy to advance Julie the money needed to make up the difference and take it out of her allowance each week until the bill was repaid. Rebecca asked Julie if she could handle seventy-five cents or a dollar a week.

Julie was caught completely off guard. She started to make excuses and her mother said, "Honey, let's just figure out how to replace the items." Julie replied, "Okay, how about a dollar each week?"

Julie's mother continued, "Someone said they saw you sharing what they thought were the missing items with your friends."

Julie began to defend herself. In the past Rebecca would tell her daughter she was lying and an ugly scene would follow. This time Rebecca said instead, "Julie, I'm sure your friends like you for who you are, not for what you give them. If you would like to entertain your friends, why don't you invite them over to make cookies and play games?"

Julie said, "Yeah, maybe," and she gave her mother a big hug as she left the room.

Julie stopped stealing when she learned she would be held accountable and have to pay for what she stole. Her mother closed the escape route of defensiveness and power struggles when she showed unconditional love and stopped labeling and shaming Julie, while dealing directly with the problem. She had also dealt with underlying issues such as improving their relationship, boosting Julie's self-esteem, and the importance of focusing on solutions instead of blame.

3. Sometimes stealing occurs because money is lying out and is too tempting. Keep your money and valuables out of sight. If you suspect one of your children is stealing from another, help the victim get a locked box for items she wishes to protect.

4. Children may steal from a sibling because they are jealous. Ask your children whether perhaps they think you favor one sibling over another. Listen to their responses for clues as to whether you are on target. Tell them that feeling jealous is natural, and that you love them very much. Discuss what you find special about them and be sure it is positive and not critical.

5. During another family meeting, help children "explore" the consequences of stealing before it happens. (If stealing has already occurred, be sure this conversation is friendly and generic instead of focused on an individual.) Do this by asking what, why, and how questions: "Why do you think someone might steal? What are the consequences of stealing? What do we need to do in our family so we can all feel trust and safety?"

6. Convey a message of unconditional love that does not include rescuing. In other words, let your children know what you will do instead of trying to control what they will do. To a teenager who steals hubcaps and car parts to support his pot habit, you might say, "If you go to jail, I will love you and I will bring you cookies, but I will not bail you out." To a ten-year-old who broke a toy he "borrowed" from a friend, you could say, "I will help you figure out how to solve the problem, but I will not solve it for you."

Life Skills Children Can Learn

Children can learn that they can save face and take care of a mistake without losing the love and respect of their parents. Their financial needs are important and their parents can help them figure out ways to get what they want without stealing. They realize that they are not bad; they have just made a mistake that can be corrected.

Parenting Pointers

1. Teens may steal for the thrill and for peer acceptance. It helps for them to get caught and be allowed to make restitution. Don't rescue them or bail them out when this happens. Otherwise they may think they are invincible and that no one can stop them.

2. Dealing with a child's hurt feelings and the pain of feeling that she doesn't belong will stop stealing quicker than punitive measures.

STEPFAMILIES

"I have two children and have recently married a woman with three children. Our children don't seem to be adjusting too well. Two of her children seem to resent me most of the time, and my son seems to resent her most of the time. It is causing a lot of strain on our relationship. We don't know what to do."

Understanding Your Child, Yourself, and the Situation

Blending families is a process that takes time. Due to the complexities of multiple changing relationships, along with day-to-day logistics that can be overwhelming, a certain amount of stress is inevitable. Children have to get used to new roles and different parenting styles. Adults often feel compared to ex-spouses or left out of the decision making altogether. Parents and new stepparents have to figure out how to merge their parenting styles and handle responsibility. Add to all of those changing relationships the fact that every day may bring a different grouping of children to the house for visitation rights, and you have a complicated set of dynamics to deal with. If you have a Brady Bunch mentality and think that everyone will be thrilled to be one big, happy family immediately, you'll be setting yourself up for a lot of disappointment.

Suggestions

1. Allow time for the process to unfold. Expect some anger, jealousy, rivalry, and grieving, but know that these will not last forever if handled sensitively. Just knowing that adjustment to change takes time can ease the frustration.

2. Allow your children (and your spouse) to express their feelings without criticism or judgment. Show understanding instead of telling them they shouldn't feel what they feel. Be a good listener, but don't try to fix things by running interference between your children and their new stepparent.

3. If there are serious issues that can't be solved just by listening, set up times to discuss them when everyone is present. Let your children know that you will help bring up the discussion if they feel too intimidated to do so but that not discussing problems with the people involved isn't an option.

4. When the kids spend time with their other parent, allow time for them to adjust when they move from family to family. You might take them out for hamburgers or let them spend time with their friends or in their room. Avoid asking questions, but be available to listen if they feel like talking.

5. Be flexible and creative in how you assign chores to accommodate the various living schedules (see Chores).

Planning Ahead to Prevent Future Problems

1. Honor the need of your children to love their original parents. Do not say bad things about them. Don't make them feel they have to choose. It is easier for children to love two sets of parents than to have to choose between parents.

2. It is important for married couples to work on agreeing that they have equal responsibility to love and discipline all children. Some people think

BOOSTER THOUGHTS When José and Marie married, they each brought three children to their newly blended family. The six children ranged in age from six to fourteen. Obviously there were many adjustments to be made.

Marie worked outside the home. She really enjoyed her new family and was anxious to get home to them after work—except for one problem. The first thing she would notice was the mess. The children would come home from school and leave their books, sweaters, and shoes all over the house. To this they would add cookie crumbs, empty milk glasses, and toys.

Marie would start nagging and cajoling. "Why can't you pick up your things? You know it upsets me. I enjoy being with you, but I get so angry when I see all this mess that I forget about joy." The children would pick up their things, but by then Marie was upset and displeased with them and with herself.

Marie finally put the problem on the agenda for their regular Monday-night family meeting. She admitted that it was her problem. It obviously didn't bother the children to have the house cluttered, but she asked that they help with her problem.

The children came up with a plan for a "safe-deposit box." This was a big cardboard box, which they would put in the garage. Anything that was left in the common rooms, such as the living room, family room, and kitchen, could be picked up by anyone who saw it and put in the safe-deposit box. It would have to stay there for a week before the owner could claim it.

The plan worked beautifully. The clutter problem was taken care of and the safe-deposit box was jammed with things. Because they came up with the rules together, they stuck to them, even when one of the kids lost his shoes to the box and had to wear his bedroom slippers to school for a week! They were brought closer by everyone getting involved with problem solving.

that discipline should be handled only by the birth parent. Others think the new stepparent should assert his or her authority by doling out discipline. Either of these scenarios creates division rather than respectful partnerships. It helps to have a united front. When discipline is nonpunitive and children are included in the problem-solving process, they are less likely to feel resentful.

3. Children will pick up your attitude. A healthy attitude to have is "I know this is hard. I understand why you feel hurt and angry. This new relationship is important to me, and I know that, with time, we can create a healthy, loving family."

4. It is a mistake for either parent to let his or her children come before their spouse or their spouse's children. This is not healthy for the relationship or for the kids. Children need to know that their parents and stepparents value their relationship and are loyal to each other. Children need to know that they are loved but that they can't manipulate their parents against each other.

5. Schedule regular family meetings where everyone can brainstorm to solve problems and create new routines. (Some children resent the word *family,* so you may wish to call these meetings or planning sessions.) Acknowledge that things were different in the original families and express your need for their help in creating new guidelines that work for this new family.

Life Skills Children Can Learn

Children can learn that it is okay and normal for them to experience hurt and anger when their lives are disrupted. They can deal with that hurt and anger in productive ways.

Parenting Pointers

1. When discipline is nonpunitive and kind and firm at the same time, either the birth parent or stepparent can handle discipline respectfully.

2. If you as the birth parent are feeling embarrassed by how your children are treating the person you love, have faith in your new spouse and your children to work out difficulties without you interfering or protecting your mate.

SUICIDE AND CUTTING

"My teenager has been threatening suicide. I'm so scared. I can't think of anything worse than losing a child to suicide."

Understanding Your Child, Yourself, and the Situation

Suicide and cutting are issues that are more prevalent with adolescents than younger children. Threats of suicide should always be taken seriously. Not every threat results in a suicide, but you don't want to take a chance with your child by ignoring the threat. Cutting and self-mutilation is usually more than a trend, though some young people self-mutilate because their friends or people they admire (entertainers, etc.) indulge in this activity. Most cutting is an effort to feel a sense of power or release pain. Adolescent hormones create wild mood swings. If the child's downswings are accompanied by a lack of confidence in their ability to live up to adult expectations, a lack of skills to solve problems that seem insurmountable, a lack of unconditional love, or drug involvement, suicide is a real danger. Children need courage, confidence, and skills to deal with the ups and downs of life.

Suggestions

1. Know the warning signs of suicide and seek professional help if you notice any of them:

   a. Verbal threats to commit suicide;
   b. Extended periods of depression, loss of appetite, sleeping more than usual, poor hygiene, spending a lot of time alone, and general despair;
   c. Acting out extreme behaviors such as stealing, setting fires, becoming physically violent, giving up in school, throwing up, abusing chemicals, or leaving drug paraphernalia around the house;
   d. Signs of suicide attempts, cutting or mutilating their bodies, getting pregnant, or staying intoxicated all the time;
   e. Getting their life in order and giving away their possessions.

2. Many teens will exhibit some of these signs as part of the turmoil of adolescence. Seek professional help if you have *any* doubt at all that the signs are serious, or if your child is cutting or self-mutilating at all. Make sure you consult with a professional who offers drug-free therapy. Putting a hormonal or drug-abusing adolescent (and you may not be aware of this if your child is hiding the information from you) on prescription medication can be a surefire way of exacerbating the situation. Studies have shown that hormonal adolescent young men who have been prescribed certain antidepressants have a higher rate of suicide.

3. When talking to children about suicide, it's important to use words like *suicide* and *death* and not shy away from them for fear of introducing an idea you think they haven't already thought about.

4. If you suspect your child is thinking about suicide, ask if he or she has a plan or has already tried. Finding out if children have a plan shows how far along they are in their thinking. If they have a plan, get professional help immediately.

5. Ask children what would change if they killed themselves. Their answers may tell you what is bothering them.

6. During some quality time with your child who has been threatening suicide or cutting herself, invite her to share with you how things are going in each of the four areas of her life: school, family, friends, and love relationships. If things are not going well in any of these areas and she is coping by attempting suicide or self-mutilating, your child may need professional help.

BOOSTER THOUGHTS The following conversation from the book *Positive Discipline for Teenagers* shows the wrong way to react when children express their feelings. We include it because, unfortunately, it is a very harmful, but very typical, parental response. It shows a lack of compassion, a judgmental attitude, and no listening.

Cliff: No one cares if I live or die.

Dad: You always feel so sorry for yourself.

Cliff: Well, you and Mom split up and you expect me to live with that disgusting person who calls herself my stepmother.

Dad: How dare you say that about your stepmother? She's doing the best she can!

Cliff: Oh, yeah? Then why does she scream and yell at me all the time?

Dad: Cliff, I know your stepmother, and I know that just isn't true. Why do you tell such lies?

Cliff: Nobody believes me. I hate you all and I wish I were dead! A lot you guys would care!

Dad: Cliff, there you go exaggerating again. You know you don't mean what you say. Now settle down and think about how you can get along with your stepmother.

Cliff didn't kill himself, but he did run away at the age of fourteen and wasn't seen again.

◎

Thirteen-year-old Shawna was caught cutting herself. Her father screamed at her. Her mother slapped her. Her siblings cried. When the cutting didn't stop, her folks sent her to a therapist.

7. If you notice signs of self-mutilation or notice that your teen wears long-sleeved clothing no matter what the temperature, say that you are worried and scared and that you want to find some help for your child asap so you can gain understanding of the issues and your child can learn healthier ways to cope. Do not punish your child for cutting.

Planning Ahead to Prevent Future Problems

1. Teach over and over again that making a mistake is just an invitation to learn and try again—no matter what the mistake. Regular practice and thinking about mistakes as opportunities reduces the perfectionist mentality—a common motivation for suicide.

During a session several issues surfaced: Shawna's friends were cutting themselves and she wanted to see what it would be like. She found she liked the way it felt because it made her stop thinking of the pain she experienced as a young adolescent and focus on the current physical pain. The therapist also found that she felt her parents hated her because they constantly nagged her about her schoolwork, slapped her when she was sassy, and banned her from going on family outings because she was always grounded for her bad behavior. She felt she no longer had a family. (Ah, the wisdom of a thirteen-year-old!) Some of Shawna's friends were being seen by therapists who diagnosed them as bipolar and put them on medication. Shawna wondered if that was her problem too.

Shawna's therapist asked for permission to discuss these issues with Shawna's parents while Shawna was present. She said that if there were any repercussions from her parents afterward, Shawna could call her and the therapist would speak to her parents.

Shawna agreed and after two very emotional sessions and lots of crying all around, the parents agreed to stop the groundings and slapping and emotional abuse, and Shawna agreed to stop cutting herself. Shawna continued seeing her therapist for several more sessions, but life was getting better for her. She felt more understood and loved, her parents hadn't retaliated for her telling the therapist about their problems, and the rest of the family was relieved that their sister had turned a corner.

2. Family meetings are an excellent inoculation against suicide because children have an opportunity to feel belonging and significance on a regular basis, and they learn to focus on solutions to problems and not feeling or placing blame.

3. Teach kids (before suicide is even an issue) that suicide is a permanent solution to a temporary problem.

4. Share with your teenagers the times you have felt discouraged, and give them the knowledge that these times pass. One mother who suspected her daughter might be thinking of suicide told her, "Honey, I remember a few times when I felt like committing suicide. I felt so bad I couldn't imagine things getting any better. But they did. I hate to think of how much I would have missed if I had killed myself. For one thing, I would have missed you."

Life Skills Children Can Learn

Children learn that it is good to have someone to talk to whom they can trust and who doesn't judge them. Children can also learn better solutions for dealing with life's ups and downs, and figure out that suicide is a permanent solution to a temporary problem, and the wrong way to go.

Parenting Pointers

1. Take children seriously. Encourage them to share their feelings with you or with someone else if they feel more comfortable. Ask them to tell you if they ever feel like hurting themselves, and that you won't blame or judge them but you'll try to help and understand.

2. One of the best ways to inoculate your children from suicide is to make sure they are involved in activities where they think about others. Their mental health improves as their ability to care for others increases.

3. Don't let your embarrassment or guilt as a parent stop you from seeking outside help. A suicidal teen is not necessarily a reflection of your parenting. Teens can be extremely upset about the loss of a friend or boyfriend or girlfriend. Don't underestimate those hormones.

SUMMER VACATION

"Summer vacation seems like it will never end. The kids are driving me crazy. They're bored and demanding and I wish school would start tomorrow. They've only been out of school a week. Help!"

Understanding Your Child, Yourself, and the Situation

Many of today's parents grew up at a time when summer meant sleeping in, playing with friends, and hanging around the house. Today 62 percent of families have two working parents or are single-parent homes. During summer vacation parents have to leave kids with relatives, home alone, with babysitters, or at day camps. Even if you'd like to provide a summer vacation for your kids like the ones you used to have, it's almost impossible, unless you have a relative who can look out for the kids or enough money to hire in-home child care. Even if you stay at home, summer vacation isn't easy. You might think it's your job to entertain the kids and make sure they have fun (see Boredom). Perhaps you alternate between trying to take care of all their needs and shooing the kids out of your way so you don't have to entertain them. Regardless of your situation, your kids need your help to make summer vacations work.

Suggestions

1. Set up and maintain a routine, even if it's different from the rest of the year. Make sure the kids are involved in planning the routine.

2. Spend some time each day alone with each child doing something that you both enjoy or just being together. If you work close enough to home, try alternating lunch dates with your children. Otherwise get the kids involved in helping with the dinner so you can have time and energy for some fun time after dinner.

3. Set up a chore time where everyone works together and forget about trying to clean during the rest of the day. (It is unrealistic to expect kids to get things done when you aren't there to follow through.) A good time for chores is before breakfast or before dinner. Usually everyone is together at those times.

4. Check your local resources for lessons, special programs, or summer activities. Be sure to involve the kids in making decisions before signing them up.

5. Do not underestimate the importance of downtime for children to meditate, contemplate, or simply rest. Most kids have a pretty hectic schedule during the school year. Remember how nice it feels to have a day or more just to do nothing. Don't be alarmed when the kids spend their day that way.

6. Involve your kids in setting limits for TV viewing and turn it off when it's not TV time. Do not let the TV be a babysitter for the kids.

Planning Ahead to Prevent Future Problems

1. With the kids, brainstorm a list of ideas for those times when they feel bored. Then when the kids complain about being bored, you can say, "Why don't you check your list for an idea of what to do."

2. Kids need to be with friends during the summer. If you don't trust the kids to have friends over if you aren't home,

you need to make arrangements for someone to stay at the house, so kids can play with their friends. Sometimes it is easy to work a trade with another family so the kids have a place to stay where there is a grown-up available.

3. If you have to leave the kids with a sitter, inform the sitter about the routines instead of expecting the sitter to work things out with the kids. Don't expect older kids to babysit without being paid or having a choice, but suggest the kids look out for each other.

4. Even though it may be difficult, it is important to spend some time with the kids when you get home from work before jumping in to do chores just to let them know you are glad to see them and check with them how their day has been. Make it clear to them that this is not complaint time, but share time.

5. Plan some special outings and rituals that are for summer only for you and the kids.

6. Talk with the kids to find out what they are thinking about how they will spend vacation. Some kids wait all year to have the time to master a video game, read a series of books, watch old movies, or just "chill." Don't be too quick to judge how they want to spend their time or think your ideas for summer fun are better than theirs. Work with them to figure out times they can do what is important to them.

7. If you don't like the idea of your children having months off, look into year-round schools. If there aren't any available in your area, lobby for instituting one.

BOOSTER THOUGHTS America is the only large, developed nation that suspends the learning process for three full months each summer so that teachers and students spend more time shutting it down and starting it up than in keeping it moving productively. The summer break started because children were needed at home to help with the summer crops, but that's outdated. We have kept the form, but lost the function. As a result our children get forty to sixty fewer days of education than the top nations.

In the future America may have year-round (trimester) education with several shorter breaks during the year. Until then consider talking to your child about working, volunteering, taking special summer courses, or any doing other productive activities during the summer.

Life Skills Children Can Learn

Kids can learn that they can either entertain themselves or just feel bored. They also learn that just because they are on vacation doesn't mean they can forget all their responsibilities around the house. Children can also learn to expect that their folks will help them be safe and have a fun summer.

Parenting Pointers

1. With so many parents working, summer vacation is not what it used to be. Many children need a break from school, but don't have opportunities to use this time productively. Planning ahead for productive use of time (including rest time) is important.

2. Some children become depressed during summer vacation for lack of a productive focus. Others handle their boredom by getting involved in shoplifting or gang activities. Children need a productive focus to avoid these pitfalls.

TATTLING

"What can be done about children who tattle? It seems like I spend half my day getting involved in settling problems tattlers bring me."

Understanding Your Child, Yourself, and the Situation

Children tattle because they lack the skills to solve their own problems or because they feel discouraged and seek undue attention by trying to prove how "good" they are. Some adults shame children for tattling. Others jump in and try to fix the situation because they think that the children are incapable of figuring out what to do. Instead of getting irritated about tattling, see it as an opportunity to teach your child important life skills.

Suggestions

1. Listen respectfully, with your mouth closed, without fixing the problem. When you avoid fixing that does not mean you're abandoning the child. When adults just listen, some children think of a solution on their own.

2. Use reflective listening to let the tattler know you understand her feelings. "I'll bet you're really angry with _____." Again you don't have to do anything else to fix the situation.

3. When the tattler arrives, you might kindly ask, "Why are you telling me?" or "How is that a problem for you?" Then quietly watch the response. This offers some children an opportunity to think about their reason and to realize they don't have a good one, or that it isn't their problem.

4. Another possibility is to take this opportunity to teach your child problem-solving skills. You might ask, "What ideas do you have to solve that problem?" or "Would you like to put the problem on the family-meeting agenda so the whole family can brainstorm for a solution?"

5. Sometimes it is enough to show faith in the child. Say, "I'm sure you can work it out." Then walk away to demonstrate your faith.

6. Assemble the children who are involved in the problem, including the tattler. Tell them, "I can see there is a problem, and I have faith in you kids to work it out. Here's a place you can talk." You can sit quietly and listen to them discuss solutions, or you can walk away and ask

them to find you and tell you how they worked it out.

7. If the kids are arguing, let them know that, until they find a solution to their problem, they can't continue doing whatever the argument is about. If they can't agree on a program to watch, they'll have to turn off the TV until they all agree on a solution.

BOOSTER THOUGHTS A young mother was taking a parenting class and decided that when kids tattled, she would just say, "I have faith in you to solve the problem." A few weeks later, she invited her nieces and nephew over to play with her kids. One of the nieces averaged six tattles an hour. Mom decided to try out her new skills and said to her niece, "I'm sure you kids can work it out." Her niece looked at her like she was the meanest, most disgusting person in the world and stomped out of the room and played by herself for about ten minutes.

An hour later she overheard a child tell the tattler, "I'm going to tell Auntie on you."

The tattler said, "I wouldn't bother. She'll just say, 'You kids can work it out,' so we may as well work it out."

"Okay," the other child said. "Let's take turns picking out a toy."

"That sounds fun," the tattler said.

Planning Ahead to Prevent Future Problems

1. Change your thinking about tattling. When your children get older, you may wish they would tell you more about what is going on in their lives. Now is the time to let them know you are interested in their concerns and will help them learn skills instead of putting them down or turning them away.

2. Don't put older kids in charge of their younger siblings. The responsibility may be too great and they may deal with problems by tattling.

3. Place an agenda on the refrigerator so children have a place to write their concerns. Then have regular family meetings so your children can practice looking for solutions instead of blame.

Life Skills Children Can Learn

Children can learn that they can talk to their parents about anything because they won't experience punishment or insults. They learn that they can work out problems or leave the scene if they don't like the way someone else is behaving. It's okay to be upset and the family meeting is a good place to talk about the things that upset them.

Parenting Pointers

1. If you want to encourage a discouraged child, you need to find ways to give recognition without reinforcing the mis-behavior. "I love you and have faith in you to solve your problems" is a good message.

2. Most kids can work out problems themselves quicker and more creatively when well-meaning adults don't get involved. Step back and give kids a chance to see what they can do on their own before getting involved.

TEMPER TANTRUMS

"What can I do when my child throws herself on the floor kicking and screaming—especially when it happens in a public place?"

Understanding Your Child, Yourself, and the Situation

Temper tantrums can be infuriating and embarrassing. Sometimes children have tantrums because they are tired and parents are dragging them to places they don't have the resources and skills to handle. Your child may have tried to let you know his wants and needs in a more subtle way that you missed. Or you may have induced a state of anxiety and aggravation within your child by giving too many commands and using too many words. Other times it helps to remember that your child's behavior may have a purpose (see Four Mistaken Goals of Behavior, page 25).

Tantrums are a form of communication. If the first tantrum was effective to engage you, obstruct you, or upset you, your child may have figured out this is the way to relate with you. To correct this mistake and be effective, you must first deal with the tantrum in a way that doesn't encourage more of them. Later you can look for the coded message of the tantrum and/or how you may have invited the tantrum in the first place.

Suggestions

1. Have faith in your child to deal with her feelings—eventually. We rob our children of opportunities to develop belief in their own capabilities when we always try to rescue them or fix everything for them. Let your child have her feelings without thinking you need to prevent or change them. Don't give in to the tantrum—stop trying to please your child in this moment. If you choose any of the following methods, do so with an attitude of empathy instead of a need to control or rescue.

2. With some children, it helps to hold them and comfort them when they have a tantrum. Validate their feelings by saying something such as, "It's okay to be upset. It happens to all of us. I'm here and I love you." Other children don't want to be held. You might want to sit close and simply give emotional support without saying anything.

3. It's okay to say no to your child, and it's okay for her to be angry. (Don't you sometimes feel angry or upset when you don't get what you want?) Say, "I know you are angry, and that's okay. You wish you could have what you want. I'd probably feel the same way." Then wait or redirect.

4. Another way to deal with a temper tantrum is to simply ignore it. Stand quietly, with an attitude of empathy, and wait until it's over.

5. Sometimes it is best to shut your mouth and act. Take your child outside and put her in the car, and let her know that it's okay that she's upset, and that you and she can try again when she calms down.

6. With young children, distractions work really well. Instead of fighting or arguing, make funny noises, sing a song, or say, "Let's go see what's over there."

7. Once the tantrum is over, it may be appropriate to say nothing about it. If your child is using a tantrum for emotional blackmail, she will soon give up if you don't buy into it. Or once your child has calmed down, you might ask if he would like your help to think of ways to deal with a similar problem in the future. You could then ask curiosity questions (see Ask "Curiosity" Questions, page 9) to help her figure out a solution.

*Planning Ahead to Prevent
Future Problems*

1. As mentioned in Suggestion 1 above, one of the biggest mistakes parents make is thinking they need to protect their children from ever feeling upset or disappointed. It could be that the best way to prevent future problems is for you to change your attitude and simply allow your child to have her feelings. When children can have their feelings, they rarely need a full-blown tantrum to make a point.

2. Ask your child at a calmer time if she would like to learn some good ways to handle frustration. If she agrees, teach her to tell you in words how she feels instead of using an emotional display.

3. Pay attention to ways you may be setting your child up to have a tantrum. You may be arguing, demanding, controlling, and fighting with her until she throws a tantrum in exasperation.

4. Create a plan together. Ask your child what she would like you to do when she is having a tantrum. Do this at a time when you can discuss it calmly. Give choices such as, "Would you like a hug, would you like me to just wait until you're over it, or would you like to go to your feel-good place (see Make Time-Out Positive, page 21) until you feel better?" She might have other ideas. Children are more receptive to a plan they have helped choose in advance.

5. Decide what you will do and inform your child in advance. For example, you may decide that you will take the child to the car and patiently read a book until she has settled down and tells you that she is ready to try again. Or you may decide that you will go home immediately and try again another day. Whatever you decide, be sure to follow through with dignity and respect. In other words, keep your mouth shut and act. The only thing you could say that would be effective is, "We can try again when you are ready" (if you just went to the car) or "We can try again tomorrow or next week" (if you decided to go home)—and it might be better to wait until everyone is calm to make either comment.

6. Role-play the plan before going to a public place. (Three- to six-year-olds will understand the word *pretend* better than role-play.) Describe the behavior that is expected and let your children pretend you are in the public place and that they are doing what is expected. Then let them have fun role-playing a temper tantrum and you can role-play what you will do per the plan you both came up with. It is fun to reverse roles. You play the child who is having the tantrum and let your child play what the parent will do.

7. Put the problem of tantrums on the family-meeting agenda and let your children brainstorm for solutions about what to do. After you have a list of sug-

BOOSTER THOUGHTS Mrs. Benito and her four-year-old daughter, Emma, had decided in advance that if Emma didn't follow her morning routine and wasn't dressed and ready for school by 7:30 A.M. when it was time to leave, Mrs. Benito would put her clothes in a paper bag and Emma could get dressed in the car after they arrived at the preschool. (She couldn't get dressed while the car was moving because of their firm seat belt rule.) Because this was discussed during a calm time, Emma was happy to agree.

Two weeks later Emma wasn't dressed on time. She was still in her pajamas. Mrs. Benito put her clothes in a paper bag and said, "It is time to leave. You can get dressed in the car after we get to school."

Emma had a mild temper tantrum. "No! I don't want to!"

Mrs. Benito said, "It is time to leave. Do you want to get into the car by yourself, or do you want me to help you?"

Emma could tell that her mom meant it, so she got into the car, still yelling, "I don't want to get dressed in the car! You are so mean. I hate you!"

Mrs. Benito said, "I don't blame you for being upset. I would be too." Then she didn't say another word. She remained silent and let Emma have her feelings.

When they arrived at the preschool, Emma was pouting (a silent temper tantrum). She refused to get out of the car. Mrs. Benito said, "I'm going into the school. Come in when you are ready." (She had parked in the driveway where she could sit in the preschool director's office and watch to make sure Emma was safe.)

Emma sat in the car and pouted for about three minutes. Then she got dressed and came into the school. All her mom said was, "Thank you for keeping our agreement. I appreciate it."

It was several weeks before Emma was late getting dressed again. This time she got into the car without having a temper tantrum. She and her mother had a nice discussion on the way to school. When they arrived, Mrs. Benito said, "Do you want me to sit here while you get dressed, or shall I wait for you in the office?" Emma said, "I want you to wait for me." Mom had let Emma know that if she dawdled, she would go into the office to wait, so Emma got dressed quickly, happily walked into the preschool with her mom, kissed her good-bye, and ran off to play with her friends.

gestions, let the child who typically has tantrums choose the suggestion she feels will help her the most.

Life Skills Children Can Learn

Children can learn that life is full of ups and downs and that they are capable of dealing with their feelings. They learn that tantrums and emotional blackmail won't get them what they want and that there are more appropriate ways to express their feelings.

Parenting Pointers

1. It is such a gift for children to know that it is okay to have their feelings, and you love and accept them even if they are having a fit.

2. Some kids (and some adults, too) like to bluster before they accept the inevitable. It's their style and doesn't hurt anyone. Once the blustering (or tantrum) is done, often they will cheerfully do what needs to be done. Keep your sail out of their wind while they bluster, and it won't rock your boat.

TERRIBLE TWOS (*SEE ALSO* NO!)

"My child is an angel, but she's almost two. I've heard so many awful things about this age that I'm living in fear of what lies ahead for us. Any suggestions?"

Understanding Your Child, Yourself, and the Situation

There can only be terrible twos in a world where parents want to control or protect rather than empower. If you welcome your child's individuation, there isn't a better time than the twos. In fact we are renaming them—the terrific twos. As your child asserts more independence, you'll find that the more you understand about the basics of positive discipline, the more fun you'll have with this age. You might find yourself getting frustrated if all you know is how to say no, use time-outs, spank, or ignore your child's acting out. Your child is feeling a sense of personal power right now, which is great, but he's still only two and not quite ready to run the family. He's looking for room to experiment while knowing where the safe boundaries are. That's your job. Our suggestions will help you turn the twos into a wonderful time of life for the whole family.

Suggestions

1. When your child looks at you with the gleam in his eye, tempting you with his next "naughty" act, don't say a word. If it's not that important, ignore it. If it is important, act without talking and do what is needed (distracting, redirecting, removing) to keep the situation safe.

2. When your child says no to everything, you are making too many demands or asking too many questions that can be

answered by yes or no. Instead give children limited choices. "Hold my hand when we cross the street," invites a big no from a two-year-old, whereas "Do you want to hold my right hand or my left hand?" invites cooperation.

3. A two-year-old understands the logic of the social order. Here's how it sounds: it's time for a bath; the clock says it's toy-pick-up time; when the timer goes off, we all have to run to the car so we won't miss the play; pants on first, shoes on next; seat belts and car seats before we can start the car; playing with food means dinner is over; etc. (see Establish Routines, page 17).

4. Lead with what your child can do instead of what he can't do. Say, "The dog is for snuggling," or "Food is for eating," or "You can push the buttons on the microwave as soon as we put the food inside." If you pay attention, you'll notice how much negativity you use with your kids instead of showing what *can* be done.

5. Two-year-olds love to help. It gives them a positive sense of power. Ask your two-year-old for help so *you* can have a rest instead of saying *she* has to nap. Ask him to stay near you on a walk to help keep you safe instead of yelling not to run ahead. Ask if he can help you by whispering instead of yelling.

6. It is amazing how much two-year-olds can understand when you talk and explain to the child as if he is a real person with an ability to comprehend. Often two-year-olds can be heard saying things like "Be patient," or "We have to whisper in the library," parroting what they have heard you say and practicing the behavior.

7. "Try again," is the magic phrase with a two-year-old. It means what he's doing now isn't working, it's a mistake, and he can have another chance . . . later!

Planning Ahead to Prevent Future Problems

1. Minimize uses of power and control and use empowerment and encouragement instead.

2. Create a schedule that is respectful of this age group that hates to rush. Leave extra time for activities so that your child can cooperate.

3. Say something once and then act. Don't threaten or repeat orders from afar.

4. If your child doesn't understand what you want or need, practice through pretend play at times when neither of you are stressed. You can pretend it's dinnertime to practice manners, or pretend it's bath time to practice how the routine needs to go.

5. Don't be afraid to let your two-year-old have feelings when he doesn't get his way. You can validate the feelings with-

BOOSTER THOUGHTS Mom separated Billie from the dog Snickers at least ten times a day saying, "The dog is for snuggling, not for kicking. Be gentle or you and Snickers will have to take a break and try again later." She hoped the dog would learn to stay away from Billie to avoid being squeezed and poked, but Snickers seemed to be a glutton for punishment, and Billie just couldn't stop playing too rough with her. Mom wasn't willing to let Billie mistreat the dog, so she continued to separate them as often as needed.

After about three weeks of this behavior, one day she heard Billie call from another room. "Mom, come see how gentle I'm being with Snickers." She went into the other room to find Billie and Snickers curled up together in Snicker's dog bed, snuggling like two old buddies. Mom realized that Billie wanted to do the right thing—it just took him a while to figure it out.

◎

Mr. and Mrs. Aguilar decided they would not say no to their twins in the hope that they would not go through a no stage. Instead they used distraction, showed the twins what they could do instead of what they couldn't, and did a lot of "acting" (quietly redirecting) instead of "talking." One day they were shocked to hear one of the two-year-old twins say, "No, no! Bad dog!" They had forgotten to avoid saying no to the dog.

out changing your mind or fixing the situation.

6. Two-year-olds have great senses of humor. If your two-year-old is pouting, you could say, "I want that face," and pretend to remove it from him and put it on you. In no time, you'll both be laughing.

7. Don't forget to spend time each day playing. Two-year-olds are still kids and need to play with you instead of rushing from one activity to another.

Life Skills Children Can Learn

Children can learn that there is room for them to experiment without getting hurt or aggravating the entire family. They can garner self-confidence and skills as they take on more activities for themselves.

Parenting Pointers

1. Do not let your two-year-old run the family. It is okay to set boundaries and follow through with them, as long as your methods are firm, kind, friendly, and few.

2. Sit back and enjoy all that your young person is learning to do. Don't interfere unless safety is involved. You'll be surprised at how much that little person has already learned.

TOUCHING THINGS

"I've told my seven-month-old child a hundred times to leave the TV dials alone, but he just won't listen. Counting to three doesn't work; neither does slapping his hand. What should I do?"

Understanding Your Child, Yourself, and the Situation

It is normal for children to want to touch things as they explore their world. It is a shame to punish children for doing what is normal. The latest brain research tells us that punishing children for doing things that are developmentally appropriate for them to do can impede optimal brain development. And punishment is likely to give them a sense of doubt and shame rather than a healthy sense of self-worth.

This does not mean they should be allowed to touch anything they want. It does mean we need to use kind and firm methods, *not* punishment, to teach children what they can and cannot touch.

Suggestions

1. Actions speak louder than words with a young child (and older ones). If you don't want your child to touch something, tell her only once not to touch it. As soon as she touches it again, kindly and firmly remove her from that object and show her what she can touch.

2. Show your child how to touch an item without hurting it or the child, that is, "We can smell the flowers, not pick them," or "You can push the spigot on the watercooler as soon as I have a cup under it."

Planning Ahead to Prevent Future Problems

1. Childproofing a house can cut down on nagging and increase optimal brain development. Put valuables out of reach, put covers over electrical outlets, and stabilize items your child can damage or get hurt on. Put items that are okay for your child to touch on lower shelves.

2. Set up a special play area where it's safe and okay for your child to play, such as a playpen or a kitchen cupboard filled with interesting things your little one can pull out and leave all over the floor. Long periods of confinement to a playpen or high chair is not healthy for toddlers.

Life Skills Children Can Learn

Children can learn that some things are out of bounds and they are treated with

BOOSTER THOUGHTS[19] "We childproofed our home when Brett was a baby. I packed up my crystal collection and put it away for a while. As he got older, I would think about putting it out again, but there was always some reason not to—clumsy walking at two, rough-and-tumble play at four, then the baseballs, footballs, and basketballs. When he went away to college, I put a few pieces out on the bookcase. My husband broke one while rushing to get the dictionary during a heated Scrabble game. I broke another while dusting. Now we have grandchildren. I think a better term for it would be "people proofing." If you want to enjoy your fragile valuables, put them in a glass-front case—even if the kids are grown and gone."

respect as they learn what they are. Their parents respect their needs by childproofing to make exploration safe.

Parenting Pointers

1. Many parents feel their children should learn not to touch things, and they refuse to make changes in the decor as children are added to the family. This indicates that the parents don't understand child development and age-appropriate behavior, and it tells children that their needs aren't important and that they are in the way.

2. By showing your children what they *can* do instead of what they can't do, you eliminate power struggles. Many items that seem interesting at one age soon lose interest as your child gets a little older.

TOYS AND TIDINESS

"It is a constant battle to get my children to pick up their toys. And it is so annoying when my child has friends who come to the house get every toy out on the floor, and then leave the room in shambles. I nag and threaten to take the toys away, but nothing is working."

Understanding Your Child, Yourself, and the Situation

Most parents dislike having their home turned into a playground. Most kids dislike cleanup. Most friends forget to help pick up when they are done playing. It's age-appropriate behavior, but you have a right to expect that your children be involved in cleanup. Instead of punishing or having unrealistic expectations, you'll have to learn how to teach kids in a way that invites cooperation.

Suggestions

1. Do not clean up the mess yourself, and do not punish your child for leaving the mess.

2. Children aged two to five usually need help. It is unrealistic to expect them to follow your demands and clean up on their own. Instead say, "I will help you pick up your toys. Which ones do you want me to pick up and which ones will you pick up?" or "Let's set the timer and see how many of these toys we can pick up before the timer goes off."

3. Young children often respond to the "Clean Up Song." All you do is ask them to sing with you, "Clean up, clean up. It's time to clean up," while they clean up their toys. They also love the cuddly stuffed lamb with a timer in its belly (available at www.focusingonsolutions.com) that can be used as a "time for clean up" reminder, or setting the amount of time they think it will take.

4. For ages six to twelve say, "The mess in your room needs to be cleaned up. Would you like to clean it up yourself, or do you want to invite your friend to help you?"

5. Ask if your child wants to clean up his own toys, or if he wants you to do it. (This only works if you have previously agreed that when you "clean" you get to put all the toys on the floor into a bag that they can have back after a week— see Planning Ahead 2.)

6. If some of your child's belongings disappear after a friend has been playing at your house, help your child call the friend's house and ask if the friend accidentally picked up one of your child's toys. Let the family know you will be happy to stop by to get the "lost" toy.

Planning Ahead to Prevent Future Problems

1. During a family meeting, ask your kids to brainstorm with you to see how many ideas you can all come up with to solve the problem in advance. Remember that kids are more motivated to follow solutions they create.

2. Decide what you will do. In advance let your children know that you will clean up if they don't . . . by picking up any toys that are on the floor and putting them into a bag in the garage or on a high shelf for a week. If you do have to follow through with this consequence, you may be surprised at how many toys the children won't miss because you have purchased way too

many that they don't care about longer than two minutes—which is really your problem.

4. For ages two to six put each toy or set of toys (especially those with small pieces) in separate plastic drawstring bags and put the bags on high hooks. Teach your children that they and their friends can have one or two bags at a time. The toy they are playing with must be picked up and put back in the bag before they can have another one.

5. When your child has friends over, let them know in advance what is expected and help them come up with a plan to accomplish it: "How much time do you think you will need to clean up? Do you want to set a timer, or would you like me to tell you when it is time to clean up?" Before your child's friend leaves, ask him or her to check the room with you and your child to make sure they have kept their agreement.

6. Create a play area for the kids either in their rooms or in a separate part of the house. Let the kids know that toys belong in this area and not in the living room. If older kids have toys with small parts that are dangerous for younger kids, keep their play areas in a separate part of the house.

Life Skills Children Can Learn

Children can learn that there is responsibility that goes along with privileges. They can learn to plan ahead with their parents' help to make sure their friends cooperate.

BOOSTER THOUGHTS One mother tells about her experience: "In our family, the kids learned early that if I said something I meant it, so they didn't bother testing me. When their friends came to play and refused to help with cleanup, I could hear the kids saying from the next room, 'You may as well start cleaning. She means it when she says it's time to clean up. She'll just come in and wait until we're done before she lets us leave the room.'

"Occasionally one of their friends would insist on testing the limits. Then my kids would come in and ask me if I would help them get their friend moving. I would sit in the center of the room and pick up one toy at a time, handing it to the recalcitrant friend. I'd say, 'Who wants to put this one away? Thanks so much for putting it away. How about this toy? Who wants to do this one?' I wouldn't leave until the last toy was cleaned up."

Parenting Pointers

1. Give up nagging, threats, and punishment. Look for solutions instead of blame.

2. Your children may be quite responsible about cleanup, but their friends may not have to do it at home. Help your children involve their friends in the process instead of assuming it is up to your children to work it out alone.

TRAVELING

"We want to take our children on vacations with us, but they are very difficult to deal with. Are there some ways to make vacations with children more fun and manageable?"

Understanding Your Child, Yourself, and the Situation

Vacations are a time for making family memories. They can be a nightmare or a lot of fun, depending on both the parents' attitude and the amount of advance planning. What you do and where you go can make or break a vacation. If you expect your kids to enjoy an adult-centered trip, guess again. Children don't stop being children just because they are on vacation. Their needs must be considered to have a successful vacation. Adults often expect their children to act like grown-ups on vacation and are disappointed when the kids behave like kids. Many adults have a picture of what a vacation should look like, and they may be both surprised and disappointed to find that other family members have a very different picture. It is important to match pictures ahead of time to improve the quality of the vacation experience.

Suggestions

1. When you take children on a vacation, sometimes you have more work to do preparing than you would if you stayed home. The more you involve the kids in the planning and the chores, the more it will be a vacation for everyone. Use the family meeting to discuss vacation plans including packing for the trip, packing the car, chores, and the special things each family member wants to do on the trip.

2. Let young children assist in packing their suitcases or pack them without your help if they are ready. You may wish to make a checklist with them or give information about the type of clothing that will be suitable for the activities you plan to do and the weather conditions.

3. Car trips can be more enjoyable if you rotate who sits in the front seat and next to each other. Leave plenty of extra time for frequent stops to run and play at a rest area or to pull over and wait quietly for children to settle down if they are

fighting or getting too rowdy for you to drive safely.

4. Don't push until everyone is overtired. Stop early and enjoy some space from each other and time to unwind.

5. Prepare a surprise sack. Wrap several inexpensive items such as a coloring book and crayons, a card game, a pack of gum, stickers, hand puzzles, etc. Tell the kids they can open a new surprise every hour.

6. At the end of a trip, take time to ask each family member what was most special for them. Let the family help put photos in a trip album together.

Planning Ahead to Prevent Future Problems

1. Get your kids used to car travel by taking them on an extended trip weekly. This could be as short as an hour ride, or even a day trip. Even though they may cry in the car when they are young, it's amazing how quickly they get used to being in their car seat. It is never too early to start this—in fact, in some families, taking the baby for a ride seems to be the only way to get her to nap.

2. Let the kids help pick out and pack a special bag to take on trips with toys they can play with on a plane or in the car. Include snacks if appropriate. You may wish to include cameras or diaries for the kids.

3. Don't just talk about taking vacations. It's discouraging to kids to hear promises with no follow-through. Vacations can be a day trip to an interesting nearby attraction, an overnight to a city close by, a family camping trip, or anything else—it doesn't have to be an overwhelming two-week stay away from home. Sometimes just spending the night in a motel with a pool in your own city can be a real treat for the kids.

4. If you are flying with infants, reserve an aisle seat and notify the airline of your need for extra help. Check as much baggage as possible, as it is a handful just to carry your child and the toys or diaper bag.

5. If you can, get a traveling video player and entertain the kids with videos while you drive.

6. Look into family cruises, family camps, or family resorts where there are special activities for kids and babysitters who can give you a break.

7. Consider making other arrangements for teens who really hate to travel with you and will make your trip a living nightmare if you insist they come along.

Life Skills Children Can Learn

Children can learn how special it is to take a trip with their family. They see other

BOOSTER THOUGHTS We traveled around the country in a van for seven months when our children were four and two years old. It was a very special time once we learned to drive short distances and then stop for the kids to play or explore. It also helped to create a routine the kids could count on. For us that included finding a camping spot by 4:00 P.M., having some physical activity before going into a restaurant, a quiet time each day when we didn't answer questions or play games in the car, taking turns to sit with the kids, and staying extra days if another family with children was camping nearby. Our kids read books from local libraries, played with a piece of rope and sticks for hours, and made forts out of picnic tables. We were on a very limited budget so we found fun things to do that didn't cost money: the beach, playgrounds, hiking, games around the fire, cooking together, coloring, fishing, etc. Traveling with kids can be a great experience once their needs are considered.

Now I spend every Thursday with my grandson, and we have turned that into a mini-vacation day. He has grown up driving long distances and is used to being in the car. We sing, play games, look for trucks, make funny noises, and even enjoy the silence. He is learning to welcome new places as well as longing to return to some of the old ones. We are making memories together. I call him "Mr. Thursday," a name he enjoys and understands, even though he is only two.

parts of the country or reconnect with relatives who can enjoy and appreciate them and help them feel special.

Parenting Pointers

1. It's okay to take some vacations without your children.

2. If you hate to camp, send your kids to camp or let them go camping with a neighbor and you stay home.

3. It is not necessary to spend a lot of money to have a good time on a vacation, but it is important to make the trip special by doing things that are different from what you would do at home.

UNMOTIVATED AND UNINTERESTED

"My child does as little as he can to 'get by' in school. He doesn't do his chores around the house. We have offered rewards and taken away privileges. Nothing seems to work. He just doesn't seem to have any interest or motivation for anything. What should we do?"

Understanding Your Child, Yourself, and the Situation

When a child lacks motivation, it is helpful to get into his world to discover the purpose of his behavior. Most unmotivated behavior is a response to having to do something the child doesn't want to do. That same child may be highly motivated in areas of his own choosing. Perhaps your child feels powerless and is trying to tell you "You can't make me," as his only way to win a power struggle. Perhaps he feels conditionally loved by your pressure and high expectations, which hurts, so he wants to hurt back by not trying. If you have been doing too much for your child it is possible that he has adopted the belief that he is incapable and has given up because it is easier to avoid trying than to face failure. Your child may be comparing himself to a sibling and trying to find belonging and significance in the family by being different, especially if one of the siblings is highly motivated. Another possibility is that he has learned many bad habits by being allowed to watch too much TV or play too many video games. Whatever the reason, a child who lacks motivation presents one of the most challenging and discouraging situations a parent faces. Typical parental responses are to do things for him, to push him harder, to try punishments, or to make him feel bad in the hope that he will change his ways. But all these responses make the situation worse. The challenge is for parents to stop doing things that don't work and take time to find ways to encourage both themselves and their children.

Suggestions

1. Take a look at your own behavior. Are you not giving your child enough quality time where you just enjoy him for who he is, causing him to seek attention? Are you so controlling that you invite power struggles and rebellion? Are your expectations so high that your child feels she can't live up to them, and feels hurt by your conditional love? Are you doing too much for your child, which may invite her to believe she is incapable? If you answered yes to any of those questions, stop the behavior immediately and choose any of the following suggestions to create a more respectful relationship.

2. Instead of expecting your child to follow through, you be the one to follow through (see Part 1) with kindness, firmness, dignity, and respect. Use one word to communicate what your child needs to do: "Homework." "Chores." Make eye contact, and try to have a firm yet kind expression. If you still get resistance, keep your mouth shut, give him a knowing smile, a wink, or a hug, and point to what needs to be done. These methods are much more motivating than words that invite a power struggle.

3. Act. Take a young child by the hand and lead her kindly and firmly to the task that she needs to do. Too many parents try talking too much or "directing from afar" and it doesn't work.

4. Offer your honest emotions: "I feel upset because you spend time on everything but your schoolwork, and I wish it was more of a priority for you."

5. Let the consequences be the teacher. (Consequences are what happen as a result of a child's choices, not something you impose.) If a child is not doing his homework, this will be reflected in poor grades and in missed opportunities. Don't underestimate the value of learning from failure. Show empathy when he experiences the consequences of his choices. Don't display an I-told-you-so attitude.

6. Follow up with "what" and "how" questions to help him explore and understand the cause and effect, and use this information to form a plan for success. "How do you feel about what happened?" "What is important to you?" "What are the benefits to you now or in the future if you do or don't do this?" "What is a plan that would work for you to accomplish your goals?" (If he says, "I don't know," say, "Why don't you think about it and get back to me later because I know you are a good problem solver.")

7. Engage in joint problem solving. Decide together what the problem is and what some possible solutions are. Begin by sharing your perspective: "I notice that you aren't making any effort to do your schoolwork or to help around the house." Then invite him to share his picture of what's happening. This is effective only if he feels you will listen without judgment. Then brainstorm together for solutions and pick the one that works for both of you.

8. Assure your child that you know he is capable of doing whatever he needs to do to be successful.

Planning Ahead to Prevent Future Problems

1. Notice when a child who usually participates abruptly stops. This may be an indication that something is happening at school or at home, such as a divorce or serious illness. Or the child could be having problems with peer relationships.

2. Help your child do some goal setting. Ask what your child would do if he had a magic wand and could do what he liked. This will give you a lot of insight into what your child's real interests are.

3. Have regular family meetings and joint problem-solving sessions. Keep three things in mind. First, when children are involved in making decisions, they are motivated to adhere to the decisions. Second, children participate more when they understand the relevance of what

they're doing. Third, children learn a valuable life skill when they participate in brainstorming for solutions that are respectful and helpful to all concerned.

4. Discuss all the things that are going well, giving your child a chance to speak first. Then ask for his opinion of what needs improvement. Brainstorm with him what he could do and what you could do that would be the most encouraging and helpful to him.

5. Create routines with (not for) your children (see Establish Routines in Part 1). When they have a say in when and how, they are more willing to do the what.

6. Build on strengths. If a child is doing well in any area, encourage her to spend more time in this area. (Don't forbid her to spend time on a subject in which she does well until she does better in another subject.) A child needs to feel encouraged in her areas of strength.

BOOSTER THOUGHTS In the eighth grade, Stuart lost interest in school. His mother would have to coax and then yell at him to get up in the morning and to go to school. Stuart would finally get up but would act angry and sullen. He refused to work hard in school and skipped classes, and his grades were slipping.

Finally his mother decided to stop engaging in the power struggles. Instead she asked Stuart to sit down with her in the family room and asked, in a friendly manner, a series of "what" and "how" questions. "What do you think will happen in your life if you don't get a good education?" she asked. Stuart replied sullenly, "There are lots of millionaires who don't have a good education." Mom acknowledged, "That is true. How many people do you know who have dropped out of school?" "A few," Stuart said. Mom asked, "How are they doing?" Stuart looked a little sheepish as he said, "One is in jail. Another one is working at McDonald's."

Mom avoided the temptation to say "Well, is that how you want to end up?" Instead she continued to invite Stuart to explore possibilities. She asked, "What kind of jobs do you think you will be able to get if you don't have an education?" Stuart said, "Well, I could be a contractor." Mom said, "I'm sure you could. What kind of jobs will you *not* be able to get without an education?" Stuart thought about it. "Well, I couldn't be an engineer or a pilot." Mom watched as Stuart figured it out. After a few minutes Stuart said, "Okay, I'll go to school, but I'm not going to like it." Mom said, "Wow. That is profound. You just discovered a success principle—to do something even if you don't like it because you see the long-range benefits."

Teach her to manage her weaknesses, and let her know that barely passing or dropping a class once in a while is okay as long as she is doing well in areas where she has strength.

7. Avoid lectures and show empathy when your child experiences failures. Teach that mistakes are wonderful opportunities to learn.

8. Let go and allow your child to work out the problem. There's a difference between letting go and giving up. Giving up means cutting all ties, which sends the message that you are no longer available. When you let go, you can stay connected while handing the responsibility for the problem back to your child.

Life Skills Children Can Learn

Children can learn that they can establish their own goals and learn the skills they need to accomplish those goals, and their parents will be there to help them. They can learn that their parents love them unconditionally and have faith in them to figure things out and to learn from their mistakes.

Parenting Pointers

1. Help your children find and maintain their courage by stressing that the problem isn't failing, but what one does after failing.

2. Remember not to live through your children. Your job is help them discover who they are and develop their own goals.

VALUES AND MANNERS

"Maybe I'm old-fashioned, but I'm concerned about the lack of values in kids today, including my own. How do I counter all the materialistic, hedonistic, and sexual messages that seem to be teaching my children more than I do? It is obvious that today's kids don't have the sexual taboos I grew up with, which may have been extreme, but is an opposite extreme healthy? How do I teach values to my children?"

Understanding Your Child, Yourself, and the Situation

Core values are the internal beliefs you hold about yourself, others, life, and how things should be. Values are learned in two different ways: by watching and observing, and by listening and learning. People's core values are formed by age five (not that they can't be updated from time to time).

The updating and expansion of core values takes place as children get older and are influenced by relatives, friends, school, church, and mass media. Most young people go through a period during their teen years when they rebel against family values, often going in the opposite direction for a few years. Usually they come back to the family's core values if you don't have a power struggle with them throughout that time.

We live in a very different world from when you grew up—things have changed radically even in the last twenty years. Instead of thinking of this in negative terms, think of it as a challenge that provides opportunities for increasing your parenting skills and your connection with your kids. It is no longer safe to trust the rearing of children to outside forces. Your kids may not be learning the values you think are important by playing computer games, watching TV, or hanging out with friends. It's up to you to decide on the values you want to teach so you have a goal in mind. When parents think about it, they usually list values such as respect, concern for others, honesty, self-reliance, resiliency, motivation to learn, generosity, responsibility, self-discipline, dependability, and good manners. We would like to add to this list social responsibility or a desire to contribute.

Keep in mind that if what you are teaching is opposite from how you are living, your children will believe what you do more than what you say, and use that to form the basis of their values.

Suggestions

1. Don't be afraid to say to your kids, "Here's how we do such and such." For instance, you could say that in your family, you don't play with gifts until you write a thank-you note. You could tell the kids that at holiday time, first you buy gifts for those who are needy and then you do your family shopping. Most younger kids will accept what you say in a matter-of-fact way. If they argue with it, welcome this as a great opportunity for discussions about values.

2. When a child is rude, you can say, "Excuse me. What do you need to remember about being polite? How could you restate that?"

3. A variation of the above would be to say, "Whoops. Would you like to start over using the wonderful manners that reflect the real you?"

4. It is okay to give gentle reminders in the moment such as: Remember to serve ladies first. Don't forget to hold your guest's chair while she is being seated at the table. What do you need to say when asking for something? (Please.) What do you need to say when someone does something for you? (Thank you.)

5. If a child calls you a name, take the child to a private place, stoop down to her level and whisper in her ear, "I don't call you that, and I don't want you to call me that name. It hurts my feelings. Please don't do it again. I love you."

Planning Ahead to Prevent Future Problems

1. Model the values you want to teach. If you want children to learn respect, be

respectful and respect yourself. Practice what you preach, because the kids will do as you do and not as you say.

2. Use discipline methods that teach values and manners. All Positive Discipline parenting tools are designed to teach valuable social and life skills for good character.

3. If you have a strong faith and you want your kids to share your beliefs, you may want to send them to religious school where they will learn values from others. When they are young, kids are very literal and tend to accept what they are told, so make sure the teachings reflect what you want your children to learn.

4. Help your kids think of steps they can take when there is a tragedy or disaster so they can lend a hand to others. Check out your local Volunteer Bureau and find ways to get involved in your community.

5. Over and over we suggest family meetings because it is one of the most powerful formats you can use to teach values. Children learn concern for others by listening to different points of view and finding helpful solutions. They learn to look for the good and to verbalize compliments. They learn to focus on solutions that are respectful and helpful to all concerned. Do not miss out on this valuable tool to teach values.

6. During family meetings, work together on limiting the amount of screen time (see the sections on Electronics: TV, Video Games, iPods, Computers, etc., *and* Cell Phones). Be sure to join them sometimes when they watch TV programs, listen to music, and play video games, so you can engage in discussions about what they think of the values that are being portrayed and have a chance to honestly express what you think about them.

7. Use curiosity questions to help children explore what the consequences of their choices might be. In this way they explore their goals and their values and how to accomplish the life they want to lead.

8. Take time to teach manners without lectures and nagging. Have a "mealtime manners night" once a week where you practice manners. Make it fun. Invite everyone to exaggerate, saying things like, "Pleeeeese pass the butter." Make a game of getting points for catching others with their elbows on the table, talking with their mouths full, interrupting, complaining, or reaching across the table. The one with the most points gets to choose the after-dinner game. Eat together at the table. Use place mats or a tablecloth, napkins, and candles to make the meal special.

9. Find stories about people who demonstrated integrity (perhaps in movies

BOOSTER THOUGHTS

Marianna came home from school in tears because her friends had teased her about her curly hair. Mom validated her feelings, saying, "Ouch. That must have really hurt."

After Marianna had calmed down, Mom decided to use this as an opportunity to help her explore some values. She asked, "Marianna, are you the only one who gets teased?"

Marianna thought about it and replied, "No, everyone gets teased about something." Lightbulbs seemed to go off in Marianna's head as she continued, "Even the popular kids get teased. Dorie is very popular, but she gets teased for her 'bunny teeth.'"

Mom asked, "How do other people handle it when they get teased?"

Marianna said, "I'm not sure. I think they get mad. I got mad, but I really felt sad too. I'll bet they feel the same way."

Mom asked, "Do you tease other kids?"

Marianna looked a little embarrassed as she said, "Sometimes. I don't start it, but sometimes I join in with the other kids. I don't mean anything by it. I didn't even think about how it might hurt them."

Mom asked, "Now that you have thought about it, how do you feel about it?"

Marianna said, "I sure don't like being teased, so I'm not going to tease others."

Mom went a step further, "Do you wish someone had stood up for you when you were being teased?"

Marianna said, "Yes. I was sad and angry when my best friend joined in the teasing. It hurt that she didn't stick up for me."

Mom asked, "Do you think you would have the courage to stand up for others who are being teased? I must warn you that if you do, others might turn on you because they feel embarrassed for being called on what they are doing."

Marianna said, "I don't care. Now that I know what it feels like, I don't want to be any part of hurting others—and I hope I have the courage to stand up for others."

This conversation was an indirect but effective way that Mom shared her values with Marianna.

or the news), such as someone who returned a wallet or someone who stood for values against all odds, such as in the movie *North Country*. Ask the questions, "What is more important than your integrity? Is money more important? How about what others think of you—is that more important than your integrity?"

10. Take time for training. Short lectures are acceptable when they are given during a calm time and with your children's permission. For example, "Would you like to know how to avoid embarrassing yourself when you are invited to dine with the rich and famous?" "Would you like to know how to be labeled a 'gentleman' instead of a 'jerk without manners' when you meet the girl of your dreams?" Once you have taken time for training, short reminders are okay, as long as they're not delivered in an angry tone. "Don't forget to say hello to Grandma when she comes. Remember to open the car door for your mother."

11. Take time to get your children involved in role-playing what they will do in certain circumstances such as when friends invite them to do drugs, steal, or engage in sex. They can also practice how to treat guests and what to do when they are a guest in someone's home. Previous practice goes a long way in being prepared to deal with the "real" situation.

Life Skills Children Can Learn

Children can learn that their lives are richer and they feel better about themselves when values and manners are a part of their lives.

Parenting Pointers

1. Children do not develop integrity and manners through osmosis. It requires time for training.

2. Alfred Adler taught that gemeinschaftsgefühl (social interest) is a measure of mental health. The more a person focuses on others and contributes, the better he or she feels.

WEANING

"My three-year-old still loves her bottle, her blanky, and her binky. I'm feeling embarrassed to take her out in public because I get so many disapproving stares, and my relatives give me a very bad time. Is it time for weaning? If so, how do I do it without traumatizing her for life?"

Understanding Your Child, Yourself, and the Situation

It is easy to understand why weaning is not easy for children. But why is it so difficult for parents? Why is it so hard for us to keep in mind that weaning is beneficial to children even when they don't like it at the time? The unfortunate paradox in loving children so much that you fail to wean them is that children inevitably resent you for it later on. Parents really think their children will appreciate all they do for them, but parents are continually hurt and disappointed when they see their children becoming spoiled brats instead of grateful and well-adjusted children. The reverse, fortunately, is also true: Children will respect and appreciate you (eventually) when you love them enough to wean them and teach them self-reliance and self-confidence, even though they don't like it in the moment. Weaning is never easy for the weanee or the weanor, but it is essential to the ultimate growth and progress of each.

Suggestions

1. Make a plan (together, if possible, depending on your child's age) with goals and timetables, remembering to take time for training in new skills. Your first goal can be leaving the blankie at home when you go out to the store, then the next goal can be to put it up in the closet for a whole day. Work on your plan when you aren't stressed or in the middle of a conflict.

2. Expect resistance and let children have their feelings. Use words like "I know you miss your bottle and you wish you still had it, but now you drink out of a sippy cup. Would you like to snuggle with me while you drink your milk from the cup?"

3. Follow through with confidence and consistency. It's torture for everyone if you are strong sometimes and give in other times.

4. Pick your battles and take small steps. You can't change a habit overnight.

Planning Ahead to Prevent Future Problems

1. Don't start your children on habits that you will dislike later. If you don't want your child in your bed, don't allow it because you are too tired to get up to feed your child or because you are too worried to let your child cry—you'll just have to wean your child from the behavior later.

2. If you plan to help your child learn to be more independent, have the items on hand that will facilitate change, for example, pants with elastic so children can learn to dress themselves, plastic dishes and cups so children can feed themselves, etc. Make learning a game.

3. Adjust your attitude and think of yourself as an empowering parent rather than a protective parent. Allow your children to try new things as they are ready, while keeping the endeavor safe for them. (We are not talking about

abandoning children or ignoring their safety, health, or genuine needs.)

4. Know the difference between wants and needs. Your child may want to bring her teddy bear with her everywhere, but she doesn't *need* it. He may want you to help him fall asleep by laying on the bed, but he doesn't need that.

Life Skills Children Can Learn

Children learn how to break old habits and learn new behaviors to replace the old, and that they can make changes one step at a time.

Parenting Pointers

1. Children need to be weaned to develop the self-reliance that will help them survive more successfully in society. The longer weaning has been delayed, the more uncomfortable everyone will feel and the longer your children may hold on to their anger.

2. The essential weaning isn't only from the breast or bottle (although most mothers can tell you that process can be tough enough)—parents must wean their children gradually and lovingly from emotional and physical dependence.

3. It may not make sense to you that loving in healthy ways is sometimes very uncomfortable, but this is a very important concept to grasp. It is much more comfortable to rescue children, give in to them, or help them feel better when they are upset. If what you are doing in the process of weaning your child *feels*

BOOSTER THOUGHTS Every animal in the animal kingdom, except humans, knows the importance of weaning. They instinctively know that young animals will not survive as adult animals unless they are weaned. Mother animals are not influenced at all by the fact that their offspring do not enjoy the weaning process (actually the mothers don't enjoy it much either). Have you ever watched a young animal try to nurse after its mother has decided it is time to wean? Every time a colt or calf tries to suckle, the mother animal uses her head to butt him away. It does not matter how hard the young animal tries; the mother knows instinctively that weaning is essential to self-reliance and survival.

good, it may be an unhealthy thing to do. If it feels uncomfortable, it just may be the most loving thing you can do for your child in the long run.

WHINING

"My child whines and it is driving me crazy. Punishment and bribery haven't worked. Does it sound like I'm whining? I'll do worse than whine if I don't get some help!"

Understanding Your Child, Yourself, and the Situation

Children do what works. If your child is whining, he or she is getting a response from you. Oddly enough, children seem to prefer punishment and anger to no response at all. Whining is usually based on the goal of seeking undue attention. This child believes "I belong only if you pay constant attention to me—one way or the other." For some children, it is the only method they know to get their needs met. Other children go through a whiny time and it then disappears as quickly as it started. Some of the suggestions here may seem contradictory, depending on whether they address the belief or the behavior. Choose the approach that feels best to you.

Suggestions

1. Every time your child whines, take him/her on your lap and say, "I bet you need a big hug." Do not say anything about the whining or what the child is whining about—just hug until you both feel better.

2. Let your child know that you love him but whining hurts your ears and that you will be happy to wait until he feels better to discuss the matter, so that he can talk in his normal voice. If he continues to whine, tell him that you love him and that you will leave the room if he continues to whine. If he continues, leave.

3. Address the problem your child is whining about by saying, "Let's put that on the family-meeting agenda and work on a solution at our next meeting when we all feel better."

4. Use your sense of humor. Take a crouching stance with your arms outstretched and fingers wiggling and say, "Here comes the tickle monster." It is likely he'll soon be laughing because you have redirected his energy.

5. Quit letting it bother you so much. This suggestion can work on its own, and it can also be an important component of all the other suggestions. Children can tell when their behavior pushes your buttons, and they'll keep doing it if they're getting a response.

Planning Ahead to Prevent Future Problems

1. Look for the hidden message beneath the whining. Perhaps your child is trying to tell you (in whining code) that she doesn't feel loved. Perhaps you have been too busy and haven't noticed how much she feels neglected. In that case, plan for regular, scheduled special time with your child to help her feel special, important, and that she belongs. On the other hand, maybe she is letting you know that she has a mistaken idea of how to get her needs met and needs some "training" in better communication skills.

2. During a happy time when there is no whining, brainstorm together for a signal about what you'll do when you hear whining. One possibility is to pull on your ear as a reminder that you hear normal voices only. Perhaps you will put your fingers in your ears and smile. Another possibility is to pat your hand over your heart as a reminder that "I love you." Let your child decide which signal works best for him. It is much more effective when he chooses the signal.

3. Tell your child, in advance, what you are going to do: "When you whine, I will leave the room. Please let me know when you are willing to talk in a respectful voice, because I enjoy listening to you when you're not whining." Still another possibility is to share "It's not that I don't hear you. I just don't

BOOSTER THOUGHTS Mrs. Jones had a little girl, Stacy, who whined incessantly and demanded almost constant attention. Mrs. Jones scolded Stacy and pushed her away, telling her she could entertain herself.

One day a friend of Mrs. Jones talked her into having her fortune told at a county fair. The fortune-teller implied that Mrs. Jones would not live to see the flowers bloom next spring. Even though Mrs. Jones didn't believe in fortune-tellers, she was plagued with the possibility that she might not live to watch her little girl grow up. Suddenly she could not get enough of Stacy. She wanted to spend time with her, hold her, read to her, play with her. Stacy loved all the attention— for a while. Then she began to feel smothered. Instead of demanding constant attention, she started pushing her mother away and demanding more independence. Stacy stopped whining when she got enough attention so she could stop demanding undue attention.

want to have a discussion with you until you use your regular voice. I don't answer whiny voices. I'm looking forward to hearing your respectful voice."

4. Whining could be a sign of discouragement that will stop when the child feels enough belonging and significance. Ignore the whining and find lots of ways to encourage your child.

Life Skills Children Can Learn

Children can learn that their parents love them but will not fall for their manipulative tactics. Children feel better about themselves when they learn effective skills to deal with their needs and wants.

Parenting Pointers

1. Some fascinating studies have been done with children of deaf parents. The researchers found that the children would make facial expressions that looked like they were crying, but they weren't making any sounds. The children had learned from experience that their deaf parents didn't respond to sounds, but did respond to their facial expressions. Children learn very quickly what works and what doesn't work.

2. A misbehaving child is a discouraged child. A cooperative child is an encouraged child who has learned respectful social skills.

WON'T TALK TO ME

"My eleven-year-old child won't talk to me. I try to show him I'm interested in him when he comes home from school by asking him questions about his day. I usually get one-word responses: 'Fine.' 'Nothing.' 'Yeah.' 'Nah.' 'Chill.' If I'm lucky I get three words, 'I don't know.' He used to talk to me. Now I think he hates me."

Understanding Your Child, Yourself, and the Situation

You have a normal preadolescent child. He doesn't hate you, but he hates the *inquisition*. This is what questioning seems like to kids this age. Some of their reasons include protecting their suddenly precious privacy; fear of your disapproval; inner turmoil as they try to sort out what they think, feel, and want; and shifting their loyalty from family to friends. Sometimes younger children don't listen because they have learned that parents don't mean what they say until they yell. Others don't listen because parents are too controlling and not listening is a passive way to have some power. Some kids may be introverts and will never be big talkers. Accepting kids unconditionally is crucial at this uncertain time of their lives.

Suggestions

1. With teens and preteens, don't take it personally. Know that it is normal and that, if you learn good listening skills, it may pass.

2. When your child does talk, *listen*. Ask her questions about what she's talking about, even if it's a video game or something you don't know much about, and show her that you're interested in the things that she does want to talk about. Many children stop talking because parents respond too quickly with disapproving looks or lectures. Learn to listen with your lips closed. Try limiting your responses to "Um-hmm. Um. Hmm." You'll be surprised how your child sometimes goes on and on when she feels listened to.

3. If you are yelling, stop. Speak with dignity and respect and then wait. Children learn what they see modeled by adults.

4. Try humor. With younger children, start wiggling your fingers in front of you and go after him/her saying, "Here comes the tickle monster to tickle sons/daughters that don't answer their mother."

5. Another possibility is to quit talking and try sign language or notes.

Planning Ahead to Prevent Future Problems

1. Sometime during the evening, invite your child to sit with you on the couch "because I need some time just to be with you." Don't ask questions. Allow your child to feel your unconditional love and acceptance.

2. Have regular family meetings where kids have an opportunity to learn communication and problem-solving skills based on mutual respect.

3. Get into your child's world. When he does talk, try to understand what he means even deeper than what he is saying. Try paraphrasing, "Are you saying _____ ?"

4. Become a closet listener. Just hang out where your kids are and keep your mouth shut. One mother sits on the edge of the tub in the morning while her daughter is getting ready for school. She doesn't ask any questions. Before long

BOOSTER THOUGHTS Sam resisted participating in "talks" with his mother, a marriage, family, and child counselor who specialized in adolescent counseling. His mom complained, "Sam, other teenagers enjoy talking with me and are willing to pay for the privilege."

Sam pointed out, "If you would talk with me the way you talk with them, I would probably enjoy it too."

All Mom could say was, "Touché!"

her daughter is babbling about her life. A father puts his paper down when his son comes into the room and says, "Hi." He keeps his paper down and resists asking questions. Sometimes his son plops down on the couch and they enjoy silent companionship. Sometimes his son starts talking about his day. Another possibility is to be there with cookies after school and don't ask questions. Driving the car pool is another great opportunity to just be available to listen.

5. Be curious. Ask only the kinds of questions that invite more talking: "I'm not sure I understand what you mean." "Could you tell me more?" "What example could you give me of that?" "When was the last time that happened?" "Anything else?" An attitude of true curiosity is essential.

Life Skills Children Can Learn

Children can learn that they are loved unconditionally. When they feel like talking, they are listened to, taken seriously, and validated for their thoughts, feelings, and ideas. They have a safe place to grow, change, and explore who they are.

Parenting Pointers

1. It is essential to the development of healthy self-esteem that children have their thoughts, feelings, and ideas listened to and taken seriously—even when their parents don't agree with them.

2. Children will listen to you only if they feel listened to.

WORKING OUTSIDE THE HOME

"I have a friend who works outside the home because she has to. I work outside the home because I want to. We both worry that our children may be harmed emotionally because they have working mothers. Please help."

Understanding Your Child, Yourself, and the Situation

It is easy to blame working parents, single parents, materialism, television, computers, and many other "situations" for the ails of the world. However we all know many children who have been raised in all kinds of circumstances and still grow into wonderful adults. And some children raised in the same circumstances grow up with all kinds of problems. What makes the difference? Kind and firm parenting isn't the only thing that can make a difference, but it is the one variable that you have control over, and it has a *huge* influence.

Recent studies have shown that children thrive when mothers give 100 percent of their energy to their jobs while they are at work and 100 percent to their families when they are at home. Ellen Galinsky[20] was brilliant enough to go to the source. She asked *children* how they felt about having a working mother. She discovered that children actually feel proud of their working mothers so long as mothers don't neglect their children when they are home. It is reasonable to assume that children would feel the same about their working fathers.

Think about it. Many mothers who stay home may be depressed, hooked on soap operas, or have such a busy social life that they neglect their children even though they're not working. Both working parents and stay-at-home parents may be too permissive, too strict, or too over-protective. Children can thrive whether their parents stay home or work outside the home—if parents use respectful parenting methods.

Suggestions

1. Give up your guilt. When your children know you have a "guilt button" they are happy to push it. Children do what works. If they can use your guilt to manipulate you, they will.

2. Do not convey the attitude that your children are deprived. Instead convey the attitude that "This is how it is in our family, and we can be grateful for our circumstances and use them to create a family atmosphere of teamwork and

contribution. Everyone is needed to do their share."

Planning Ahead to Prevent Future Problems

1. Involve children in plans for how they can be contributing members of your family team. They can help create routines and divide up the chores.

2. Make special time a priority. During every family meeting, take time to plan and schedule family fun time. Also list the children's events, such as soccer games, dance recitals, plans, and school events, and make your attendance a priority. Also spend individual special one-on-one time with each child on a regular basis.

3. Have faith that your children will benefit from their circumstances when they are treated with dignity and respect and you treat yourself with dignity and respect.

BOOSTER THOUGHTS[21] Being a working mother can be beneficial to your children— and it can be harmful. It all depends on how you handle the following factors of working parents.

Harmful Factors	Beneficial Factors
Feeling guilty	Feeling confident
Poor child care	Quality child care
Misunderstanding children's motives	Understanding why children misbehave
Pampering	Allowing children to develop self-reliance
Punishing, demeaning, or underestimating children	Effective parenting skills
Lack of organization and routines	Organizing and creating routines *with* your children
Neglecting children	Planning for and spending special time with children
Workaholism	Balancing family and work

☙

This story continues one mother's experience with working and guilt, begun in the Booster Thoughts in the Crying entry.

"When my children became teenagers, my guilt button about working reappeared. This time I decided I would stop working for a while so I could be home during their teen years. I announced my decision at a family meeting. I mentioned that this would mean tightening our belts a little—a small reduction in allowances, fewer pizza nights, and a budget vacation.

I was surprised at the kids' reaction: "No way. We don't want you to stop working. We are proud of you and all you do. What a drag it would be to have a stay-at-home mom nagging us all the time." (I don't know where they got that idea.)

I didn't miss out on this great opportunity. I said, "Well then, if you want to enjoy the opportunities of having a working mother, you will need to take more responsibilities around the house to help me out. I know you have been doing chores, but I would like help with the bigger jobs, like scrubbing floors and deep cleaning."

They said, "No problem."

4. Have interests apart from your family, whether it is a part-time job, a hobby, volunteer work, or a full-time career. While it is challenging to juggle home and work, it is worse to define yourself completely through your children and live your life vicariously through theirs. Being a parent is only one aspect of your personality.

Life Skills Children Can Learn

Children can learn the satisfaction of feeling capable and responsible when they are needed to make meaningful contributions.

Parenting Pointers

1. It is not respectful to you or to your children if you feel you need to give them material things or to be permissive to make up to them for working.

2. Too many parents have the mistaken belief that being a good parent means they should always be present and take care of their children's every need. This actually robs their children of the opportunity to learn self-reliance and cooperation.

3. Listen to your heart and follow it instead of listening to what friends or extended family members tell you about whether or not to work. Trust yourself to make the right decision for yourself and your immediate family.

ZITS

"My children are starting to get zits and you would think the world is coming to an end. How can I help them? I tried to tell them that it would help if they watched their diet, stopped drinking soda pop and eating chocolate and got more sleep. They just rolled their eyes and walked away."

Understanding Your Child, Yourself, and the Situation

Most parents worry that their children might be unhappy and unpopular if they have less than perfect skin. Often so do their children. Acne can be embarrassing during the adolescent years, even though it is quite common due to the buildup of more oil and bacteria, which happens when hormone levels increase. Parents want to help their children by fixing the situation. One of the most popular ways parents have for "helping" their children is to give them a lecture. But kids have lecture antennas: as soon as parents start lecturing, they immediately tune them out.

Suggestions

1. Stop lecturing. You can change a lecture to sharing valuable information just by asking for permission first. "I have some information on pimples. Would you like to hear it?" If your child says yes, she will

be willing to listen. If she says no, there is no point in sharing—unless you enjoy having your valuable ideas rejected.

2. Ask your child, "Do you want my help, or would you like to make an appointment with a dermatologist or someone who does facials?"

3. If your child says he would like your help, offer one suggestion at a time. Keep it simple. For instance, "Let's do some research on the Internet and find some legitimate resources for information." Then be a copilot while your child navigates the Web.

4. Ask your child if she is the only one in her school with this problem. This helps her see that it is normal at this age to have skin problems and that she isn't a freak.

5. Instead of telling kids what not to do, tell them what will work. For instance, mention that washing skin twice a day with a mild soap works better than squeezing.

6. Many over the counter remedies will help, but it usually takes four to six weeks to show improvement.

7. If the problem becomes severe, take your child to a dermatologist. However when medications are recommended, be sure to do your homework. Years ago dermatologists recommended some treatments

and medications that were later found to have long-term negative effects.

Planning Ahead to Prevent Future Problems

1. Invite your child to join you in a skin-care routine that includes regular facials as part of your special time together.

2. Teach your children to drink a lot of water. When they become teens, this habit will help keep acne from getting out of control.

3. Always check to make sure that cosmetics or moisturizers aren't oily or greasy.

Life Skills Children Can Learn

Children can learn to do research among their friends, on the Internet, and with specialists (doctors) and their parents to find solutions to problems that seem beyond their control. They can also learn that they can survive what seem like major tragedies in life.

Parenting Pointers

1. If the problem is beyond your ability to help, it's okay to take your child for professional help, but only if he or she is willing.

2. There are many times when you can't protect your children, nor should you. Don't underestimate the value of a loving, listening ear.

BOOSTER THOUGHTS Nancy was hysterical about a zit she discovered while getting ready for the prom. Her mother invited Nancy to stand in front of the full-length mirror. She stripped to her underwear to display cellulite and sagging flesh and asked Nancy, "Want to trade—my sags for your zit?"

Nancy burst out laughing, covered her pimple with makeup, and went to the prom.

NOTES

1. Ilg, Frances L., and Louise Bates Ames. *The Gesell Institute's Child Behavior from Birth to Ten* (New York: Harper & Row, 1955), 330.

2. Kline, Kris, and Stephen Pew, Ph.D. *For The Sake of the Children* (Roseville, CA: Prima Publishing, 1992).

3. Story from *Positive Discipline for Parenting in Recovery* by Jane Nelsen, Riki Intner, and Lynn Lott, 2005; e-book available at www.focusingonsolutions.com.

4. Gentile, D. A., and D. A. Walsh. "A Normative Study of Family Media Habits," *Applied Developmental Psychology,* 23 (Jan. 28, 2002), 157–178.

5. Office of Educational Research and Improvement. "National Education Longitudinal Study of 1988" (Washington, DC: Government Printing Office, 1988).

6. Dreikurs, Rudolf, and Vicki Soltz. *Children: The Challenge* (New York: Dutton, 1964), 36.

7. Glenn, H. Stephen. *Developing Healthy Self-esteem* (Orem, UT: Empowering People Books, Tapes, and Videos, 1989, videocassette).

8. Redlich, Fritz, and June Bingham. *The Inside Story—Psychiatry and Everyday Life* (New York: Alfred A. Knopf, 1953), 145ff.

9. Glenn, H. Stephen and Jane Nelsen. *Raising Self-Reliant Children in a Self-Indulgent World* (New York: Three Rivers Press, 2000), 127–128.

10. Björklund, Barbara R. and David F. Björklund. *Parents Book of Discipline* (New York: Ballantine Books, 1990), 211.

11. May, Rollo. *Love and Will* (New York: Norton, 1969), 630.

12. Glenn, H. Stephen, and Michael Brock. *7 Strategies for Developing Capable Students* (New York: Three Rivers Press, 1998).

13. Stolmaker, Laurie. "The Truth about Consequences: Boy and His Pet Rat," Family Education Centers Newsletter (Fall 1992).

14. See Chapter 3 on birth order in Jane Nelsen, *Positive Discipline* (New York: Ballantine, 2006) for exceptions to this rule and for more information on birth-order beliefs.

15. NICHD Early Child Care Research Network. "Characteristics of Infant Child Care: Factors Contributing Positive Care-giving," *Early Childhood Research Quarterly,* 11 (1996), 267–306.

16. Ilg and Ames, *The Gesell Institute's Child Behavior from Birth to Ten,* 142.

17. Frieden, Wayne, and Marie Hartwell Walker. *Songs for Elementary Emotional Development—Family Songs,* available at www.focusingonsolutions.com.

18. Ferber, Richard, M.D. *Solve Your Child's Sleep Problems* (New York: Simon & Schuster, 1986).

19. Björklund and Björklund, *Parents Book of Discipline,* 33.

20. Galinsky, Ellen. *Ask the Children* (New York: William Morrow, 1999).

21. Excerpt from *Positive Discipline for Working Parents* by Jane Nelsen and Lisa Larson Fitch (New York: Three Rivers Press), which includes a full chapter on each of these factors.

SELECTED BIBLIOGRAPHY

Glenn, H. Stephen, and Nelsen, Jane. *Raising Self-Reliant Children in a Self-Indulgent World* (New York: Three Rivers Press, 2000).

Lott, Lynn, Jane Nelsen, and Therry Jay. *Pup Parenting* (New York: Rodale, 2006).

Lott, Lynn, Jane Nelsen, and Rick Naymark. *Madame Dora's Fortune Telling Cards* (Gloucester, MA: Fair Winds Press, 2003).

————, and Riki Intner. *Chores Without Wars: Turning Housework into Teamwork.* (Previously published as *The Family That Works Together . . .* and *Family Work: Whose Job Is It?*) (Pennsylvania: Taylor Trade Publishing, 2006).

————, Riki Intner, and Barbara Mendenhall. *Do-It-Yourself Therapy: How to Think, Feel, and Act Like a New Person in Just 8 Weeks,* available at www.empoweringpeople.com.

————, and Dru West. *Together and Liking It.* (Previously published as *Married and Liking It*) (Petaluma, CA: The Practical Press, 1990).

————, Marilyn Matulich Kentz, and Dru West. *To Know Me Is To Love Me: Steps for Raising Self-Esteem.* (Previously published as *To Know Me Is to Love Me*) (Petaluma, CA: The Practical Press, 1990).

Nelsen, Jane. *Positive Discipline,* 4th ed. (New York: Ballantine, 2006).

————. *Understanding Serenity: What Thoughts Are You Willing to Give Up Your Happiness For?* (Previously published as *Understanding: Eliminating Stress and Finding Serenity in Life and Relationships* and *From Here to Serenity)* (Lehi, Utah: Empowering People, 2006).

————. *Positive Time-Out: And Over 50 Ways to Avoid Power Struggles in the Home and the Classroom* (New York: Three Rivers Press, 2000).

————, and Lynn Lott. *Positive Discipline for Teenagers,* Revised Edition (New York: Three Rivers Press, 2000).

————, Lynn Lott, and H. Stephen Glenn. *Positive Discipline in the Classroom,* 3rd ed. (New York: Three Rivers Press, 2000).

————, Cheryl Erwin, and Carol Delzer. *Positive Discipline for Single Parents* (New York: Three Rivers Press, 1999).

————, Cheryl Erwin, and Roslyn Duffy. *Positive Discipline for Preschoolers,* 3rd ed. (New York: Three Rivers Press, 2007).

————, Cheryl Erwin, and Roslyn Duffy. *Positive Discipline: The First Three Years,* 2nd ed. (New York: Three Rivers Press, 2007).

————, Linda Escobar, Kate Ortolano, Roslyn Duffy, and Debbie Owen-Sohocki. *Positive Discipline: A Teacher's A–Z Guide* (New York: Three Rivers Press, 2001).

————, and Cheryl Erwin. *Parents Who Love Too Much* (New York: Three Rivers Press, 2000).

————, and Cheryl Erwin. *Positive Discipline for Child Care Providers* (New York: Three Rivers Press, 2002).

————, Cheryl Erwin, Michael Brock, and Mary Hughes. *Positive Discipline for Christian Families* (New York: Three Rivers Press, 2002).

————, and Lisa Larson. *Positive Discipline for Working Parents* (New York: Three Rivers Press, 2003).

RESOURCES

Manuals, Facilitators' Guides, and Workbooks

Lott, Lynn, and Jane Nelsen. *Teaching Parenting the Positive Discipline Way Manual* (Empowering People Books, Tapes, and Videos, 2007). Available at www.empoweringpeople. com.

Nelsen, Jane, and Lynn Lott. *Positive Discipline in the Classroom Facilitator's Guide* (Empowering People Books, Tapes, and Videos, 1992). Available at www.empoweringpeople.com.

E-Books

Nelsen, Jane. *UNDERSTANDING SERENITY: What thoughts are you willing to give up your happiness for?* (Formerly *UNDERSTANDING: Eliminating Stress and Finding Serenity in Life and Relationships* and *From Here to Serenity.*) E-book available at www.focusingonsolutions. com.

———, Lynn Lott, and Riki Intner. *Positive Discipline for Parenting in Recovery,* 1996. E-book available at www.focusingonsolutions.com.

———, Cheryl Erwin, and H. Stephen Glenn. *Positive Discipline for Your Step Family,* 2000. E-book available at www.focusingonsolutions.com.

Books and lectures on CDs and/or MP3

Nelsen, Jane. *Positive Discipline Birth to Five,* 2006, two-hour lecture, available at www. focusingonsolutions.com.

———. *UNDERSTANDING SERENITY: What thoughts are you willing to give up your thoughts for?,* 2006, unabridged book read by the author, available at www. focusingonsolutions.com.

———. *Positive Discipline: Empowering Teens* 2005, two-hour lecture available at www. focusingonsolutions.com.

FOR MORE INFORMATION

Jane Nelsen and Lynn Lott are popular keynote speakers for conferences (parents, psychologists, therapists, social workers, nurses, school counselors, and teacher in-service).

Lynn and Jane are the developers of two popular two-day workshops that are now facilitated by certified Positive Discipline associates:

Teaching Parenting the Positive Discipline Way
Positive Discipline in the Classroom

For more information go to www.positivediscipline.com or contact Jane Nelsen at jane@positivediscipline.com.

Lynn Lott is a family therapist in private practice in Sonoma County, California. For more information go to www. lynnlott.com. For appointments, e-mail lynnlott@sbcglobal.net or call 707-526-3141.

ACKNOWLEDGMENTS

We'd like to acknowledge Rudolf Dreikurs and Alfred Adler for lighting the way for generations of parents. Special appreciation to our editor, Lindsey Moore, who gets it. You helped us make our third edition a better book. Thanks always to our husbands who give us the space to write, and write, and write. And to our kids, stepkids, and grandchildren, who constantly teach us what it means to be a parent.

INDEX

ABOUT THE AUTHORS

JANE NELSEN, Ed.D., coauthor of the bestselling Positive Discipline series, is the mother of seven children and grandmother to twenty—and still counting. She is a California-licensed marriage, family, and child therapist and an internationally known speaker. Jane and her husband, Barry, now divide their time between San Clemente, California, and South Jordan, Utah. She has appeared on numerous TV shows, including *Oprah, Sally Jesse Raphael,* and *CBS This Morning.* Her books have sold over two million copies.

LYNN LOTT, M.A., M.F.T., is a therapist and author of eighteen books and manuals, including four in the Positive Discipline series. Her private practice is located in Santa Rosa, California. Lynn is mother of two, stepmom to two, and grandmother of three. She has appeared on *The Joan Rivers Show, The Today Show, The Home Show,* and *Phil Donahue.* Lynn and her husband, Hal, divide their time between California and Florida.

H. STEPHEN GLENN, Ph.D., is the coauthor of the bestselling classics *Raising Self-Reliant Children in a Self-Indulgent World* and *7 Strategies for Developing Capable Students* with Mike Brock. He developed the popular Developing Capable People program. Steve passed away in 2004. He will be missed, yet he still lives on through his books, programs, and popular DCP CDs.